KOREAN
FOLKTALES
for Language Learners

KOREAN FOLKTALES
for Language Learners

전래 동화로 배우는 한국어와 한국 문화

Sukyeon Cho
Yeon-Jeong Kim
Andrew Killick

Illustrated by **Minjee Kim**

TUTTLE Publishing

Tokyo | Rutland, Vermont | Singapore

To Access the Audio Recordings:

1. Check that you have an internet connection.
2. Type the URL below into your web browser:

   https://www.tuttlepublishing.com/korean-folktales-for-language-learners

For support you can email us at info@tuttlepublishing.com.

Contents

How to Use This Book

In this book you'll find a collection of well-known folktales that are much loved by Koreans, featuring wily animals and wise animals, fighting families and loving families, humor, horror and magic, as well as legends about the creation of Korea.

Each story is presented with parallel Korean and English text on facing pages. You can challenge yourself by reading the stories in Korean, using the English text as a guide if needed, or you can simply enjoy the English stories. For students who are unfamiliar with the Hangul alphabet, this is presented on pages 10–11, followed by reading and writing exercises that will allow you to master the basics.

The book goes from short, simple stories to longer, more complex ones. To tell the stories clearly we use some grammatical forms that are considered "intermediate" even in the first part of the book. As far as possible we use expressions that are common today rather than old-fashioned forms, to be of practical use to the Korean language learner. English translations aim to be faithful to the original, but where a literal translation would sound awkward, a freer translation has been given. Each chapter also contains the following elements:

Vocabulary
A comprehensive list gives key words from the story in Hangul and English.

Selected grammar points
Key grammar points from the story are explained, along with example sentences.

After reading the story
Comprehension questions encourage your deeper understanding of the story and reinforce the vocabulary and grammar presented in each lesson.

Let's talk!
Students working with a teacher can use the prompts as a starting point for discussion. Self-study students can explore issues from the story in writing.

Notes on Korean culture
Notes on the cultural background to each story help you gain valuable insights into Korean society.

An English-Korean glossary is provided at the end of the book.

Each story is available as an online audio recording made by native Korean speakers, via the link on page 4.

The Korean Language:
an Overview

The Korean Language   한국말

Korean belongs to a family of languages that is thought to include Japanese and possibly even Mongolian, Finnish and Hungarian. Although Korean has no structural relationship with the Chinese language, a large portion of Korean vocabulary has cognates in Chinese.

In contrast with some European languages, in Korean the verb always comes at the end of the sentence, with the basic sentence structure being: subject – object – verb. So a sentence would be structured as, for example, "My friend the book reads" rather than "My friend reads the book."

In addition, particles are added to nouns to indicate their function in the sentence. In Korean you would say: My friend (+ subject particle) the book (+ object particle) reads.

In Korean, verbs must change their forms in order to show tense and mood. The tense of a verb indicates whether the action or state is taking place in the present, future or past. There are five moods in Korean, which are declarative (statements), interrogative (questions), imperative (commands), propositive (suggestions) and exclamatory (exclamations).

Perhaps one of the most interesting features of Korean is the extensive use of honorific language. When speaking in Korean, you must use a level of respect appropriate to the person being addressed or the person being discussed. The language used to address a small child will differ significantly from that used to a friend, and that too will be different from the level of speech used to a senior colleague or elderly relative. There are some verbs and nouns which have their own honorific equivalents: for example, the word for one's own wife is *urijipsaram* while another person's wife is referred to as *buin*. Other verbs rely on infixes (syllables attached directly to the verb stem) or honorific verb endings.

The Korean Alphabet   한글

Before the invention of the Korean alphabet in the fifteenth century, people in Korea borrowed Chinese characters when they wanted to write something.

However, learning Chinese characters is quite difficult because of their complexity and quantity. As a result, most ordinary people, and even some noblemen, were illiterate.

However, in 1443, a new Korean alphabet called Hangul (also spelled Hangeul) was promulgated by the fourth ruler of the Joseon Dynasty, King Sejong the Great, who is unquestionably the most loved king in all of Korean history. Hangul was developed as a means of transcribing the sounds of Korean, which made reading and writing the language easier and accessible to all the Korean people. King Sejong the Great called the alphabet Hunmin Jeongeum or "Proper Sounds to Instruct the People." In his *Introduction to Hunmin Jeongeum*, he wrote, "Talented people will learn Hangul in a single morning and even foolish people will understand it in ten days"—a point to be borne in mind by all would-be students of the Korean alphabet!

Even after the introduction of Hangul, Korean scholars and officials were reluctant to abandon the use of Chinese characters, which had for so long been a symbol of learning and status in Korean society. However, from the seventeenth century, the Hangul alphabet was used both in court circles and among the ordinary people, and its use was encouraged by the Progressive Movement in the late nineteenth century. The first Hangul newspaper, *The Independent* was published in 1896, but during the Japanese colonial period (1910–1945), the use of the Korean language was severely restricted and from 1938 it was forbidden to use Korean in schools. Following liberation from Japanese rule in 1945, the Korean language flourished again; such is the Koreans' pride in their language and their alphabet in particular that in 1945, October 9th was established as Hangul Day (한글날), a national holiday. For a while, a mixture of Hangul and Chinese characters was used but these days Hangul is used almost exclusively both in South Korea and North Korea.

The Hangul alphabet has 40 characters (letters) that are combined in all sorts of different ways to form words. In modern Hangul, there are 19 consonants and 21 vowels, including compound vowels. Vowels and consonants have different shapes so they are easy to distinguish visually.

Hangul is an alphabet in that it has vowels and consonants like the Roman alphabet, but at the same time it is a syllabic writing system like Chinese characters. When you see an unfamiliar English word, you don't know how many syllables it has unless you know how to pronounce it. But with Hangul, one block of letters is one syllable. This, in addition to the fact that Hangul pronunciation is fully predictable from the spelling, makes Hangul relatively easy to read compared to other languages. That is why Hangul is admired as the world's most efficient alphabet by many linguists.

2.1 Consonants

There are ten basic consonants in Korean, of which four are aspirated (pronounced with a breath of air) and five are tense (pronounced with a "hard" sound). Each symbol is practically a diagram of how to pronounce it. For example, the shapes of five of the consonants reflect the shape of the mouth and tongue. The remaining consonants are adaptations of these letters. The pronunciation of many of the consonants changes when they come between vowels or in combination with other consonants.

ㄱ is the shape of the tongue just before the moment of pronunciation as the tongue blocks the passage of air.

ㄴ is designed to look like the tongue touching the front of the mouth which is how you make that sound.

ㅅ is the shape of the teeth and tongue when making this sound.

ㅁ is the shape of a closed mouth.

ㅇ is the shape of the opening to the throat.

Letter	ㄱ	ㄴ	ㄷ	ㄹ	ㅁ	ㅂ	ㅅ	ㅇ	ㅈ	ㅎ
Sound value	[g]	[n]	[d]	[l]	[m]	[b]	[s]	[ng]	[j]	[h]
Letter	ㅋ		ㅌ			ㅍ			ㅊ	
Sound value (aspirated)	[kʰ] [k]		[tʰ] [t]			[pʰ] [p]			[cʰ] [ch]	
Letter	ㄲ		ㄸ			ㅃ	ㅆ		ㅉ	
Sound value	[kk]		[tt]			[pp]	[ss]		[jj]	

2.2 Vowels

There are eight simple vowels and thirteen compound vowels in the Korean alphabet. The compound vowels are formed by combining two simple vowels in a new form.

The vowels were designed to represent the three basic components of the universe; Sky (Sun), Earth and Human. A short stroke represents the sun in the sky, the essence of yang, when written with a brush. A horizontal line symbolizes the flat earth, the essence of yin. A vertical line indicates an upright human, the neutral mediator between Sky and Earth. These three components—Sky, Earth and Human—are considered fundamental in many East Asian philosophies. By combining these very simple letters, you get various combinations of different vowels.

Letter	ㅏ	ㅓ	ㅗ	ㅜ	—	ㅣ	ㅔ	ㅐ	ㅚ	ㅟ
Sound value	[a]	[eo]	[o]	[u]	[eu]	[i]	[e]	[ae]	[oe]	[wi]
Letter	ㅑ	ㅕ	ㅛ	ㅠ			ㅖ	ㅒ		
Sound value	[ya]	[yeo]	[yo]	[yu]			[ye]	[yae]		
Letter	ㅘ	ㅝ			ㅢ		ㅞ	ㅙ		
Sound value	[wa]	[wo]			[ui]		[we]	[wae]		

2.3 Syllable Construction

A key feature of the Korean alphabet is the grouping of initial, middle and final letters into syllables which then combine to form words. You start with the initial consonant and then you add the vowel needed to make a syllable, either to the right of the consonant if the vowel is based on a vertical line or beneath if it's based on a horizontal line. Then, if there's a consonant at the end of the syllable, you put it beneath everything else. And then you write these syllable blocks left to right. And that's it.

Thus, the letters ㅎ (h), ㅏ (a) and ㄴ (n) are grouped to form the syllable 한. Similarly, the letters ㄱ (g), ㅜ (u) and ㄱ (k) are grouped to form the syllable 국. Written side by side, these two syllables form the word 한국, which means Korea. This is very different from English, where the letters are written in horizontal succession.

When writing Korean syllables, it is useful to imagine that you are writing each syllable to fit inside a small square; indeed, Korean children learn to write using squared paper. As regards the order in which the strokes are written, the general rule is to work from top to bottom and from left to right.

Reading and Writing Korean Words

1. Practice reading and writing the following words that end in a vowel.

Consonant + Vertical Vowel

나 **na** I

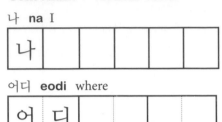

어디 **eodi** where

바다 **bada** sea

자리 **jari** seat

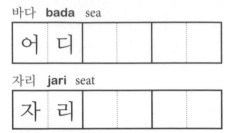

Consonant + Horizontal Vowel

오 **o** five

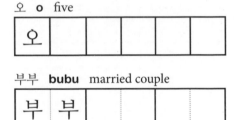

부부 **bubu** married couple

누구 **nugu** who

호수 **hosu** lake

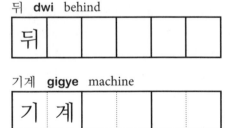

Consonant + Complex Vowel

왜 **wae** why

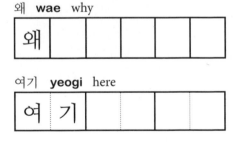

여기 **yeogi** here

뒤 **dwi** behind

기계 **gigye** machine

Aspirated Consonant + Vowel

크게 **keuge** widely

치마 **chima** skirt

부터 **buteo** from

피하다 **pihada** to avoid

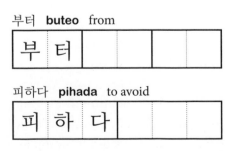

Double Consonant + Vowel

또 **tto** again

또				

오빠 **oppa** older brother

오	빠			

아가씨 **agassi** young lady

아	가	씨		

도깨비 **dokkaebi** goblin

도	깨	비		

2. Practice reading and writing the following words that end in a consonant.

Consonant + Vowel + Consonant(s)

목 **mok** neck

목				

꽃 **kkot** flower

꽃				

발 **bal** foot

발				

집 **jip** house

집				

친구 **chingu** friend

친	구			

그림 **geurim** painting

그	림			

여동생 **yeodongsaeng** younger sister

여	동	생		

값 **gap** price

값				

많이 **mani** a lot

많	이			

젊은이 **jeolmeuni** young person

젊	은	이		

3. Practice reading and writing the following words, phrases and sentences.

안녕하세요. **Annyeonghaseyo.** Hello.

안	녕	하	세	요			

고마워요. **Gomawoyo.** Thank you.

고	마	워	요				

만나서 반가워요. **Mannaseo bangawoyo.** Nice to meet you.

만	나	서	반	가	워	요

제 이름은 김연정이에요. **Je ireumeun kimyeonjeongieyo.** My name's Kim Yeon-Jeong.

제	이	름	은	김	연	정	이	에	요

저는 한국 사람이에요. **Jeoneun hanguk saramieyo.** I am Korean.

저	는	한	국	사	람	이	에	요

한국어 선생님이에요. **Hangugeo seonsaengnimieyo.** I'm a Korean language teacher.

한	국	어	선	생	님	이	에	요

제 취미는 독서예요. **Je chwimineun dokseoyeyo.** My hobby is reading.

제	취	미	는	독	서	예	요

스님은 열심히 공부했어요. **Seunimeun yeolsimhi gongbuhaesseoyo.**
The monk studied hard.

스	님	은	열	심	히	공	부	했	어	요

정말이에요? **Jeongmarieyo?** Is it true?

정	말	이	에	요				

막걸리 한 잔 주세요. **Makgeolli han jan juseyo.** Give me a cup of makgeolli.

막	걸	리	한	잔	주	세	요

옛날에 선비가 살았어요. **Yennare seonbiga sarasseoyo.**
Long ago, there lived a scholar.

옛	날	에	선	비	가	살	았	어	요

맛있게 드세요. **Masitge deuseyo.** Enjoy your food.

맛	있	게	드	세	요		

한국 옛날 이야기가 재미있어요! **Hanguk yennal iyagiga jaemiisseoyo!**
Korean folktales are fun!

한	국	옛	날	이	야	기	가	재	미	있	어	요

부부는 아이가 없었어요. **Bubuneun aiga eopseosseoyo.**
A couple didn't have any children.

부	부	는	아	이	가	없	었	어	요

걱정하지 마세요. **Geokjeonghaji maseyo.** Please don't worry.

걱	정	하	지	마	세	요	

그는 팥죽을 먹고 싶었어요. **Geuneun patjugeul meokgo sipeosseoyo.**
He wanted to eat the porridge.

그	는	팥	죽	을	먹	고	싶	었	어	요

만나서 반가워요
Mannaseo Bangawoyo

만나서 반가워요. **Mannaseo bangawoyo.**
제 이름은 조숙연이에요. **Je ireumeun josugyeonieyo.**
한국 사람이에요. **Hanguk saramieyo.**
한국 옛날 이야기가 재미있어요. **Hanguk yennal iyagiga jaemiisseoyo.**

☆ ☆ ☆

Pleased to Meet You!

Pleased to meet you!
My name is Cho Sukyeon.
I'm Korean.
Korean folktales are fun!

☆ ☆ ☆

Vocabulary
만나서 반가워요. **Mannaseo bangawoyo.** Pleased to meet you.
제 **je** [humble] my
이름 **ireum** name
이다 **ida** is, am, are
한국 **hanguk** Korea
사람 **saram** person
옛날 이야기 **yennal iyagi** folktales
재미있다 **jaemiitda** to be interesting, fun

Selected grammar points
- 은/는 **eun/neun Topic particle**
  This identifies the topic of a sentence. 은 **eun** is used after nouns ending in consonants and 는 **neun** is used after nouns ending in vowels.
  제 이름은 조숙연이에요. **Je ireumeun josugyeonieyo.**
  My name is Cho Sukyeon.

- 예요/이에요 **yeyo/ieyo Informal style of** 이다 **ida**
  This is used with a noun to identify a person or an object. Nouns ending in a vowel take 예요 **yeyo** and nouns ending in a consonant take 이에요 **ieyo**.
  한국 사람이에요. **Hanguk saramieyo.**
  I'm Korean.
- 아/어요 **a/eoyo Present tense polite informal verb ending**
  아요 **ayo** is used if the vowel in the final syllable of the verb stem is ㅏ **a** or ㅗ **o** and 어요 **eoyo** is used after all other verb stems.
  한국 옛날 이야기가 재미있어요. **Hanguk yennal iyagiga jaemiisseoyo.**
  Korean folktales are fun!

After reading the story
1. 이 사람의 이름은 뭐예요? **I saramui ireumeun mwoyeyo?**
   What is this person's name?
2. 이 사람은 어느 나라 사람이에요? **I sarameun eoneu nara saramieyo?**
   What country is this person from?

Let's talk!
자기의 이름을 한국어로 말해 보세요. **Jagiui ireumeul hangugeoro malhae boseyo.**
Tell someone your name in Korean.

Notes on Korean culture
In Korea, people usually bow their head when they greet each other. Sometimes they just tilt their head a little, but when greeting elders, they may bow deeply, using their whole back. The deeper you bow, the more respect it shows, so there are times when people bow down almost a full 90 degrees! When shaking hands, Koreans show respect by supporting the "shaking" hand with the other hand and bending the back slightly. How do you express respect in your culture?

자기소개
Jagisogae

한국어 선생님이에요. **Hangugeo seonsaengnimieyo.**
저는 30 (서른) 살이에요. **Jeoneun seoreunsarieyo.**
제 취미는 독서예요. **Je chwimineun dokseoyeyo.**
지금부터 한국의 옛날 이야기를 읽어 드릴게요.
Jigeumbuteo hangugui yennal iyagireul ilgeo deurilgeyo.

☆ ☆ ☆

A Self-Introduction

I'm a Korean language teacher.
I'm 30 years old.
My hobby is reading.
From now on, I'm going to read you some old folktales of Korea.

☆ ☆ ☆

Vocabulary

자기소개 **jagisogae** self-introduction
저 **jeo** [humble] I
한국어 **hangugeo** Korean language
선생님 **seonsaengnim** teacher
살 **sal** years of age

취미 **chwimi** hobby
독서 **dokseo** reading
지금 **jigeum** now
부터 **buteo** from
읽다 **ikda** to read

Selected grammar points

- 부터 **buteo** Particle meaning "from"

  This is attached to time nouns to indicate when a particular situation starts.
  지금부터 한국의 옛날 이야기를 읽어 드릴게요.
  Jigeumbuteo hangugui yennal iyagireul ilgeo deurilgeyo.
  From now on, I'm going to read you some old folktales of Korea.

- 의 ui **Possessive particle "of"**

  This is added to nouns to indicate something belongs to somebody or something.

  지금부터 **한국의** 옛날 이야기를 읽어 드릴게요.

  Jigeumbuteo hangugui yennal iyagireul ilgeo deurilgeyo.

  From now on, I'm going to read you some Korean folktales.

- 을/를 eul/reul **Object particle**

  This particle indicates the object of an action verb. It takes the form 을 when attached to nouns ending in a consonant and 를 when attached to nouns ending in a vowel.

  지금부터 한국의 옛날 **이야기를** 읽어 드릴게요.

  Jigeumbuteo hangugui yennal iyagireul ilgeo deurilgeyo.

  From now on, I'm going to read you some Korean folktales.

- (으)ㄹ게요 (eu)lgeyo **"(I) will (do)"**

  This pattern is used when the speaker wants to express a decision or intention to another person, similar to a promise, and also when actually making a promise to do something with the other person.

  지금부터 한국의 옛날 이야기를 읽어 **드릴게요**

  Jigeumbuteo hangugui yennal iyagireul ilgeo deurilgeyo.

  From now on, I'm going to read you some old folktales of Korea.

After reading the story

1. 이 사람의 취미는 뭐예요? **I saramui chwimineun mwoyeyo?**

   What is this person's hobby?

2. 이 사람은 몇 살이에요? **I sarameun myeot sarieyo?**

   How old is this person?

Let's talk!

자신의 취미와 직업을 말해 보세요. **Jasinui chwimiwa jigeobeul malhae boseyo.**

Talk about your hobby and job.

Notes on Korean culture

In Korea, age is very important. What to call someone and what form of speech to use with them often depends whether they are older than you. So when introducing yourself, it's usual to state your age, and when meeting someone for the first time, one of the most common questions is "How old are you?" To a Westerner, this may seem rude, but in Korea it's very important to know!

산과 바다가 된 이야기

옛날에 하늘과 땅이 있었어요. 그리고 한 장수가 살았어요.
어느 날 하느님이 하늘에서 반지를 땅에 떨어뜨렸어요.
하느님이 말했어요.
"반지를 찾아와."
장수는 땅에서 반지를 찾으려고 큰 손으로 흙을 팠어요. 그곳은 바다가
되었어요. 그리고 옆에 그 흙을 놓았어요. 그곳은 산이 되었어요.

☆ ☆ ☆

How the Mountains and the Sea Were Made

A long time ago, there was just the sky and the Earth. And there lived a big strong man.

One day God dropped a ring down to the Earth from the sky.

God said, "Find me the ring."

The strong man dug the soil with his big hands to find the ring in the Earth. That place became the sea. And beside it he put the soil. That place became the mountains.

Vocabulary

산 **san** mountain

바다 **bada** sea

되다 **doeda** to become, be formed

이야기 **iyagi** story

옛날에 **yennare** a long time ago

하늘 **haneul** sky

땅 **ttang** Earth

있다 **itda** there is, to have

그리고 **geurigo** and then

한 **han** kind of, one

장수 **jangsu** strong person

살다 **salda** to live

어느 날 **eoneunal** one day

하느님 **haneunim** God

반지 **banji** ring

떨어뜨리다 **tteoreotteurida** to drop

말하다 **malhada** to say, to speak, to tell

찾다 **chatda** to find

큰 손 **keun son** big hands

흙 **heuk** soil

파다 **pada** to dig

그곳 **geugot** in that place

옆 **yeop** side

놓다 **nota** to put

Selected grammar points

- 에 **Time particle, meaning "at a time," "on a date"**
  This is attached to the time phrase to indicate the time at which something happens.
  옛날에 하늘과 땅이 있었어요.
  A long time ago, there was the sky and the Earth.

- 와/과 **Companion particle "and"**
  This particle is used to connect two or more nouns and attached directly to the first noun; any other particles relating to the string of nouns are then attached to the final noun in the list. 과 is attached to nouns ending in a consonant. 와 is attached to nouns ending in a vowel.
  하늘과 땅이 있었어요.
  There was the sky and the Earth.

- 이/가 **Subject particle**
  This particle indicates the subject of a sentence or clause, that is, the "doer" of an action or the person or thing being described. 이 is attached to nouns ending in a consonant and 가 is attached to nouns ending in a vowel.
  땅이 있었어요.
  There was the Earth.

- 았/었어요 **Past tense verb ending**
  The past tense is created by attaching the infix 았 or 었 to the stem of the verb. 았어요 is used when the vowel in the final syllable of the verb stem is ㅏ or ㅗ. 써어요 is used when the verb stem ends in a vowel. 었어요 is used after all other verb stems.
  땅이 있었어요.
  There was the Earth.

- 에 **Location particle "at a place," "to a place"**
  This is used to indicate the location of things or people.
  하느님이 하늘에서 반지를 **땅에** 떨어뜨렸어요.
- 에서 **Location particle "at a place," "from a place"**
  This is to show where an action takes place.
  하느님이 **하늘에서** 반지를 땅에 떨어뜨렸어요.
  God dropped a ring down to the Earth from the sky.

After reading the story

1. 하느님이 무엇을 떨어뜨렸어요?
   What did God drop?
2. 어떻게 바다가 되었어요?
   How was the sea formed?
3. 어떻게 산이 되었어요?
   How were the mountains formed?

Let's talk!

세상이 어떻게 만들어졌는지에 대한 여러분 나라의 이야기를 소개해 보세요.
Tell a story from your country about how the world was created.

Notes on Korean culture

The Korean peninsula is surrounded on three sides by the sea and 70 percent of the land is mountainous. As a result, Korean cuisine makes great use of seafood and a wide variety of edible mountain plants are used in cooking, alongside cultivated vegetables. In addition, the climate has four distinct seasons, each with its own distinctive foods.

도깨비 씨름

옛날에 어떤 할아버지가 친구 집에서 술을 많이 마셨어요. 그날 밤 할아버지는 혼자서 집에 돌아가고 있었어요. 그런데 산 속에 도깨비 고개가 있었어요.

"여기가 도깨비 고개구나. 아이고, 무서워. 빨리 가야지."

할아버지는 갑자기 무서워졌어요. 그런데 정말 도깨비가 나타났어요. 할아버지는 무서웠지만 도망가지 않았어요. 용기를 내서 도깨비와 씨름을 했어요. 그리고 도깨비를 나무에 묶어 놓았어요. 그리고 집으로 돌아왔어요.

다음날 아침에 할머니와 같이 도깨비를 보러 갔어요. 그런데 그것은 도깨비가 아니었어요. 빗자루였어요!

☆　☆　☆

Wrestling with a Goblin

Long ago, a certain old man drank a lot of alcohol at his friend's house. That night, the old man was going home by himself. But in the mountains there was a goblins' hill.

"This is the goblins' hill. Oh my, it's scary! I'd better go quickly."

The old man suddenly grew scared. Then a goblin actually appeared. Although he was scared, the old man didn't run away. He plucked up his courage and wrestled with the goblin. And he tied the goblin to a tree. Then he went home.

The next morning, he went back with his wife to see the goblin. But it wasn't a goblin. It was only a broom!

Vocabulary

도깨비 **dokkaebi** goblin

씨름을 하다 **ssireumeul hada**
to wrestle

어떤 **eotteon** one, a certain

할아버지 **harabeoji** grandfather,
old man

친구 **chingu** friend

집 **jip** house, home

술 **sul** alcohol

많이 **mani** a lot

마시다 **masida** to drink

그날 밤 **geunal bam** that night

혼자 (서) **honja(seo)** alone

돌아가다 **doragada** to go back

속 **sok** inside, in

고개 **gogae** hill

여기 **yeogi** here

아이고 **aigo** Oh my!

무섭다 **museopda** to be scary

빨리 **ppalli** quickly, fast

가다 **gada** to go

갑자기 **gapjagi** suddenly

무서워지다 **museowojida** to get scared

정말 **jeongmal** actually

나타나다 **natanada** to appear

도망 (을) 가다 **domang(eul) gada**
to escape, to run away

용기를 내다 **yonggireul naeda** to pluck
up one's courage

나무에 묶다 **namue mukda** to tie
(something) to a tree

다음 **daeum** next

날 **nal** day

아침에 **achime** in the morning

할머니 **halmeoni** grandmother,
old woman

보다 **boda** to see, to watch

그런데 **geureondae** but, by the way

그것 **geugeot** that, it

빗자루 **bitjaru** broom

Selected grammar points

- **ㅂ Irregular verbs**

  Many verbs with a verb stem ending in the consonant ㅂ drop the final ㅂ and add 우.
  무서워.
  It's scary!

- **지만 Connecting two sentences that express contrast, "but"**

  Simply add 지만 to the verb stem, the future infix 겠 or the past infixes 았/었, to give
  the meaning "but."
  할아버지는 **무서웠지만** 도망가지 않았어요.
  Although he was scared, the old man didn't run away.

- **지 않다 Negative verb form**

  For negation, 지 않다 is added to the verb stem.
  할아버지는 무서웠지만 **도망가지 않았어요**.
  Although he was scared, the old man didn't run away.

- 와/과 같이 **"together with"**
  By adding the word 같이or 함께 to the 와/과 particle, these expressions mean "with (a person)."
  할머니와 같이 도깨비를 보러 갔어요
  He went with his wife to see the goblin.
- (으)러 가다/오다 **"to go/come (in order) to . . ."**
  할머니와 같이 도깨비를 보러 갔어요
  He went with his wife to see the goblin.
- 이/가 아니다 **Negative form of** 이다
  이 아니다 is used when the noun ends in a consonant. 가 아니다 is used when the noun ends in a vowel.
  그것은 도깨비가 아니었어요.
  It wasn't a goblin.

After reading the story

1. 할아버지는 누구 집에 갔어요?
   Whose house did the old man go to?
2. 할아버지는 도깨비를 만났을 때 도망갔어요?
   Did the old man run away when he met the goblin?
3. 할아버지와 할머니가 아침에 도깨비를 보러 갔어요. 그런데 그곳에서 무엇을 봤어요?
   The old man and woman went to see the goblin in the morning. But what did they see there?

Let's talk!

무서웠던 경험에 대해서 이야기해 보세요.
Talk about a scary experience you've had.

Notes on Korean culture

Korean-style wrestling is called 씨름 **ssireum.** Two men grab each other's loincloths and try to throw each other to the ground. The first one to fall is the loser. In this style of wrestling, strength is less important than keeping your balance. If your mind is not settled and your balance is unsteady, it's easy to feel impatient and cause yourself to fall. You can also fall when rushing to throw your opponent down. Wrestling cultivates the ability to keep your balance, both physically and mentally.

아기 보는 호랑이

옛날에 어느 마을에 아주 착한 며느리가 있었어요. 남편이 일찍 죽어서 며느리는 돈을 벌어야 했어요. 하지만 시아버지를 모시고 아기를 키우며 열심히 살았어요.

어느 날 시아버지가 이웃 마을 친구집에 가셨어요. 그런데 밤 늦게까지 집에 안 돌아오셨어요. 며느리는 걱정이 되어서 아기를 등에 업고 시아버지 마중을 나갔어요. 그런데 산에 시아버지가 쓰러져 계셨어요. 그리고 그 옆에 호랑이가 있었고요.

"아이고, 호랑이가 우리 시아버님을 먹으려고 하는구나."

며느리는 놀라서 시아버지를 안고서 집으로 달려 돌아왔어요. 그런데 집에 와 보니까 등에 업은 아기가 없는 거예요. 며느리는 호랑이가 아기를 잡아 먹은 줄 알고 너무 놀랐어요.

그때 밖에서 호랑이 소리가 났어요. 호랑이 등에는 아기가 타고 있었어요. 등에서 떨어진 아기를 데려다 준 거예요.

The Tiger That Saved a Child

Long ago, in a certain village, there lived a very kind-hearted daughter-in-law. Her husband had died young, so she had to work for a living. But she lived very diligently with her father-in-law while raising her child.

One day, the father-in-law went to a friend's house in a neighboring village. But he didn't come home even when it got late. The daughter-in-law got worried and went to look for her father-in-law, carrying her child on her back. She found her father lying passed out in the hills. And beside him was a tiger.

"Oh, no! The tiger is going to eat my father-in-law!" she cried.

Frightened, she lifted up her father-in-law and rushed back home. But when she got home, she realized the child that she had been carrying on her back was not there. Thinking the tiger had preyed on her child, she was deeply shocked.

Then, from outside, there came the sound of a tiger. And the child was riding on the tiger's back. The tiger had brought the child that had fallen from its mother's back.

Vocabulary

아기를 보다 **agireul boda** to take care of a baby

호랑이 **horangi** tiger

어느 **eoneu** one, a certain

마을 **maeul** village, town

아주 **aju** very, so

착하다 **chakada** to be kind-hearted

며느리 **myeoneuri** daughter-in-law

남편 **nampyeon** husband

일찍 **iljjik** early, soon

죽다 **jukda** to die

돈을 벌다 **doneul beolda** to make money

하지만 **hajiman** but, however

시아버지를 모시다 **siabeojireul mosida** to live with one's father-in-law

키우다 **kiuda** to raise

열심히 **yeolsimhi** hard, diligently

이웃 **iut** neighbor, neighboring

밤 **bam** night

늦게까지 **neugekkaji** till late

돌아오다 **doraoda** to come back

걱정이 되다 **geokjeongi doeda** to get worried

등 **deung** back (of a person or animal)

업다 **eopda** to carry on one's back

마중을 나가다 **majungeul nagada** to go to meet, to look for

쓰러지다 **sseureojida** to pass out

우리 **uri** our

먹다 **meokda** to eat

놀라다 **nollada** to be frightened, to be surprised

안다 **anda** to hold (a person)

달려 돌아오다 **dallyeo doraoda** to rush back

잡아먹다 **jabameokda** to prey on

너무 **neomu** very, so

그때 **geuttae** that time

밖에서 **bakkeseo** outside

소리가 나다 **soriga nada** to sound

타다 **tada** to ride

떨어지다 **tteoreojida** to fall

데려다 주다 **deryeoda juda** to bring (a person) back

Selected grammar points

- 아/어서 **Giving a reason: "so," "therefore"**
  This connective ending is used with the verb stem to indicate the reason or cause of the next clause.
  남편이 일찍 죽어서 며느리는 돈을 벌어야 했어요.
  Her husband had died young, so she had to work for a living.

- 아/어야 하다 **"to have to do X"**
  This verb form is used to indicate an obligation or need to perform an action.
  남편이 일찍 죽어서 며느리는 돈을 **벌어야 했어요**.
  Her husband had died young, so she had to work for a living.

- 고 **"do A and do B," "is A and is B"**
  This is the simplest way of connecting two or more clauses in Korean; a way to list actions or qualities without implying any connection or comparison between them.
  시아버지를 모시고 아기와 같이 열심히 살았어요.
  She lived very diligently with her father-in-law while raising her child.

- **(으)시 Honorific infix**

  To make an honorific verb stem, we simply add the honorific infix 시 or 으시 to the verb stem, adding 시 if the stem ends in a vowel and 으시 if it ends in a consonant.

  시아버지가 이웃 마을 친구집에 **가셨어요**.

  The father-in-law went to a friend's house in a neighboring village.

- **까지 Particle expressing "to," "as far as"**

  It is attached to time or place to indicate when a particular situation ends.

  밤 늦게까지 집에 안 돌아오셨어요.

  He didn't come home even when it got late.

- **안 For general negation**

  안 is a shorter way of making negative sentences and is placed in front of the verb.

  집에 **안** 돌아오셨어요.

  He didn't come home.

- **고 있다 "is doing" (currently, at this moment)**

  This verb form expresses the progression or continuation of an action and is the equivalent of "-ing" in English.

  호랑이 등에는 아기가 **타고 있었어요**.

  The child was riding on the tiger's back.

After reading the story

1. 며느리는 왜 돈을 벌어야 했어요?

   Why did the daughter-in-law have to earn money?

2. 며느리는 누구와 같이 살았어요?

   Who did the daughter-in-law live with?

3. 며느리가 집에 왔을 때 왜 놀랐어요?

   Why was the daughter-in-law shocked when she got home?

4. 누가 아기를 집에 데려다 주었어요?

   Who brought the child home?

Let's talk!

지금은 한국에서 야생 호랑이를 거의 찾아 보기 어렵지만 예전에는 가장 크고 무서운 동물이었습니다. 여러분 나라에서는 어떤 동물이 가장 크고 무서운 동물인가요?

Nowadays, it's hard to find a wild tiger in Korea, but in olden times the tiger was the biggest and scariest animal around. What is the biggest and scariest animal in your country?

Notes on Korean culture

In Korea, devotion to your parents is considered very important. Koreans were even taught to prioritize their parents above their own children. In this story, even the tiger is moved by the daughter-in-law living so diligently with her father-in-law. That's why the tiger looks after both the father-in-law and the child. And Koreans have always thought of the tiger as the scariest of animals.

은혜 갚은 황새

옛날에 어떤 농부가 나무 위에서 황새들이 우는 것을 보았어요. 나무 위를 보니까 큰 뱀 한 마리가 황새 새끼를 먹으려고 하는 거예요. 농부는 새끼들이 불쌍했어요. 그래서 창으로 뱀을 찔렀어요. 그러니까 뱀이 죽었어요.

몇 달 후 농부는 잉어 한 마리를 잡았어요. 그것을 집에 가지고 와서 요리해서 먹었어요. 그러자 농부의 몸이 시퍼렇게 변했어요. 의사도 치료할 수 없어서 농부는 곧 죽을 것 같았어요. 그런데 갑자기 많은 황새들이 날아와서 이 농부의 몸을 쪼았어요. 그 황새 중에는 농부가 살려 준 새끼 황새도 있었어요. 농부의 몸에서 나쁜 피가 나왔어요. 그것은 독이었어요. 농부는 다시 건강해졌어요.

농부는 잉어를 요리한 솥을 다시 봤어요. 그곳에는 창 조각이 들어있었어요. 농부는 생각했어요.

"아, 창으로 뱀을 찔러 죽였는데 그 뱀이 복수하려고 잉어로 태어났구나. 그걸 알고 황새가 와서 나를 살려 준 거야."

☆ ☆ ☆

A Grateful Stork

Long ago, a farmer heard the squawking of some storks in a tree. Looking up to the tree, he saw a big snake that was going to eat one of the stork chicks. The farmer felt sorry for the chicks, so he stabbed the snake with his spear and it died.

A few months later, the farmer caught a carp. He brought it home, cooked it and ate it. Then the farmer's body turned blue. The doctor couldn't cure him and it looked as if the farmer would die soon.

But suddenly a lot of storks came flying and pecked at the farmer's body. Among those storks was the chick that the farmer had saved. Some bad blood came out of the farmer's body. It was venom. And the farmer got well again.

The farmer looked again at the cauldron in which he had cooked the carp. In it was a piece of his spear.

"Oh, so I killed that snake with my spear and it was reborn as a carp to get revenge," thought the farmer. "The stork knew that, so it came to save me."

Vocabulary

은혜를 갚다 **eunhereul gapda** to repay one's kindness
황새 **hwangsae** stork
농부 **nongbu** farmer
나무 위에서 **namu wieseo** in the tree
울다 **ulda** to cry, squawk, etc. (animal sound)
큰 뱀 **keun baem** big snake
한 **han** one
마리 **mari** counter for animals
새끼 **saekki** young (animals)
불쌍하다 **bulssanghada** to pity
그래서 **geuraeseo** so, therefore
창 **chang** spear
찌르다 **jjireuda** to poke, to stab
그러니까 **geureonikka** so, then
몇 **myeot** several
달 **dal** month
후 **hu** after
잉어 **ingeo** carp
잡다 **japda** to fish, to catch
가지고 오다 **gajigo oda** to bring (something)
요리하다 **yorihada** to cook
그러자 **geureoja** (and) then
몸 **mom** body

시퍼렇다 **sipeoreota** to be blue
변하다 **byeonhada** to turn
의사 **uisa** (medical) doctor
고치다 **gochida** to treat, to cure
곧 **got** soon
많다 **manta** to be many, to be much
날아오다 **naraoda** to fly
쪼다 **jjoda** to peck
중에는 **jungeneun** between, among
살려 주다 **sallyeo juda** to save
나쁘다 **nappeuda** to be bad
피 **pi** blood
나오다 **naoda** to come out
독 **dok** venom
다시 건강해지다 **dasi geonganghaejida** to regain one's health
솥 **sot** Korean traditional cast-iron cauldron
조각 **jogak** piece
들어있다 **deureoitda** to be contained
생각하다 **saenggakhada** to think
복수하다 **boksuhada** to get revenge
태어나다 **taeeonada** to be born
알다 **alda** to know
오다 **oda** to come

Selected grammar points

- 는 것 **Changing verbs to nouns**
  Some action verbs can change into nouns by simply adding 는 것to the verb stem.
  농부가 황새들이 우는 것을 보았어요.
  A farmer heard the squawking of some storks.

- (으)려고 하다 **"intend to"**
  This form is used to talk about plans or intentions.
  큰 뱀 한 마리가 황새 새끼를 먹으려고 하는 거예요.
  A big snake that was going to eat one of the stork chicks.

- (으)로 **Instrument particle "by," "with/using," "from"**
  This is used for means of transport, or tools and materials used to make or do something. 으로 is added to nouns ending in a consonant except ㄹ. 로 is added to nouns ending in vowels or ㄹ.

창으로 뱀을 찔렀어요.

He stabbed the snake with his spear.

- **(으)ㄹ 수 있다/없다 "can/can't"**

These forms express ability or possibility. When someone or something is able to do something, or when something is possible, (으)ㄹ 수 있다 is used, and when someone or something is not able to do something, or when something is not possible, (으)ㄹ 수 없다 is used.

의사도 **치료할 수 없어서** 농부는 곧 죽을 것 같았어요.

The doctor couldn't cure him and it looked as if the farmer would die soon.

- **도 Inclusive particle "also"**

This particle attaches directly to nouns and other particles to give the meaning "also," "too," in "addition."

농부가 살려 준 **새끼도** 있었어요.

There was the chick that the farmer had saved as well.

- **(으)려고 "in order to"**

This expresses doing one thing in order to/intending to do something else.

뱀이 **복수하려고** 잉어로 태어났구나.

It was reborn as a carp to get revenge.

After reading the story

1. 농부는 왜 뱀을 찔렀어요?

   Why did the farmer spear the snake?

2. 농부가 잉어를 먹자 어떻게 되었어요?

   What happened when the farmer ate the carp?

3. 황새들이 왜 왔어요?

   Why did the storks come?

4. 농부의 몸에서 무엇이 나왔어요?

   What came out of the farmer's body?

Let's talk!

여러분은 도움을 받은 적이 있지요? 도움을 준 사람한테 무엇을 해 줬는지 이야기해 보세요.

Have you ever been helped by someone? How did you repay the person who helped you?

Notes on Korean culture

In Korean the word 보은 **boeun** (requital) refers to repaying kindness. There's an important teaching that people have a duty to remember the kindness they've received and pay it back. In this story, the stork remembered the kindness of the farmer that saved it and in return came to save the farmer when he was sick. Through stories like this, children learn to be thankful for what they receive and to want to give something in return.

세상에서 제일 무서운 것

어떤 할아버지가 도깨비와 친구가 되었어요. 하지만 할아버지는 자기도 도깨비가 될까 봐 걱정이 되었어요. 할아버지가 도깨비한테 물었어요.

"너는 이 세상에서 무엇이 제일 무섭니?"

"저는 빨간 피가 제일 무서워요."

이번에는 도깨비가 할아버지한테 물었어요.

"그럼, 할아버지는 무엇이 제일 무서우세요?"

"나는 세상에서 돈이 제일 무서워. 돈 때문에 사람들이 죽기도 하고 살기도 하니까 말이야."

도깨비가 돌아간 후에 할아버지는 돼지 피를 마당에 뿌려 놓았어요. 밤에 할아버지를 만나러 온 도깨비는 빨간 피를 보고 놀라서 도망을 갔어요.

"착한 도깨비야, 미안해. 너는 도깨비이고 나는 사람이라서 어쩔 수가 없어." 할아버지는 마음 속으로 사과했어요.

그런데 다음 날 밤에 도깨비가 또 다시 나타났어요. 그리고 돈이 있는 자루를 던지고 갔어요.

☆ ☆ ☆

The Scariest Thing in the World

An old man became friends with a goblin. But the old man grew worried that he would turn into a goblin himself.

The old man asked the goblin, "What's the scariest thing in the world to you?"

"For me, the scariest thing is red blood."

Then the goblin asked the old man, "So, what's the scariest thing to you?"

"I think money is the scariest thing in the world, because people live and die for money."

After the goblin went home, the old man spread some pig's blood in the yard. When the goblin came to see him at night, it saw the red blood and ran away in fright.

In his mind, the old man apologized. "I'm sorry, kindly goblin. It can't be helped, because you're a goblin and I'm a man."

However, the next night, the goblin appeared again. It threw down a bag of money and went away.

☆ ☆ ☆

Vocabulary

세상 **sesang** world
제일 **jeil** the most
자기 **jagi** oneself
도 **do** too, also, as well
묻다 **mutda** to ask (a question)
너 **neo** you
이 **i** this
무엇 **mueot** what
빨갛다 **ppalgata** to be red
이번 **ibeon** this time
그럼 **geureom** then
돈 **don** money
때문에 **ttaemune** because of

사람들 **saramdeul** people
돼지 **dwaeji** pig
마당 **madang** yard
뿌려 놓다 **ppuryeo nota** to spread
미안하다 **mianhada** to be sorry
나 **na** I
어쩔 수(가) 없다 **eojjeol su(ga) eopda**
   to be inevitable
마음 **maeum** heart, mind
사과하다 **sagwahada** to apologize
또, 다시 **tto, dasi** again
자루 **jaru** bag
던지다 **deonjida** to throw

Selected grammar points

- 이/가 되다 **"to become an X"**

  When we want to say that something or someone becomes something or someone else we add the subject particle 이/가 to the second noun and use the final verb 되다. In these sentences it is common to find two subject particles in the same sentence.

  할아버지가 도깨비와 친구가 되었어요.

  An old man became friends with a goblin.

- 한테/에게 **Particles meaning "to"**

  This pair of particles is used to express the idea of "to (a person or thing)" or "from (a person)."

  도깨비한테 물었어요.

  He asked the goblin.

- 제일/가장 **"the most . . . of all/among all the . . ."**

  제일 or 가장 can be placed in front of a descriptive verb or adverb to create a superlative: the biggest, the best, the highest and so on.

  저는 빨간 피가 제일 무서워요.

  For me, the scariest thing is red blood.

- (으)ㄴ 후에 **"after"**

  This pattern means "after a certain period of time" or "after some action" and corresponds to "after" or "later" in English.

  도깨비가 돌아간 후에 할아버지는 돼지 피를 마당에 뿌려 놓았어요.

  After the goblin went home, the old man spread some pig's blood in the yard.

After reading the story

1. 할아버지는 무엇이 걱정이 되었어요?
   What was the old man worried about?
2. 도깨비는 무엇이 제일 무섭다고 했어요?
   What did the goblin say was the scariest thing?
3. 할아버지는 무엇이 제일 무섭다고 했어요? 그렇게 말한 이유는 뭐예요?
   What did the old man say was the scariest thing? Why did he say that?
4. 도깨비는 왜 도망을 갔어요?
   Why did the goblin run away?
5. 도깨비는 그 다음 날에 다시 왔을 때 무엇을 가지고 왔어요?
   When the goblin came back the next day, what did it bring?

Let's talk!

여러분은 이 세상에서 무엇이 제일 무서운가요?
What do you think is the scariest thing in the world?

Notes on Korean culture

A goblin, known as 도깨비 **dokkaebi**, is a kind of spirit that likes to use its extraordinary powers and abilities to enchant people and play tricks on them. It's a supernatural being rather similar to the Western concept of a fairy. Koreans think of goblins not just as frightening spirits, but rather as familiar beings like our human neighbors. The image of a goblin, benefiting humans through its foolishness and simplicity, must have eased the fear that people felt about the mysterious world of the spirits.

원앙새

사냥꾼이 새를 잡으러 갔는데 새가 별로 없었어요. 그런데 호수에서 원앙새 두 마리가 놀고 있었어요. 그래서 한 마리를 잡아서 집으로 가지고 왔어요.

그날 밤 꿈에 원앙새 한 마리가 나타나서 말했어요.

"왜 오늘 제 남편을 죽였어요? 저는 남편이 없으면 살고 싶지 않아요. 내일 저도 죽여 주세요."

다음 날 사냥꾼은 그 호수로 다시 갔어요. 호수에는 원앙새 한 마리가 슬프게 울고 있었어요. 그래서 사냥꾼은 원앙새를 활로 쏘았어요.

사냥꾼은 새들이 서로를 그렇게 사랑하는 것을 보고 감탄했어요. 그래서 두 마리를 같이 묻어 주었어요.

☆　☆　☆

Two Mandarin Ducks

A hunter went to kill some birds, but there weren't many birds around. There were only two mandarin ducks swimming on a lake. So the hunter killed one of them and took it home.

That night, a mandarin duck appeared to the hunter in a dream and said, "Why did you kill my husband today? I don't want to live without my husband. Tomorrow, please kill me too."

The next day, the hunter went back to the lake. There, a lone mandarin duck was weeping sadly. So the hunter shot the duck with an arrow.

The hunter was impressed to see how much the two birds loved each other. So he buried them both together.

Vocabulary

원앙새 **wonangsae** mandarin duck
사냥꾼 **sanyangkkun** hunter
새 **sae** bird
잡다 **japda** to catch, to kill
별로 **byeollo** especially, particularly
없다 **eopda** there is none, not to have
호수 **hosu** lake
두 (둘) **du (dul)** two
놀다 **nolda** to play
꿈 **kkum** dream
왜 **wae** why
오늘 **oneul** today

죽이다 **jugida** to kill
내일 **naeil** tomorrow
슬프게 **seulpeuge** sadly
활로 쏘다 **hwallo ssoda** to shoot with a bow
서로 **seoro** each other
그렇게 **geureoke** like that
사랑하다 **saranghada** to love
감탄하다 **gamtanhada** to be impressed
같이 **gachi** together
묻다 **mutda** to bury

Selected grammar points

■ (으)러 가다/오다 **"to go/come to (do something) . . ."**
사냥꾼이 새를 잡으러 갔는데 새가 별로 없었어요.
A hunter went to kill some birds, but there weren't many birds around.

■ (으)ㄴ/는데 **"and . . . ," "but . . ."**
This verb form is used to link two independent or loosely related clauses, with a variety of meanings ranging from "and" to "but."
사냥꾼이 새를 잡으러 갔는데 새가 별로 없었어요.
A hunter went to kill some birds, but there weren't many birds around.

■ (으)면 **Indicating assumption or supposition: "if," "when"**
This verb form is used to express the idea of "if (something happens or is so)" or "when (something happens or is so)."
저는 남편이 **없으면** 살고 싶지 않아요.
I don't want to live without my husband.

■ 고 싶다 **Expressing the wish or hope: "want to"**
This is used with an action verb stem to indicate the speaker's desire, wish or hope.
저는 남편이 없으면 살고 싶지 **않아요**.
I don't want to live without my husband.

■ 아/어 주다/드리다 **Doing and asking for favors**
These verb forms can be used to ask someone to do you a favor or to offer to do a favor for someone else. 아/어 주다 (neutral) can be used in reference to yourself and others of the same status. 아/어 드리다 (humble) is used when referring or speaking to someone of higher status.
저도 **죽여 주세요**.
Please kill me too.

After reading the story

1. 원앙새가 어디에 있었어요?
   Where were the mandarin ducks?
2. 원앙새가 꿈에 나타나서 뭐라고 했어요?
   What did the mandarin duck say when it appeared in the dream?

Let's talk!

여러분 나라에서 결혼한 부부의 사랑의 상징은 무엇인가요?

Are there any symbols for a married couple's love in your country?

Notes on Korean culture

Mandarin ducks are known for being devoted to their mates. A pair will live together for their whole lives and when the first one dies, the other one is said to stop eating and starve to death thinking of its mate. That's why, in a traditional Korean wedding, a pair of wooden mandarin ducks was always on display.

쌀 나오는 구멍

어떤 스님이 산에서 열심히 공부를 하고 있었어요. 그런데 배가 고파서 먹을 것을 찾으러 나갔어요. 그런데 어느 작은 구멍 앞에 쌀이 많이 있었어요.

"이상하다, 왜 여기에 쌀이 있지?"

스님은 쌀을 가지고 와서 밥을 해 먹었어요. 며칠 후에 그곳에 다시 갔는데 이번에도 구멍 앞에 또 쌀이 있었어요.

"참 이상한 일이네. 내가 공부를 할 수 있도록 부처님께서 이렇게 선물을 주셨나 봐."

스님은 이렇게 생각하고 더 열심히 공부했어요.

같이 사는 욕심쟁이 스님이 이 이야기를 들었어요.

"이 구멍은 쌀이 나오는 구멍이구나. 구멍 속에는 쌀이 정말 많을 거야."

욕심쟁이 스님은 삽으로 구멍을 파기 시작했어요. 하지만 쌀은 나오지 않았어요. 너무 파니까 흙이 쏟아지면서 구멍이 막혀 버렸어요. 그리고 그 다음부터는 다시는 쌀이 나오지 않게 되었어요.

☆ ☆ ☆

Rice from a Hole

A monk was studying hard in the mountains. Growing hungry, he went out to get something to eat. He found a lot of uncooked rice next to a little hole in the ground.

"That's strange, why is there rice here?" he asked himself.

The monk took the rice, cooked it and ate it.

A few days later he went back to the same place and again there was rice outside the hole.

"This is really strange. Buddha must have sent me this gift to help me study."

With that thought, the monk studied all the harder.

A greedy monk who lived in the same temple heard the story.

"So this is the hole where rice comes out," he thought. "There must really be a lot of rice inside the hole."

The greedy monk began to dig out the hole with a spade. But no rice came out. Because he dug too much, the soil fell in and the hole became blocked. And after that, no more rice came out.

Vocabulary

쌀 **ssal** uncooked rice

구멍 **gumeong** hole

스님 **seunim** monk

공부를 하다 **gongbureul hada** to study

배가 고프다 **baega gopeuda** to be hungry

나가다 **nagada** to go out

작다 **jakda** to be small

앞 **ap** in front of, next to

이상하다 **isanghada** to be strange, unusual

밥을 하다 **babeul hada** to cook rice

며칠 **myeochil** a few days

후에 **hue** after

참 **cham** really

이상한 일 **isanghan il** unusual thing

내가 **naega** I

부처님 **bucheonim** Buddha

이렇게 **ireoke** like this

선물 **seonmul** present, gift

욕심쟁이 **yoksimjaengi** greedy person

듣다 **deutda** to hear, to listen

삽 **sap** shovel, spade

시작하다 **sijakhada** to start, to begin

쏟아지다 **ssodajida** to pour (out of)

막히다 **makida** to be plugged, to be blocked

Selected grammar points

- (으)ㄴ/는/(으)ㄹ **Modifier**

  In Korean, modifiers function like adjectives in English.

  작은 구멍 앞에 쌀이 많이 있었어요.

  He found a lot of uncooked rice next to a little hole.

- 나 보다 **"it seems that," "I think that"**

  This indicates a conjecture after witnessing a certain situation.

  부처님께서 이렇게 선물을 주셨나 봐.

  Buddha must have sent me this gift.

- ㄹ **Irregular verbs**

  For a few verb stems that end in ㄹ, ㄹ is omitted when adding an ending that begins with ㄴ, ㅂ or ㅅ. But when used with vowels, ㄹ is not omitted.

  같이 사는 욕심쟁이 스님이 이 이야기를 들었어요.

  A greedy monk who lived in the same temple heard the story.

- ㄷ **Irregular verbs**

  For a few verb stems that end in ㄷ, ㄷ changes to ㄹ when added to an ending that begins with a vowel.

  같이 사는 욕심쟁이 스님이 이 이야기를 들었어요.

  A greedy monk who lived in the same temple heard the story.

- (으)니까 **"because"**

This connective ending (으)니까 is used with the verb stem to indicate the reason or cause of the next clause.

너무 **파니까** 흙이 쏟아지면서 구멍이 막혀 버렸어요.

Because he dug too much, the soil fell in and the hole became blocked.

- 아/어 버리다 **"gets it (all) done," "does to my disappointment," "does to my relief"**

This is used to indicate that nothing is left, a burden is relieved, or there is a sense of regret and sorrow once an action is completed.

너무 파니까 흙이 쏟아지면서 구멍이 **막혀 버렸어요**.

Because he dug too much, the soil fell in and the hole became blocked.

After reading the story

1. 스님은 어디에서 공부를 하고 있었어요?

   Where was the monk studying?
2. 스님은 구멍 앞에서 무엇을 발견했어요?

   What did the monk find next to the hole?
3. 욕심쟁이 스님은 왜 구멍을 팠어요?

   Why did the greedy monk dig out the hole?
4. 구멍이 어떻게 되었어요?

   What happened to the hole?

Let's talk!

만족을 모르고 너무 욕심을 부리다가 가지고 있던 것도 잃게 되는 경우가 있지요? 이런 경우에 대해서 이야기해 봅시다.

By not being satisfied and trying to get more, there are times when we lose what we already had. Can you think of an example of this?

Notes on Korean culture

Among traditional Korean folktales, there are many stories about greedy people being punished. In these stories, people lose everything by being too greedy. Satisfying our desires to a reasonable extent makes us happy, but if we want too much, we end up regretting it. This message surely has resonance in today's materialistic society, when we are never satisfied and always wanting more.

독수리가 된 왕

한 나라가 날아다니는 기계를 발명했어요. 그 이야기를 이웃 나라의 왕이 들었어요. 그런데 날아다니는 사람이 있다고 잘못 들었어요. 그래서 날아다니는 기계를 만든 나라의 왕한테 편지를 보냈어요.

"날아다니는 사람을 보내라. 그렇지 않으면 전쟁을 할 것이다."

편지를 받은 왕은 걱정이 되었어요. "날 수 있는 사람은 없는데 어떡하지?"

그때 어떤 사람이 입으면 날아다닐 수 있는 외투를 도깨비에게서 받았어요. 이 사람은 이것을 가지고 이웃 나라로 갔어요. 그리고 이웃 나라의 왕 앞에서 이 외투를 입고 위로 날아올랐어요.

왕이 말했어요. "나도 날아 보고 싶어."

이 사람은 왕한테 외투를 입혀 주었어요. 그런데 왕은 단추를 떼면 다시 땅으로 내려온다는 것을 배우기 전에 하늘로 올라갔어요. 그래서 그 왕은 하늘에서 내려올 수 없었어요. 결국 왕은 날아다니다가 독수리가 되고 말았어요.

☆ ☆ ☆

The King Who Became an Eagle

A certain country invented a flying machine. The king of a neighboring country heard about it, but he misunderstood and thought that there was a flying *person*. He sent a letter to the king of the country that had made the flying machine.

"Send me the flying man. Otherwise I will declare war."

The king who received the letter was worried. "There is no flying man—what should I do?"

Then someone received from a goblin a coat that would enable the wearer to fly. This person took the coat to the neighboring country and in front of the king he put the coat on and flew up.

"I want to try flying too," said the king.

The man put the coat on the king. But the king flew up into the sky before learning that he had to take off a button to come back down to the ground. So the king couldn't come down from the sky. In the end, the king just flew around until he turned into an eagle.

☆ ☆ ☆

Vocabulary

독수리 **doksuri** eagle

왕 **wang** king

나라 **nara** nation, country

날아다니다 **naradanida** to fly

기계 **gigye** machine

발명하다 **balmyeonghada** to invent

잘못 **jalmot** wrongly, mistake

만들다 **mandeulda** to make

한테 **hante** to (a person)

편지 **pyeonji** letter

보내다 **bonaeda** to send

그렇지 않으면 **geureochi aneumyeon** otherwise

전쟁을 하다 **jeonjaengeul hada** to make war

받다 **batda** to receive

어떡하지? **eotteokhaji** what should (I) do?

입다 **ipda** to wear

에게서 **egeseo** from (a person)

이것 **igeot** this

가지고 가다 **gajigo gada** to take (something)

위로 **wiro** upwards

날아오르다 **naraoreuda** to fly high

외투 **oetu** coat

입혀 주다 **ipyeo juda** to help someone on with their clothes

단추 **danchu** button

떼다 **tteda** to take off

내려오다 **naeryeooda** to come down

배우다 **baeuda** to learn

전에 **jeone** before

올라가다 **ollagada** to go up, to rise

결국 **gyeolguk** in the end

Selected grammar points

■ 한테서/에게서 **Animate source particles meaning "from"**

These particles mark the source of an action or an item.

외투를 도깨비에게서 받았어요 . . .

Someone received from a goblin a coat . . .

■ 아/어 보다 **"try to," "attempt to"**

This form expresses trying out or experiencing an action. In general, when used with the present tense, it expresses trying something.

나도 날아 보고 싶어.

I want to try flying too.

■ 기 전에 **"before"**

This pattern means "before a certain period of time" or "before some action," and corresponds to "before" or "ago" in English.

왕은 단추를 떼면 다시 땅으로 내려온다는 것을 배우기 전에 하늘로 올라갔어요.

The king flew up into the sky before learning that he had to take off a button to come back down to the ground.

- 고 말다 **"unfortunately/unintentionally ended up V-ing"**
  This expression refers to an unplanned event or action that continued until it was
  completed or thoroughly finished in a way undesired by the speaker.
  결국 왕은 날아다니다가 독수리가 **되고 말았어요**.
  In the end, the king just flew around until he turned into an eagle.

After reading the story

1. 무엇을 발명했어요?
   What was the new invention?
2. 이웃 나라의 왕은 무엇을 발명했다고 생각했어요?
   What did the king of the neighboring country think had been invented?
3. 이 사람은 어떻게 날 수 있었어요?
   How was a man able to fly?
4. 이웃 나라의 왕은 왜 하늘에서 내려올 수 없었어요?
   Why couldn't the king of the neighboring country come down from the sky?
5. 이웃 나라의 왕은 무엇이 되었어요?
   What happened to the king of the neighboring country?

Let's talk!

날아다닐 수 있는 옷과 같이 신기한 물건을 가질 수 있다면 여러분은 무엇을 가지고
싶습니까? 그것으로 무엇을 하고 싶습니까?
If you could own a magical object such as clothing that enabled you to fly, what would
you like to have? What would you do with it?

Notes on Korean culture

It seems that people have always longed to be able to fly like a bird. Koreans of old in-
dulged in this dream by flying kites. Kite-flying was a traditional pastime all over Korea
around Lunar New Year. Korean kites were rectangular in shape, with a round hole in
the middle so that a strong wind could blow through and not damage the kite. They
could fly high and move around freely. Contests were held where one kite would try to
cut another's string using friction. These games became village festivals that attracted
crowds of spectators as well as kite-flyers.

거저 먹은 술

옛날에 막걸리 장수가 막걸리를 가지고 팔러 다녔어요. 하지만 한 잔도 팔지 못했어요.

날이 더워서 나무 아래에 앉아서 잠깐 쉬기로 했어요.

그때 동동주 술장수도 더워서 그곳에 쉬려고 앉았어요.

"저는 오늘 한 잔도 못 팔았어요."

"저도요. 아침부터 다녔는데 한 잔도 못 팔았네요."

막걸리 장수는 술을 마시고 싶었어요. 그렇지만 자기 막걸리는 팔아야 되기 때문에 먹고 싶은 마음을 꾹 참고 있었어요. 그런데 마침 동동주 장수가 왔으니까 동동주를 한 잔 사 마시기로 했어요.

"그렇지 않아도 술 한잔 마시고 싶었는데 잘 됐네요. 동동주 한 잔만 주세요."

"아, 좋지요. 여기 있습니다. 맛있게 드세요."

동동주 장수는 돈을 받고 술을 따라 주었어요. 막걸리 장수는 동동주를 맛있게 마셨어요.

Free Drinks

Long ago, a merchant went around trying to sell *makgeolli* rice wine. But he couldn't even sell a single cup. It was a hot day and he decided to sit down under a tree and rest for a while.

Then a *dongdongju* rice-wine seller also sat down there to rest from the heat.

"I haven't been able to sell a single cup today."

"Me neither. I've been going around since the morning, but I couldn't sell a single cup."

The makgeolli seller wanted to drink some wine. But as his own makgeolli was for selling, he was firmly suppressing his desire to drink. But now that the dongdongju seller had come along, he decided to have a cup of dongdongju.

"I wanted to have a drink anyway, so this is lucky. Give me just one cup of dongdongju."

"OK. Here it is. Enjoy it."

The dongdongju seller received the money and poured out the wine. The makgeolli seller enjoyed his drink of dongdongju.

그것을 보니 동동주 장수도 술이 마시고 싶어졌어요. 그리고 또 술을 팔았기 때문에 돈이 생겨서 기분도 좋았어요.

동동주 장수가 막걸리 장수에게 말했어요.

"저도 한잔 해야겠어요. 막걸리 한 잔만 주세요."

동동주 장수는 막걸리 장수에게서 받은 돈을 주고 막걸리 한 잔을 사서 맛있게 마셨어요.

이것을 보고 막걸리 장수도 더 마시고 싶어졌어요.

"저는 한 잔으로 부족하네요. 저도 이제 돈을 좀 벌었으니 한 잔만 더 주세요."

막걸리 장수는 동동주 장수에게서 받은 돈을 다시 주고 동동주 한 잔을 더 사 마셨어요.

이번에는 동동주 장수가 말했어요.

"저도 아무래도 한 잔으로는 부족하군요. 저도 한 잔 더 해야겠어요."

동동주 장수는 자기가 받은 돈을 다시 막걸리 장수에게 주고 막걸리를 한 잔 받아서 마셨어요.

이렇게 두 사람은 하루 종일 서로 돈을 주고 받으면서 술을 다 마셔 버렸어요.

그런데 오늘은 정말 운이 좋은 하루인 것 같았어요.

술도 다 팔았고 돈을 하나도 쓰지 않고도 술을 사 마실 수 있었기 때문이에요. 두 사람은 행복해져서 웃으면서 자기 집으로 돌아갔어요.

☆ ☆ ☆

Vocabulary

거저 먹다 **geojeo meokda** to eat/drink for free

막걸리 **makgeolli** makgeolli rice wine

장수 **jangsu** seller, merchant

가지다 **gajida** to have

팔다 **palda** to sell

다니다 **danida** to go around

한 잔 **han jan** a glass of (alcohol)

날 **nal** day

덥다 **deopda** to be hot

나무 **namu** tree

아래 **arae** under

앉다 **antta** to sit

잠깐 **jamkkan** for a while

쉬다 **shida** to rest

동동주 **dongdongju** dongdongju rice wine

그렇지만 **geureochiman** but, however

꾹 참다 **kkuk chamda** to bear patiently

마침 **machim** just in time

Seeing that, the dongdongju seller started to want a drink too. And as he had just sold some wine, he had some money and was in a good mood.

The dongdongju seller said to the makgeolli seller, "I'll have a drink too. Give me just one cup of makgeolli."

The dongdongju seller gave back the money he had received from the makgeolli seller to pay for the cup of makgeolli, which he drank with pleasure.

Seeing this, the makgeolli seller wanted to drink some more.

"One cup is not enough for me. Now I've made some money too, so give me just one more cup."

The makgeolli seller gave back the money he had received from the dongdongju seller to buy another cup of dongdongju, which he drank.

This time, the dongdongju seller spoke.

"One cup doesn't seem to be enough for me either. I'll have to have another cup too."

The dongdongju seller gave the money he had received back to the makgeolli seller, received a cup of makgeolli and drank it.

In this way, the two men spent the whole day giving the money back and forth to each other until they had drunk up all the wine.

This did seem a lucky day for them. They had sold all their wine and they'd been able to drink without spending any money at all. The two men were so happy that they went home laughing.

☆ ☆ ☆

잘 됐다 **jal dwaetda** That's great!
  This is lucky!
따라 주다 **ttara juda** to pour
맛있게 마시다 **masitge masida**
  to enjoy (a drink)
돈이 생기다 **doni saenggida** to get
  money
기분이 좋다 **gibuni jota** to be in a
  good mood
주다 **juda** to give
더 **deo** more
부족하다 **bujokhada** to be insufficient

아무래도 **amuraedo** it seems
한 잔 더 하다 **han jan deo hada** to have
  another drink
하루 종일 **haru jongil** all day
다 **da** all
운이 좋다 **uni jota** to be lucky
하나도 **hanado** even one
쓰다 **sseuda** to use, to spend
사다 **sada** to buy
행복하다 **haengbokhada** to be happy
웃다 **utda** to laugh

Selected grammar points

- 지 못하다 **"not being able to"**

  This pattern can be attached to the verb stem of any action verb and indicates that the subject of the sentence lacks the ability to carry out the action or that some external circumstance prevents him/her from doing it.

  한 잔도 팔지 못했어요.

  He couldn't even sell a single cup.

- 기로 하다 **"decide to do X"**

  잠깐 쉬기로 했어요.

  He decided to rest for a while.

- 못 **"not being able to"**

  This is a shorter form of 지 못하다, in which 못 is placed before the verb.

  한 잔도 못 팔았어요.

  He couldn't even sell a single cup.

- ㅂ니다/습니다 **Formal style verb ending**

  To make the present statement form of any Korean verb in the formal style, take the verb stem and add ㅂ니다 or 습니다. ㅂ니다 is added to verb stems ending in a vowel. 습니다 is added to verb stems ending in a consonant.

  여기 있습니다.

  Here it is.

- 만 **Exclusive particle "only," "just"**

  This particle expresses the choosing of one thing to the exclusion of the other things.

  동동주 한 잔만 주세요.

  Give me just one cup of dongdongju.

- 기 때문에 **"because"**

  This verb form is used in the first clause to explain the reason for what happens in the second. It cannot be used if the second clause ends in a command or suggestion: in these cases you must use (으)니까.

  술을 팔았기 때문에 돈이 생겨서 기분도 좋았어요.

  As he had just sold some wine, he had some money and was in a good mood.

After reading the story

1. 왜 막거리 장수는 자기의 막걸리를 마시지 않았어요?
   Why didn't the makgeolli seller drink his own makgeolli?
2. 동동주 장수가 동동주를 판 돈으로 무엇을 했어요?
   What did the dongdongju seller do with the money he had made from selling dong-dongju?
3. 두 사람은 술을 팔아서 돈을 벌었나요?
   Did the two men make money from selling their wine?
4. 두 사람은 왜 운이 좋다고 느꼈어요?
   Why did the two men feel that they were lucky?

Let's talk!

여러분 나라의 전통 술에는 무엇이 있나요?
What kinds of traditional liquor are there in your country?

Notes on Korean culture

Dongdongju (동동주) and **makgeolli** (막걸리) are two similar kinds of wine made by fermenting rice. Ordinary people used to make and drink them at home or make a lot and go around the villages selling it. This rather ridiculous story tells of two men who were happy because they were able to drink without spending any money. Does their happiness mean that the story ends well? One can't help but wonder what their wives will say to them when they get home!

느티나무 총각

어느 마을에 할아버지하고 할머니가 사셨어요. 어느 해 겨울에 눈이 너무 많이 와서 산에 가서 땔나무를 해 올 수가 없었어요. 그래서 아궁이에 불을 피울 수가 없어서 너무 추웠어요.

그런데 이 마을에는 아주 오래된 느티나무가 있었어요.

마을의 젊은이들이 말했어요. "추워서 얼어 죽겠어요. 저 느티나무라도 베어서 땔나무로 사용합시다."

할아버지는 그것을 보고 말씀하셨어요.

"저 나무는 오랫동안 우리와 같이 살아온 나무인데 어떻게 벨 수 있겠는가?"

"땔나무는 없고 눈은 이렇게 많이 오는데, 그럼 어떻게 해요?"

"그러면, 나무는 베지 말고 우리 집 행랑채를 뜯어서 써."

옆에 있던 할머니가 걱정을 하셨어요. "내년 봄에는 머슴이 살아야 할 텐데 행랑채가 없으면 우리는 어떻게 해요?"

할아버지는 대답하셨어요.

"그래도 살아있는 나무를 함부로 베면 안 돼."

이렇게 행랑채는 없어지고 느티나무는 베이지 않게 되었어요.

The Zelkova Tree Bachelor

An old man and woman lived in a certain village. One winter, it snowed so much that they couldn't go out to the hills to gather firewood. So they couldn't light a fire in their hearth and they were terribly cold.

In this village there was a very old zelkova tree. The young people of the village said, "It's so cold we're freezing to death. Let's at least cut down that zelkova tree and use it for firewood."

Hearing this, the old man said, "That tree has lived beside us for ages—how can you cut it down?"

"Then what are we to do when there's no firewood and so much snow?"

"Don't cut the tree down, just take apart the servants' quarters of our house and use that."

The old woman, who was beside him, got worried. "The farmhands will need to sleep there in the spring—how can we manage without servants' quarters?"

The old man answered, "Even so, you can't just thoughtlessly cut down a living tree."

And so the servants' quarters were dismantled and the zelkova tree was not cut down.

봄이 되었어요. 그런데 행랑채가 없어서 머슴을 살겠다고 오는 사람이 없었어요.

그런데 어느 날 총각 한 명이 와서 머슴을 살겠다고 했어요.

"우리 집에는 행랑채가 없어. 그래서 잘 곳이 없어."

"괜찮습니다. 낮에 와서 일하고 밤에는 우리 집에 가서 잘게요."

"그럼, 돈을 얼마나 주어야 할까?"

"저는 일을 잘 할 줄 모릅니다. 그래서 일 배우는 셈치고 시키는 일만 할 테니까 돈 걱정은 하지 마세요."

이렇게 해서 총각이 일을 하게 되었어요. 총각은 놀지 않고 일을 아주 열심히 했어요. 그래서 농사가 아주 잘 되었어요.

가을이 되어 농사가 다 끝났어요.

"이제 더 이상 할 일이 없으니 저는 이제 집으로 돌아가겠습니다."

이 말을 들은 할아버지는 총각에게 돈을 주려고 하셨어요.

"그동안 열심히 일 해 줘서 고마워. 많지는 않지만 이 돈을 받아 가지고 가."

하지만 총각이 말했어요.

"저는 돈을 벌려고 온 것이 아니에요. 할아버지가 저를 살려 주셔서 은혜를 갚으려고 일한 거예요. 그러니까 걱정하지 마세요."

이 총각은 바로 느티나무 신령이었어요. 마을 사람들은 느티나무를 아끼면서 잘 살았어요

☆ ☆ ☆

Vocabulary

느티나무 **neutinamu** zelkova tree

총각 **chonggak** bachelor, unmarried man

해 **hae** year

겨울 **gyeoul** winter

눈이 오다 **nuni oda** to snow

땔나무를 하다 **ttaellamureul hada** to gather firewood

아궁이 **agungi** fireplace, hearth

불을 피우다 **bureul piuda** to make a fire

춥다 **chupda** to be cold

오래되다 **oraedoeda** to be old

젊은이 **jeolmeuni** young person

얼다 **eolda** to freeze

베다 **beda** to cut

사용하다 **sayonghada** to use

말씀하다 **malsseumhada** [honorific] to say, to speak

오랫동안 **oraetdongan** for a long time

우리와 **uriwa** with us

살아오다 **saraoda** to live

그러면 **geureomyeon** then

행랑채 **haengnangchae** servants' quarters

The spring arrived. But no one came to work as a farmhand as there were no servants' quarters.

Then one day, an unmarried man came saying he wanted to work as a farmhand.

"Our house has no servants' quarters, so there's nowhere to sleep."

"That's OK. I'll come to work in the daytime and go home to sleep at night."

"Then, how much will we have to pay you?"

"I don't know how to do the work well. Let's just say I'm learning the job and I'll do whatever work you give me, so don't worry about money."

In this way, the bachelor came to do the work. He worked very hard, without shirking. As a result, the farming was very successful.

In the autumn, the farm work was finished.

"There's no more work to do, so I'll go home now."

On hearing this, the old man was about to give the bachelor some money.

"Thank you for working so hard all this time. It's not much, but take this money with you."

But the bachelor said, "I didn't come here to earn money. I worked to repay the kindness you showed when you saved me. So don't worry about anything."

For this bachelor was none other than the spirit of the zelkova tree. After this, the villagers lived well, cherishing their zelkova tree.

☆ ☆ ☆

뜯다 **tteutda** to take (something) apart
걱정하다 **geokjeonghada** to worry
내년 **naenyeon** next year
봄 **bom** spring (season)
머슴 **meoseum** servant
대답하다 **daedaphada** to answer
함부로 **hamburo** carelessly, thoughtlessly
명 **myeong** counter for a person
잘 곳 **jal got** a place to sleep
괜찮다 **gwaenchanta** to be alright
낮 **nat** daytime
일하다 **ilhada** to work
자다 **jada** to sleep

얼마나 **eolmana** how much
놀다 **nolda** to idle, shirk
농사가 잘 되다 **nongsaga jal doeda** to have a good harvest
가을 **gaeul** autumn
끝나다 **kkeunnada** to finish
이제 더 이상 **ije deo isang** no longer
그동안 **geudongan** all the while
고맙다 **gomapda** to thank
바로 **baro** the very, none other than
신령 **sillyeong** spirit
아끼다 **akkida** to cherish

Selected grammar points

- **(이)라도 "even if only," "at least"**

  This form can be used when something is not ideal, but is acceptable for now.

  저 느티나무라도 베어서 땔나무로 사용합시다.

  Let's at least cut down that zelkova tree and use it for firewood.

- **(으)ㅂ시다 "let's"**

  This verb ending can be used in a formal situation in which the speaker is suggesting or inviting a group of people to do something, or when the listener is younger or of lower status than the speaker.

  저 느티나무라도 베어서 땔나무로 사용합시다.

  Let's at least cut down that zelkova tree and use it for firewood.

- **(으)ㄹ 텐데 "I expect that X will happen," "it will be X"**

  In the first clause of the sentence, a strong intention or expectation about a future event or situation is given and in the second clause, following (으)ㄹ 텐데, a statement either related or contrary to the first clause given.

  머슴이 살아야 할 텐데 행랑채가 없으면 우리는 어떻게 해요?

  The farmhands will need to sleep there in the spring—how can we manage without servants' quarters?

- **다고 하다 Reported speech: "(somebody) says that . . ."**

  To turn direct into indirect speech, simply add 고 하다 to the plain form.

  총각 한 명이 와서 머슴을 살겠다고 했어요.

  An unmarried man came saying he wanted to work as a farmhand.

- **(으)ㄹ 줄 알다/모르다 "knows/does not know how to do X"**

  This pattern expresses whether one knows how, or has the ability, to do something.

  저는 일을 잘 할 줄 모릅니다.

  I don't know how to do the work well.

- **(으)ㄴ/는 셈 치다 "let's just say . . ." "to assume"**

  This is used when considering a certain state of affairs to be true when they haven't occurred in reality.

  일 배우는 셈 치고 시키는 일만 할 테니까 돈 걱정은 마세요.

  Let's just say I'm learning the job and I'll do whatever work you give me, so don't worry about money.

- **지 마세요 "please don't . . ."**

  This is used for negative commands, expressing prohibition.

  돈 걱정은 하지 마세요.

  Don't worry about money.

After reading the story

1. 마을의 젊은이들은 왜 느티나무를 베고 싶어했어요?
   Why did the young people of the village want to cut down the zelkova tree?
2. 할아버지는 느티나무 대신 무엇을 쓰라고 했어요?
   What did the old man tell them to use instead of the zelkova tree?
3. 할머니는 할아버지의 말씀을 듣고 무슨 걱정을 했어요?
   What did the old woman worry about after hearing her husband's words?
4. 머슴을 살겠다고 온 총각은 잠을 어디에서 자겠다고 했어요?
   Where did the bachelor who came to work as a farmhand say he was going to sleep?
5. 할아버지가 총각에게 돈을 주려고 했을 때 총각은 뭐라고 했어요?
   What did the bachelor say when the old man was going to give him some money?

Let's talk!

여러분은 자연 보호에 대해서 어떻게 생각합니까? 자연 보호를 위해서 무엇을 하고 있나요?

What are your views on nature conservation? Do you do anything to help protect the environment?

Notes on Korean culture

In olden times, Koreans believed that even trees had spirits. In particular, the oldest tree in a village was believed to have a spirit that watched over the village. Also, when throwing hot water away on the ground, people would first shout a warning so that the living things in the ground could run away. Regarding all living things as precious, and humanity as part of nature, Koreans lived in harmony with nature and didn't harm the environment.

건달 농사꾼

어느 마을에 형제가 살았어요. 두 사람은 결혼을 한 후에도 같은 마을에서 농사를 지으면서 살았어요. 그런데 형은 부지런하지만 동생은 게을렀어요. 그래서 형은 갈수록 부자가 되고 동생은 갈수록 가난해졌어요. 겨울이 되면 동생은 먹을 것이 없어서 형에게서 곡식을 빌려다가 먹어야 했어요. 어느 해 봄에 또 동생 집에 곡식이 떨어졌어요. 그래서 할 수 없이 형을 찾아갔어요.

"형님, 농사를 지어야 하는데 밭에 뿌릴 씨도 없어서 큰일이에요. 미안하지만 조 한 자루만 빌려 주세요."

형은 동생에게 아주 좋은 조를 골라 주면서 말했어요.

"이건 우리 집에서 제일 좋은 조이니까, 가을에 수확을 하면 꼭 이렇게 좋은 것으로 갚아야 해."

동생은 형의 이야기를 듣고 서운했어요. 전에는 갚으라고 하지 않고 그냥 주었으니까요. 기분이 나빴지만 할 수 없이 가지고 왔어요.

그것을 밭에 뿌려 농사를 지었어요. 형의 말을 듣고 기분이 나빴기 때문에 전보다 조금 더 부지런히 일을 했어요. 그래서 가을에 수확한 조를 가지고 형을 찾아갔어요.

The Good-for-Nothing Farmer

Two brothers lived in a village. Even after they were both married, they went on living and farming in the same village. The elder brother was hardworking, but the younger brother was lazy. As time went by, the elder brother grew richer and the younger brother poorer. In winter, the younger brother had no food and had to borrow grain to eat from his brother. One spring, the younger brother's household ran out of grain again, so he had no choice but to go to his brother.

"Brother, I need to grow crops but I'm in big trouble because I haven't got any seeds to sow in the field. I'm sorry, but will you give me just one bag of millet?"

The elder brother chose some very good millet and gave it to his brother.

"This is the best millet in our house," he said. "When you harvest it in the autumn, be sure to repay me with grain that's equally good."

The younger brother was upset by this, because in the past his brother had just given him things without asking him to pay anything back. Although his feelings were hurt, he had no option but to take the grain.

He sowed the seeds in his field and tended to his crop. Because his brother's words had hurt his feelings, he worked a little harder than before. In the autumn, he took the grain that he had harvested to his brother.

"형님, 봄에 빌려 간 것을 가지고 왔어요."

"그래? 잘했다. 형제라도 빌려 간 것은 갚아야지. 한번 보자. 그런데 왜 이렇게 껍질만 있는 것도 있지? 내년에 농사를 더 잘 지어서 가지고 와."

동생은 화가 났어요. 다른 때보다 더 열심히 일을 했는데 형이 안 좋다고 했으니까요. 그래서 다음 해에는 농사를 더 열심히 지었어요. 그리고 가을에 다시 수확한 것을 가지고 형한테 갔어요. 형은 이번에도 가지고 온 조를 살펴보더니 말했어요.

"눈으로만 보면 알 수 없으니까 물에 담가 보자."

그러더니 조를 물에 담그는 거예요. 그랬더니 대부분 물에 가라앉았지만 물에 둥둥 뜨는 것도 있었어요. 형이 또 말했어요.

"이것도 별로 안 좋아. 다음에는 더 좋은 것으로 가지고 와."

동생은 너무나 화가 났어요. 그래서 다음 해에는 더욱더 열심히 농사를 지었어요. 그랬더니 농사가 정말 잘 되었어요. 동생은 다시 가을에 수확한 조를 가지고 형을 찾아갔어요.

"형님, 조 받으세요. 이제부터는 굶어죽더라도 다시는 형님한테 도와 달라고 하지 않겠어요."

형은 동생이 가지고 온 조를 살펴보고 말했어요.

"이번에는 정말 농사를 열심히 지었구나. 이 조는 다시 가지고 가서 가족들과 먹어라. 내가 조를 받으려고 한 게 아니야. 네가 너무 건달농사를 지어서 그 버릇을 고치려고 한 거지. 이제 어떻게 하는지 배웠으니 이제부터는 그렇게 농사를 짓고 살면 돼."

동생도 이제 형의 뜻을 알게 되었어요. 그 다음부터는 동생도 형처럼 열심히 농사를 지어서 같이 행복하게 잘 살았대요.

☆ ☆ ☆

"Brother, I've brought back what you lent me in the spring."

"Really? Well done. Even brothers must pay back what they borrow. Let's take a look. But why does some of it have only a husk like this? Grow your crops better next year and bring me some then."

The younger brother was angry, because he had worked harder than before and yet his brother said the crop wasn't good. Nevertheless, he worked even harder at his farming the following year. And in the autumn he came back to his brother again with the crop he had harvested. Once more, his brother examined the millet that he had brought.

"You can't tell just by looking, so let's soak it in water," said the elder brother.

So he soaked the millet in water. Most of it sank in the water, but some of it floated on the surface. The elder brother spoke again.

"This is not very good either. Next time, bring some better grain."

The younger brother was terribly angry. So the following year, he worked harder than ever at his farming. As a result, the crop grew really well. In the autumn, he brought the crop that he had harvested to his brother yet again.

"Brother, take this millet. From now on, I won't ask you to help me again even if I starve to death."

The elder brother examined the millet that his younger brother had brought.

"This time you've really worked hard at your farming," he said. "Take this millet back and eat it with your family. I never wanted to take your millet. I just wanted to break your habit of being a good-for-nothing farmer. Now you've learned how to do it, so from now on just go on farming like this."

Now the younger brother understood what his elder brother meant. From then on, he worked as hard as his brother at his farming and they lived happily together.

Vocabulary

건달 **geondal** wastrel, good-for-nothing

농사꾼 **nongsakkun** farmer

형제 **hyeongje** brother

결혼을 하다 **gyeolhoneul hada**
to marry

농사를 짓다 **nongsareul jitda** to farm

형 **hyeong** older brother

동생 **dongsaeng** younger brother

부지런하다 **bujireonhada** to be diligent

게으르다 **geeureuda** to be lazy

갈수록 **galsurok** as time goes by

부자 **buja** rich person

가난하다 **gananhada** to be poor

곡식 **goksik** grain

빌리다 **billida** to borrow

곡식이 떨어지다 **goksigi tteoreojida**
to run out of food

할 수 없이 **hal su eopsi** unavoidably,
without a choice

찾아가다 **chajagada** to visit

밭 **bat** field, farm

씨를 뿌리다 **ssireul ppurida** to sow
seeds

큰일이다 **keunirida** to be in trouble

조 한 자루 **jo han jaru** a bag of millet

빌려주다 **billyeojuda** to lend

좋다 **jota** to be good

고르다 **goreuda** to choose, to select

수확을 하다 **suhwageul hada** to harvest

꼭 **kkok** surely

갚다 **gapda** to pay back

서운하다 **seounhada** to be disappointed

전에는 **jeoneneun** in the past

그냥 주다 **geunyang juda** to give for free

기분이 나쁘다 **gibuni nappeuda** to be in
a bad mood

조금 **jogeum** a little

부지런히 **bujireonhi** diligently

껍질 **kkeopjil** husk

만 **man** only

화가 나다 **hwaga nada** to be angry

다른 때보다 더 **dareun ttaeboda
deo** more than usual

살펴보다 **salpyeoboda** to examine

눈 **nun** eye

물 **mul** water

담그다 **damgeuda** to soak (something)
in water

가라앉다 **garaanda** to sink

둥둥 뜨다 **dungdung tteuda** to float

별로 안 좋다 **byeollo an jota** It's not very
good.

너무나 **neomuna** too, excessively

더욱더 **deoukdeo** even more

그랬더니 **geuraetdeoni** then

굶어죽다 **gulmeojukda** die of hunger

도와 달라고 하다 **dowa dallago hada**
to ask for help

가족 **gajok** family

버릇을 고치다 **beoreuseul gochida**
to break a habit

어떻게 하는지 **eotteoke haneunji**
how to do

이제 **ije** now

뜻 **tteut** meaning

Selected grammar points

- **ㅅ Irregular verbs**

  For a few verb stems that end in ㅅ, ㅅ is omitted when followed by a vowel.

  농사를 **지으**면서 살았어요.

  They went on living and farming.

- **르 Irregular verbs**

  For verb stems that end in 르, the ㅡ of 르 is omitted when followed by a vowel and an additional ㄹ is added.

  형은 부지런하지만 동생은 **게을렀**어요.

  The elder brother was hardworking, but the younger brother was lazy.

- **(으)ㄹ수록 "the more . . . the more," "more and more"**

  This is attached to an action verb, a descriptive verb or a "noun+이다," indicating something is gradually changing as it is repeated or continued.

  형은 **갈수록** 부자가 되고 동생은 **갈수록** 가난해졌어요.

  As time went by, the elder brother grew richer and the younger brother grew poorer.

- **아/어다가 "and then . . . ," "so that . . ."**

  This form is used to indicate that an action is performed in a specified place and its result is used to carry out the action of the following statement in another place.

  형에게 곡식을 **빌려다가 먹어야** 했어요.

  He had to borrow some grain to eat from his brother.

- **보다 "than"**

  When we want to compare two things or people in Korean we attach 보다 directly to the noun being compared – the noun to which "than" refers in English sentences.

  전보다 조금 더 부지런히 일을 했어요.

  He worked a little harder than before.

- **더라도 "even if"**

  This is used to indicate that the first statement is followed by a conflicting one, while the situation described in the first statement can be assumed or admitted.

  굶어죽더라도 다시는 형님한테 도와 달라고 하지 않겠어요.

  I won't ask you to help me again even if I starve to death.

- **처럼/같이 "like"**

  We use the phrase 처럼/같이 when we want to make a comparison in the sense of "doing something like X does," "doing something as well as X does," "is as . . . as X."

  동생도 **형처럼** 열심히 농사를 지어서 같이 행복하게 잘 살았대요.

  The younger brother worked as hard as his elder brother at his farming, and they lived happily together.

After reading the story

1. 형은 왜 갈수록 부자가 되고 동생은 갈수록 가난해졌어요?
   Why did the elder brother grow richer and the younger brother grow poorer as time went by?

2. 왜 동생은 형에게 곡식을 빌려야 했어요?
   Why did the younger brother have to borrow grain from his elder brother?

3. 형은 동생에게 조를 공짜로 주었나요?
   Did the elder brother give the millet to his younger brother for nothing?

4. 동생은 빌려 온 곡식을 형에게 갚으러 몇 번을 갔나요?
   How many times did the younger brother go to pay back the grain that he had borrowed to his elder brother?

5. 형은 왜 그렇게 행동했어요?
   Why did the elder brother act as he did?

Let's talk!

영어로 "being cruel to be kind" 라는 표현이 있지요? 여러분이 형이고 게으름뱅이 동생이 있었다면 어떻게 했을 것 같아요?

In English, there is the expression "being cruel to be kind." What would you have done if you were the elder brother and you had a lazy younger brother like this?

Notes on Korean culture

Long ago, millet was a staple food in Korea, but today its place has been taken by rice. Koreans often eat rice for breakfast, lunch and dinner on the same day. That's why rice is the main agricultural crop. Growing rice is very hard work. When the seedlings reach a certain size they have to be transplanted, working in a flooded field. Some scholars believe that the tradition of cultivating rice has made Koreans particularly hardworking.

시아버지 팥죽땀

어느 집에 시아버지하고 며느리가 살았어요. 시아버지는 며느리 앞에서 어른처럼 행동하려고 조심하고, 며느리도 시아버지 앞에서 버릇없이 보이지 않으려고 조심하면서 살았어요.

어느 겨울 날에 며느리가 따뜻한 팥죽을 만들었어요. 그리고는 잠깐 밖에 나갔어요. 그런데 그 사이에 시아버지가 부엌에 들어갔어요. 부엌에는 맛있어 보이는 팥죽이 있었어요. 시아버지는 배가 고팠기 때문에 팥죽을 너무 먹고 싶었어요.

"아, 너무 맛있겠다. 그런데 며느리가 언제 올지 알 수도 없고, 그렇다고 나 혼자 먹다가 며느리가 보면 그것도 창피하고 . . . 어떻게 하지? 안되겠다. 집 뒤에 가서 아무도 모르게 먹어야지."

시아버지는 며느리가 오기 전에 몰래 먹으려고 팥죽을 그릇에 담았어요. 그리고 집 뒤로 가지고 갔어요. 혹시 며느리가 일찍 돌아와서 자기가 팥죽을 먹는 것을 보면 창피하니까요.

그 사이에 며느리가 집에 돌아왔어요. 시아버지에게 드리려고 팥죽을 가지고 갔는데 방에 안 계신 거예요.

The Man Who Sweat Porridge

In a certain house lived a daughter-in-law and her father-in-law. The father-in-law was always careful to behave like an elder in front of his daughter-in-law, while the daughter-in-law took care not to appear rude before her father-in-law.

One winter's day, the daughter-in-law cooked some warm red bean porridge. Then she went out for a while. In the meantime, her father-in-law went into the kitchen, where he saw the tasty-looking red bean porridge. The father-in-law was hungry and he badly wanted to eat the porridge.

"Ah, this will be so tasty. But I don't know when my daughter-in-law might come back and if she sees me eating this by myself, it'll be embarrassing... What should I do? It's no good. I'll have to go behind the house and eat it without anyone knowing."

The father-in-law put some of the red bean porridge in a bowl to eat it secretly before his daughter-in-law came back. And he took it behind the house, because he would be embarrassed if his daughter-in-law should come back soon and see him eating the porridge.

Meanwhile, the daughter-in-law came home. She took some of the red bean porridge to give to her father-in-law, but he wasn't in his room.

"아, 어떡하지? 아버님이 어디에 가셨나 봐. 나도 팥죽을 먹고 싶은데 기다릴 수도 없고, 그렇다고 먹다가 아버님이 갑자기 돌아오셔서 내가 먼저 먹는 것을 보면 그것도 안 되고 . . . 안 되겠다. 빨리 집 뒤에 가서 먹어야지." 며느리도 팥죽을 들고 집 뒤로 갔어요.

집 뒤에서는 시아버지가 팥죽을 맛있게 먹고 있었어요. 그런데 갑자기 며느리가 나타났어요. 시아버지는 놀라서 팥죽을 숨기려고 했는데 잘못해서 머리에 뒤집어썼어요. 그래서 팥죽이 얼굴로 줄줄 흘러내렸어요.

며느리는 시아버지 몰래 팥죽을 먹으려고 갔는데 시아버지가 보였어요. 며느리는 당황해서 말했어요.

"아버님, 팥죽 드세요."

그러니까 시아버지는, "고맙다, 그런데 나는 팥죽만 보면 이렇게 팥죽땀이 줄줄 흐르는구나." 했어요.

이렇게 며느리는 팥죽 그릇을 내밀고 서 있고, 시아버지는 팥죽 그릇을 뒤집어쓴 채 팥죽땀을 흘리고 서 있었대요.

☆ ☆ ☆

Vocabulary

팥죽 **patjuk** red bean porridge

땀 **ttam** sweat

어른처럼 **eoreuncheoreom** like an adult/elder person

행동하다 **haengdonghada** to act, to behave

조심하다 **josimhada** to be careful

버릇없이 **beoreuteopsi** rudely

보이다 **boida** to be seen, to appear

따뜻하다 **ttatteuthada** to be warm

그 사이에 **geu saie** in the meantime

부엌 **bueok** kitchen

들어가다 **deureogada** to enter

맛있다 **masitda** to be tasty

언제 **eonje** when

그렇다고 **geureotdago** be that as it may

창피하다 **changpihada** to be embarrassed

뒤 **dwi** behind

아무도 모르게 **amudo moreuge** without anyone knowing

몰래 **mollae** secretly

"Oh, what should I do? Father must have gone somewhere. I want to eat some porridge too and I can't wait, but it won't do if father suddenly comes back while I'm eating and sees that I've started before him . . . It's no good. I'll have to go and eat it quickly behind the house."

So the daughter-in-law, too, took some porridge and went behind the house.

There, her father-in-law was enjoying his red bean porridge when his daughter-in-law suddenly appeared. The father-in-law was startled and tried to hide the porridge, but by mistake he tipped it over his head. So the porridge poured down his face.

The daughter-in-law had gone to eat the porridge without her father-in-law's knowledge, but suddenly there he was. She spoke in embarrassment.

"Father, have some red bean porridge."

Then the father-in-law said "Thank you, but just seeing red bean porridge, makes me sweat porridge like this."

And so the daughter-in-law stood holding out a bowl of red bean porridge while her father-in-law stood sweating porridge with the bowl upside down on his head.

☆ ☆ ☆

그릇 **geureut** bowl
담다 **damda** to put in
혹시 **hoksi** by any chance
에게 **ege** to (a person)
방 **bang** room
계시다 **gyesida** [honorific] there is
(a person)
어디 **eodi** where
기다리다 **gidarida** to wait
들다 **deulda** to hold
숨기다 **sumgida** to hide
잘못해서 **jalmothaeseo** by mistake

머리에 뒤집어쓰다 **meorie
dwijibeosseuda** to tip (something)
on the head
얼굴 **eolgul** face
줄줄 흘러내리다 **juljul
heulleonaerida** to pour down
당황하다 **danghwanghada** to be
embarrassed
내밀다 **naemilda** to hold out
서다 **seoda** to stand
흘리다 **heullida** to shed

Selected grammar points

- 아/어 보이다 **"it looks like . . ." "it looks as if . . ."**

  This is used to indicate one's conjecture or feelings based on the outward appearance of a person, thing or event.

  맛있어 보이는 팥죽이 있었어요.

  There was some tasty-looking red bean porridge.

- 겠 **Suffix showing conjecture, supposition**

  The suffix 겠 can be used to express a supposition about a certain situation or state, corresponding to "looks like," "sounds" or "appears" in English.

  아, 너무 맛있겠다.

  Ah, this will be so tasty.

- (으)ㄴ/는/(으)ㄹ지 알다 **"(someone) knows when / where / who / what / how / why / how much, etc."**

  This form is used to express something that one knows. These patterns are used with 언제, 어디, 누구, 무엇, 어떻게, 왜, 몇, etc.

  며느리가 언제 올지 알 수도 없었어요.

  He didn't know when his daughter-in-law might come back.

- 다가 **Interrupted action**

  This form is used to indicate that one action has been interrupted and a different action is now taking place or has taken place.

  나 혼자 **먹다가** 그것을 며느리가 보면 창피하고 . . . 어떻게 하지?

  If she sees me eating this by myself, it'll be embarrassing . . . What should I do?

- (으)ㄴ 채(로) **"while (in the state of) . . ."**

  This is attached to a verb stem, indicating that the second action is being made while the preceding action is completed and maintained.

  시아버지는 팥죽 그릇을 **뒤집어쓴 채** 팥죽땀을 흘리고 서 있었대요.

  The father-in-law stood sweating porridge with the bowl upside-down on his head.

After reading the story

1. 부엌에 어떤 음식이 있었어요?
   What kind of food was in the kitchen?
2. 시아버지는 왜 부엌에서 팥죽을 먹지 않았어요?
   Why didn't the father-in-law eat the porridge in the kitchen?
3. 시아버지는 팥죽을 가지고 어디로 갔어요?
   Where did the father-in-law take the porridge?
4. 왜 팥죽이 시아버지 얼굴로 줄줄 흘러 내렸어요?
   Why was the porridge dripping over the father-in-law's face?

Let's talk!

여러분이 몰래 하려다가 들켜서 당황했던 일이 있나요?

Have you ever been discovered when you were trying to do something secretly?

Notes on Korean culture

Today, when Koreans get married they usually set up a separate household, but in the past, when a woman got married she would live with her husband's family. A daughter-in-law would always watch her behavior in front of her father-in-law because he was an elder. But the father-in-law also felt that he had to preserve his dignity in front of his daughter-in-law, so the two took care to watch their behavior around each other. In that context, if they were both discovered trying to eat red bean porridge in secret, imagine their embarrassment!

누런 소와 검은 소

옛날에 황희라고 하는 정승이 있었습니다. 황희 정승은 지식이 많고 똑똑했지만 늘 다른 사람의 잘못이나 단점을 이야기하곤 해서 사람들은 그를 좋아하지 않았습니다. 어느 날 황희 정승은 다른 정승들과 문제가 생겨서 일을 쉬어야 했어요. 황희 정승은 일을 쉬는 동안을 여행하면서 새로운 것을 경험하기로 했습니다.

황희 정승이 남쪽지방을 여행하고 있을 때였습니다. 하루 종일 걷느라고 너무 피곤해진 황희 정승은 잠깐 쉬었다가 가기로 했습니다. 나무 그늘에 앉아서 쉬고 있는데 길 건너편에서 늙은 농부가 소 두 마리를 데리고 논을 갈고 있는 것이 보였습니다. 한 마리는 누런 소였고 다른 한 마리는 검은 소였습니다.

황희 정승은 누런 소와 검은 소가 일하는 것을 보다가 늙은 농부에게 큰 소리로 물었습니다. "두 소 중에서 어느 소가 일을 더 잘합니까?"

그러자 늙은 농부는 갑자기 논을 갈던 것을 멈추고 황희 정승에게 걸어왔습니다. 그리고는 몸을 숙여 귓속말로 이야기했습니다.

"누런 소가 검은 소보다 일을 더 잘합니다."

황희 정승은 늙은 농부의 행동에 당황해서 물었습니다.

"그 얘기를 뭐 여기까지 와서 하십니까?"

The Yellow Ox and the Black Ox

A long time ago, there was a chief minister called Hwang Hui. He was knowledgeable and smart, but people didn't like him because he was always pointing out other people's mistakes or weaknesses. One time, he had to stay away from work because of conflicts with his colleagues. During his leave from work, he decided to travel the entire country to experience new things.

One day, he was traveling in the southern part of Korea. He had been walking all day and he was feeling very tired, so he decided to take some rest before going on. While he was resting in the shade of a tree, he saw an old farmer who was ploughing a rice field with two oxen across the road. One ox was yellow and the other was black.

After watching the oxen working, Hwang Hui asked the farmer in a loud voice: "Which ox works better?"

The farmer suddenly stopped ploughing and walked toward Hwang Hui. Then he bent forward and said in a whisper, "The yellow ox works better than the black one."

Puzzled by the farmer's behavior, Hwang Hui asked him, "Why did you come right across here to say that?"

그러자 늙은 농부가 대답했습니다.

"두 마리 소 모두 열심히 일하고 있는데 한 마리만 일을 잘한다고 하면 다른 한 마리는 실망할까 봐 그랬습니다. 아무리 짐승이라도 그런 이야기를 들으면 기분이 나쁘지 않겠습니까?"

황희 정승은 농부의 말을 듣고서 자신이 부끄러워졌습니다. 황희 정승은 농부에게 인생의 중요한 교훈을 알려줘서 고맙다고 말하면서 큰절을 했습니다.

그때부터 황희 정승은 절대로 다른 사람의 단점을 이야기하지 않았고, 훌륭한 정승으로 많은 일을 해서 지금까지 존경을 받고 있습니다.

☆ ☆ ☆

Vocabulary

누런 소 **nureon so** yellow ox
검은 소 **geomeun so** black ox
라고 하다 **rago hada** to call
정승 **jeongseung** chief minister
지식 **jisik** knowledge
똑똑하다 **ttokttokhada** to be smart, intelligent
늘 **neul** always
다른 **dareun** other
단점 **danjeom** shortcomings
이야기하다 **iyagihada** to talk
좋아하다 **joahada** to like
문제가 생기다 **munjega saenggida** a problem arises
동안 **dongan** while
전국 **jeonguk** entire country
여행하다 **yeohaenghada** to travel
새로운 것 **saeroun geot** something new
경험하다 **gyeongheomhada** to experience
남쪽지방 **namjjokjibang** southern province

걷다 **jeotda** to walk
피곤하다 **pigonhada** to be tired
나무 그늘 **namu geuneul** shade of a tree
길 건너편 **gil geonneophyeon** the opposite side of the street
늙다 **nukda** to be old
논을 갈다 **noneul galda** to plough a rice field
큰 소리로 **keun soriro** loudly
잘하다 **jalhada** to do something well
멈추다 **meomchuda** to stop
걸어오다 **georeooda** to come on foot
숙이다 **sugida** to bend
귓속말 **gwitsongmal** a whisper
행동 **haengdong** behavior
얘기, 말 **yaegi, mal** talk
실망하다 **silmanghada** to be disappointed
아무리 **amuri** no matter how, even though
짐승 **jimseung** animal
부끄럽다 **bukkeureopda** to be embarrassed

The farmer answered, "Both of them were working hard and I was afraid that if I said the yellow one was working better, the black one would be disappointed. Even though it's an animal, wouldn't it be upset if it heard that?"

When he heard this, Hwang Hui felt ashamed of himself. He went down on his knees and made a deep bow to the farmer, thanking him for a valuable lesson in life.

After that, Hwang Hui never talked about other people's shortcomings and did a lot of good work as chief minister. He was highly respected from that time onwards.

☆ ☆ ☆

인생 **insaeng** life
중요한 교훈 **jungyohan gyohun** important lessons
알려주다 **allyeojuda** to let (a person) know

큰절을 하다 **keun jeoreul hada** to make a deep bow
절대로 **jeoldaero** never
훌륭하다 **hullyunghada** to be great
존경을 받다 **jongyeongeul batda** to receive respect

Selected grammar points

- 이나 "or"

  This can be added to nouns to express a choice between nouns.

  다른 사람의 **잘못이나** 단점을 이야기하곤 해서 사람들은 그를 좋아하지 않았습니다.

  People didn't like him because he was always pointing out other people's mistakes or weaknesses.

- 곤 하다 "to do habitually"

  다른 사람의 잘못이나 단점을 **이야기하곤 해서** 사람들은 그를 좋아하지 않았습니다.

  People didn't like him because he was always pointing out other people's mistakes or weaknesses.

- 느라(고) "because," "due to"

  하루 종일 **걷느라고** 너무 피곤해진 황희 정승은 잠깐 쉬었다가 가기로 했습니다.

  He'd been walking all day and was very tired, so he decided to take some rest.

- 았/었다(가) **"and then," "before [doing]"**

  This indicates that after the completion of an event, a different action happens.

  하루 종일 걷느라고 너무 피곤해진 황희 정승은 잠깐 **쉬었다가** 가기로 했습니다.

  He'd been walking all day and was very tired, so he decided to take some rest before going on.

- 아/어도 **"even if," "regardless of"**

  This construction expresses that the situation in the second clause occurs regardless of what was described in the first clause. It can be strengthened by using 아무리 to make the concessive meaning clearer.

  아무리 짐승이라도 그런 이야기를 들으면 기분이 나쁘지 않겠습니까?

  Even though it's an animal, wouldn't it be upset if it heard that?

- 고서 **"(does) and then…"**

  The addition of 서 to 고 in this pattern has the effect of tightening the relationship between the preceding and following clause, and implying that the contents of the second clause are a natural and closely linked follow-on to those of the first.

  황희 정승은 농부의 말을 **듣고서** 자신이 부끄러워졌습니다.

  When he heard this, Hwang Hui felt ashamed of himself.

After reading the story

1. 사람들은 왜 황희정승을 좋아하지 않았습니까?

   Why didn't people like Hwang Hui?

2. 황희정승은 일을 쉬는 동안 무엇을 하기로 결심했습니까?

   What did Hwang Hui decide to do during his leave from work?

3. 늙은 농부는 왜 황희정승의 질문에 귓속말로 대답했습니까?

   Why did the old farmer answer in a whisper?

4. 왜 황희정승은 늙은 농부에게 큰절을 했습니까?

   Why did Hwang Hui make a deep bow to the old farmer?

Let's talk!

다른 사람에게서 배운 인생의 중요한 교훈이 무엇이고 그 교훈을 누구에게서 배웠는지 이야기하세요.

Talk about a valuable life lesson that you've learned from other people, and the people who taught you the lesson.

Notes on Korean culture

The word 절 **jeol** is a traditional Korean greeting in which you go down on your knees and bow deeply to show respect to somebody who is older or of higher status. These days Koreans practice jeol only on very formal occasions such as New Year's Day or their wedding day. In the past, Koreans used to offer jeol regardless of where they met if they needed to show respect. Can you imagine them bowing on a muddy road? They must have had to wash their clothes after that!

꼬리가 얼어붙은 호랑이

추운 겨울이었어요.

"아이고! 배 고파, 어흥!" 호랑이는 열심히 잡아 먹을 동물을 찾아봤지만 추운 겨울이라서 아무것도 찾지 못했어요.

"아이고, 배 고파 죽겠네, 물이라도 마셔야지." 호랑이가 물을 마시려던 참이었어요.

작고 하얀 토끼 한 마리가 깡총깡총 뛰어왔어요. 토끼도 목이 말라서 물을 마시러 나온 거예요.

토끼를 본 호랑이는 너무 기뻤어요.

"어흥, 토끼야, 배 고픈데 너 마침 잘 만났다."

"아이고, 깜짝이야."

토끼는 무서워서 도망가고 싶었지만 호랑이가 너무 빨라서 도망갈 수 없었어요. 호랑이는 토끼를 삼키려고 입을 크게 벌렸어요. 그런데 토끼가 웃으며 이렇게 말하는 거예요.

"산 속의 왕이신 호랑이님이 이렇게 작은 저를 잡아 먹는다고 배가 부르시겠어요? 제가 물고기를 배가 터질 만큼 드실 수 있는 방법을 알거든요. 그런데 그 방법을 못 알려 드리고 죽으니 그게 너무 아쉽네요."

How the Tiger Froze Its Tail

It was a cold winter.

"Oh my! I'm hungry! Grrr!" The tiger looked hard for some animal to catch and eat, but because it was so cold, he couldn't find a thing.

"Oh my, I'm starving! I'll drink some water, at least."

The tiger was just going to drink some water, when a small white rabbit came hopping along. The rabbit was thirsty too and had come to drink the water.

On seeing the rabbit, the tiger was overjoyed.

"I'm glad to meet you, because I'm hungry."

"Oh my, what a surprise!"

The rabbit was scared and wanted to run away, but the tiger was too fast for him. The tiger opened his mouth wide to swallow the rabbit. But the rabbit just spoke with a smile.

"If a tiger, the king of the mountains, eats a little creature like me, do you think you'll be full? I know a way that you can eat fish until your stomach bursts. It'll be a great shame if I die without teaching you that method."

"맛있는 물고기를 배가 터질 만큼 먹을 수 있다고? 그게 정말이야?"

"그럼요, 저기에 작은 강이 보이지요? 그 강에 맛있는 물고기가 정말 많아요. 그 물고기만 잡으면 호랑이님은 다시는 배 고플 일이 없을걸요."

호랑이는 토끼의 말이 맞다고 생각했어요.

"토끼야, 그럼, 나한테 그 좋은 방법을 알려 줄 수 있겠니?"

"그럼요, 제가 좋은 방법을 가르쳐 드릴 테니까 저만 따라오세요."

토끼와 호랑이는 강으로 갔어요. 강물은 얼어 있었어요. 토끼는 돌로 얼음을 깨뜨려 구멍을 냈어요.

"호랑이님, 꼬리를 이 구멍에 넣으세요. 그럼, 물고기들이 꼬리에 달라붙을 거예요. 그때 그 꼬리만 들어올리면 물고기들이 달려 나올 거예요. 그럼 그걸 드시면 돼요. 낚시하는 것처럼요."

"아, 그거 정말 좋은 방법이구나."

호랑이는 꼬리를 강물 속에 넣었어요.

"호랑이님, 잘 하셨어요. 계속 그렇게 하고 계세요. 저는 강 위쪽으로 가서 물고기를 이쪽으로 몰아 올게요."

토끼는 강 위쪽으로 뛰어갔어요.

호랑이는 가만히 앉아서 물고기가 꼬리에 달라붙기를 기다렸어요. 그런데 아무리 기다려도 물고기는 안 잡히고 토끼도 돌아오지 않았어요. 그러는 사이에 호랑이 꼬리는 강물 속에서 얼어 버렸고요. 그때서야 호랑이는 속았다는 걸 알았답니다.

☆ ☆ ☆

Vocabulary

꼬리 **kkori** tail

얼어붙다 **eoreobutda** to be frozen

어흥 **eoheung** growl

동물 **dongmul** animal

찾다 **chatda** to look for

아무것도 **amugeokdo** nothing

하얗다 **hayatda** to be white

토끼 **tokki** rabbit

깡총깡총 뛰어오다
  **kkangchongkkangchong
  ttwieoooda** to hop

목이 마르다 **mogi mareuda** to be thirsty

기쁘다 **gippeuda** to be glad

만나다 **mannada** to meet

깜짝이야 **kkamjjagiya** Oh my! What a
  surprise!

삼키다 **samkida** to swallow

입을 벌리다 **ibeul beollida** to open one's
  mouth

크게 **keuge** widely

배가 부르다 **baega bureuda** to be full

물고기 **mulgogi** fish

"You say I can eat enough tasty fish to make my stomach burst? Is that true?"

"Certainly! You see that little river over there? There are plenty of tasty fish in that river. If you can catch those fish, you'll never need to go hungry again."

The tiger thought the rabbit's words were right.

"Then, rabbit, can you teach me that good method?"

"Certainly, just follow me and I'll teach you the way."

The rabbit and the tiger went to the river. The water of the river was frozen. The rabbit broke the ice with a stone to make a hole.

"Tiger, sir, put your tail through this hole. The fish will cling to your tail. Then you just lift your tail out and the fish will come out with it. And then you can eat them. It's just like fishing."

"Ah, that's really a good method!"

The tiger put his tail in the water.

"Well done, tiger, sir. Keep doing that. I'll go upstream and drive the fish in this direction."

And the rabbit ran off up the river.

The tiger sat still and waited for the fish to take hold of his tail. But no matter how he waited, he didn't catch any fish and the rabbit didn't come back either. Meanwhile, the tiger's tail became frozen in the river. Only then did the tiger realize that he had been tricked.

☆ ☆ ☆

배가 터지다 **baega teojida** stomach bursts

드시다 **deusida** [honorific] to eat

방법 **bangbeop** way, means

아쉽다 **aswipda** to be regrettable, a shame

정말이다 **jeongmarida** to be true

그럼요 **geureomyo** certainly

저기에 **jeogie** there

강 **gang** river

맞다 **matda** to be right

가르치다 **gareuchida** to teach

따라오다 **ttaraoda** to follow

강물 **gangmul** river water

돌 **dol** stone

얼음 **eoreum** ice

깨뜨리다 **kkaetteurida** to break

구멍을 내다 **gumeongeul naeda** to make a hole

넣다 **neotda** to put (something) in

달라붙다 **dallabutda** to stick to

들어올리다 **deureoollida** to lift

달려 나오다 **dallyeo naoda** to come out with it

낚시하다 **naksihada** to fish
위쪽 **wijjok** the upper side
이쪽 **ijjok** this way
몰아오다 **moraoda** to drive
뛰어가다 **ttwieogada** to run
가만히 **gamanhi** still

잡히다 **japida** to catch
그러는 사이에 **geureoneun saie** in the meantime
그때서야 **geuttaeseoya** only then
속다 **sokda** to be fooled, tricked

Selected grammar points

- (이)라서 **"because it is X"**
  Often used in conversational Korean and has the same meaning as (이)어서.
  추운 겨울이라서 아무것도 찾지 못했어요.
  Because it was so cold, he couldn't find a thing.

- (으)려던 참이다 **"I was just about to . . ."**
  호랑이가 물을 마시려던 참이었어요.
  The tiger was just going to drink some water.

- (으)ㄹ 만큼 **"to the extent of," "so much that . . ."**
  제가 물고기를 배가 터질 만큼 드실 수 있는 방법을 알거든요.
  I know a way you can eat fish until your stomach bursts.

- 지요 **Confirming information: "right?"**
  This is used when the speaker wants to confirm with the listener or to obtain the listener's agreement about something already known. It functions like a tag question, e.g. "isn't/aren't . . . ?" in English.
  저기에 작은 강이 보이지요?
  You see that little river over there [right]?

- (으)ㄹ걸요 **"it is probably," "I think," "I bet . . ."**
  그 물고기만 잡으면 호랑이님은 다시는 배 고플 일이 없을걸요.
  If you can catch those fish, you'll [probably] never need to go hungry again.

- (으)ㄹ 테니까 **"because one expects that/intends to . . ."**
  The second clause contains the speaker's suggestion or statement of advice to the listener, while the first clause provides the speaker's reason for giving such a suggestion or advice.

  제가 좋은 방법을 가르쳐 **드릴 테니까** 저만 따라오세요.
  Just follow me and I'll teach you the way.

After reading the story

1. 호랑이는 먹을 것을 찾기가 왜 어려웠어요?
   Why was it difficult for the tiger to find anything to eat?
2. 토끼는 왜 도망가지 않았어요?
   Why didn't the rabbit run away?
3. 토끼가 호랑이에게 무엇을 가르쳐 줬어요?
   What did the rabbit teach the tiger?
4. 호랑이는 물고기를 배가 터질 만큼 먹을 수 있었나요?
   Was the tiger able to eat enough fish to make his stomach burst?

Let's talk!

토끼처럼 위험에 처했을 때 꾀를 사용해 위기를 모면하는 이야기를 해 보세요.
Tell a story about escaping from danger by using one's wits.

Notes on Korean culture

Regardless of time and place, there are always the strong and the weak. In this story, the physically weak rabbit uses its wits to play a funny trick on the strong tiger. In traditional folktales, the rabbit often appears as a small but cunning character and the tiger as the strongest of all the animals. In many Korean folktales, the weak common people defeat their strong oppressors as the rabbit does in this story: not by strength but by their wits.

한평생 쓰고도 남는 물건

어떤 마을에 부자가 살았어요. 이 사람은 부자인데도 자기가 가진 것에 만족하지 못했어요. 어느 날 어떤 나그네가 시냇물 속에서 무엇인가를 찾고 있는 것을 보았어요.

부자가 궁금해서 물었어요. "무엇을 잃어버리셨나요?"

"아니에요. 별 것 아니에요."

나그네는 그렇게 대답하고는 계속 열심히 찾았어요.

부자는 더 궁금해졌어요.

"무엇을 잃어버렸길래 그렇게 열심히 찾으시나요?"

나그네가 대답했어요.

"그렇게 알고 싶다면 알려 드리지요. 그 물건은 제가 한평생 쓰고도 남을 물건이랍니다."

부자는 "한평생 쓰고도 남을 물건이라면 굉장한 보물인가 봐. 틀림없이 비싼 걸 거야."라고 생각했어요.

"그럼, 저도 같이 찾아볼까요?"

부자는 물 속에 들어가서 나그네가 찾고 있는 것을 같이 찾기 시작했어요.

"한평생 쓰고도 남는 물건이라면 뭘까? 돈인가? 비싼 보석인가? 내가 찾으면 내가 얼른 가져야지." 이렇게 생각하면서 신이 나서 찾았어요.

A Tool That Outlives the User

In a certain village there lived a rich man. Although he was rich, this man was never satisfied with what he had.

One day, he saw a traveler looking for something in the water of a stream.

Curious, the rich man asked, "Have you lost something?"

"No, it's nothing important," the traveler answered. But he went on searching busily.

The rich man grew more curious.

"I wonder if you're searching so hard because you've lost something?"

The traveler answered, "If you're so eager to know, I'll tell you. It's something that will still remain even if I use it all my life."

The rich man thought, "Something that still remains even after using it all your life must be a terrific treasure. It's sure to be valuable."

"Then, shall I look for it with you?" he said.

The rich man went into the water and began to look for the thing that the traveler was searching for.

"If it's a thing that remains even after using it all your life, what can it be? Money? Precious jewels? If I find it, I'll take it right away!" With that thought, he searched excitedly.

한참 후에 나그네가 물 속에서 무엇을 주웠는지, "아이고, 이제야 찾았네." 하고 몸을 일으켰어요.

부자는 그 물건이 도대체 무엇일까 궁금해서 보니 그것은 바로 붓이었어요.

부자는 실망하고 화가 나서 말했어요.

"아니, 그게 한평생 쓰고도 남는 물건이라고요?"

나그네는 웃으면서 대답했어요.

"맞아요. 이게 내가 한평생 쓰고도 남을 물건이지요. 이걸 가지고 한평생 글을 쓰다가 죽으면 아들에게 물려줄 거랍니다."

부자는 아직도 화가 났어요.

"그럼 처음부터 붓을 잃어버렸다고 했어야지요. 한평생 쓰고도 남을 물건이라고 해서 나도 괜히 쓸데없이 고생만 했잖아요!"

나그네가 어이가 없어서 대답했어요.

"내가 언제 당신한테 찾아 달라고 부탁을 했습니까? 당신이 갑자기 남의 일에 뛰어들어서 한 거지요."

이렇게 말하고 나그네는 계속 길을 갔어요. 부자는 욕심 때문에 고생만 한 거지요.

☆　☆　☆

Vocabulary

한평생 **hanphyeongsaeng** one's whole life

남다 **namda** to remain

물건 **mulgeon** object, item, thing

만족하다 **manjokada** to be satisfied

나그네 **nageune** traveler

시냇물 **sinaenmul** stream

궁금하다 **gunggeumhada** to wonder

잃어버리다 **ireobeorida** to lose

별 거 아니다 **byeol geo anida** It's nothing special

계속 **gyesok** continuously

굉장하다 **goengjanghada** to be magnificent

보물 **bomurida** treasure

틀림없이 **teullimeopsi** certainly

비싸다 **bissada** to be expensive, valuable

보석 **boseok** jewel

얼른 **eilleun** immediately, right away

신이 나다 **sini nada** to be excited

한참 **hancham** for some time

줍다 **jupda** to pick up

A little later, the traveler seemed to pick something up out of the water. "Aha, at last I've found it!" he said as he straightened himself up.

Wondering what on earth this object could be, the rich man looked. It was nothing but a writing brush!

The rich man was disappointed and spoke angrily.

"What, is that the thing that remains after using it all your life?"

The traveler answered with a smile.

"That's right. This is a thing that will still remain even if I use it all my life. If I die after writing with this all my life, I will leave it to my son."

The rich man was still angry.

"Then you should have said from the beginning that you had lost your brush. Because you said it was a thing that would remain after using it all your life, I've gone to a lot of trouble for nothing."

Flabbergasted, the traveler replied, "When did I ask you to look for it? You just suddenly barged in on someone else's business."

With these words, the traveler went on his way. The rich man had gained nothing but trouble from being greedy.

☆ ☆ ☆

이제야 **ijeya** finally
일으켜다 **ireukyeoda** to raise
도대체 **dodaeche** [what] on earth
붓 **but** brush
글 **geul** writing
쓰다 **sseuda** to write
물려주다 **mullyeojuda** to pass down
아직도 **ajikdo** still
처음부터 **cheoeumbuteo** from the beginning
괜히 **gwaenhi** in vain
쓸데없이 **sseuldeeopsi** unnecessarily

고생을 하다 **gosaengeul hada** to suffer hardship
어이가 없다 **eoiga eopda** dumbfounded, flabbergasted
당신 **dangsin** you
부탁을 하다 **butageul hada** to ask a favor
남의 일 **namui il** other people's business
뛰어들다 **ttwieodeulda** to jump into
계속 길을 가다 **gyeosok gireul gada** to continue on a journey
욕심 **yoksim** greed

Selected grammar points

- (으)ㄴ/는데도 **"although . . . ," "despite . . . ," "but"**

  This expression is used to present a contrast.

  이 사람은 부자인데도 자기가 가진 것에 만족하지 못했어요.

  Although he was rich, this man was never satisfied with what he had.

- 나요? **Softer interrogative form: "I wonder?"**

  This is used to ask somebody a question politely and gently.

  무엇을 잃어버리셨나요?

  Have you lost something?

- 고도 남다 **"even after . . .ing, there is something remaining or left over"**

  그 물건은 제가 한평생 쓰고도 남을 물건이랍니다.

  It's something that will still remain even if I use it all my life.

- (으)ㄹ까요? **"shall we (I) . . . ?"**

  This verb form is used to ask tentative questions. In the first person, it means "shall I . . . ?" or "shall we . . . ?" with the sense of "How about doing . . . ?" In the third person, this pattern is used to ask someone's opinion: "Will it be . . . , do you think?" or "Do you suppose it will be . . . ?"

  저도 같이 찾아 **볼까요**?

  Shall I look for it with you?

- (으)ㄴ가 보다 **"it seems that," "I think that"**

  This indicates a conjecture after witnessing a certain situation.

  한평생 쓰고도 남을 물건이라면 굉장한 **보물인가 봐**.

  Something that still remains even after using it all your life must be a terrific treasure.

- 기 시작하다 **"to start . . . ing"**

  물 속에 들어가서 나그네가 찾고 있는 것을 같이 **찾기 시작했어요**.

  He went into the water and began to look for the thing that the traveler was searching for.

After reading the story

1. 나그네는 무엇을 잃어버렸다고 했어요?
   What did the traveler say he had lost?
2. 부자는 왜 찾는 것을 도와줬어요?
   Why did the rich man help him look for it?
3. 부자는 왜 실망했어요?
   Why was the rich man disappointed?

Let's talk!

여러분에게 소중한 물건을 소개해 보세요.
Talk about an object that's precious to you.

Notes on Korean culture

In Korea, great importance has always been attached to education. A poor family would even sell their land to pay for their children's education. This story, too, emphasizes the importance of education, represented by the writing brush. It's because of this tradition of valuing education that Korea has been able to grow into one of the world's top ten economic powers over the last seventy years despite having little land, few natural resources and being devastated by the Korean War.

힘 센 농부

어떤 마을에 힘이 센 농부가 살았어요.

"저 농부는 우리나라에서 제일 힘이 센 사람이 틀림없어요."

사람들의 칭찬을 많이 들으니까 농부는 자기가 최고라는 생각이 들었어요. 그래서 큰 도시로 가서 인정을 받고 싶어졌어요.

걸어가다가 피곤해서 잠깐 나무 밑에서 쉬고 있는데 말을 탄 선비와 하인이 왔어요.

심심했던 농부는 두 사람을 만나서 반가웠어요.

"큰 도시에 가시는군요. 잠깐 쉬고 나서 같이 갑시다."

"그럽시다."

그런데 그때 갑자기 도둑들이 나타났어요.

"가지고 있는 것을 다 내놓아라! 그렇지 않으면 다 죽이겠다."

"아이고, 우리는 가진 게 아무것도 없습니다. 살려 주세요."

하인은 놀라서 손이 발이 되도록 빌었어요. 하지만 농부는 겁먹기는커녕 눈을 크게 뜨고 소리쳤어요.

"다 덤벼라!"

농부는 옆에 있는 큰 나무를 뽑아서 지팡이처럼 휘둘렀어요.

그것을 본 도둑들은 깜짝 놀라서 도망가 버렸어요.

The Strong Farmer

In a certain village lived a farmer who was very strong.

"That farmer must be the strongest man in the country."

Hearing a lot of praise from other people, the farmer came to think he was the greatest. So he wanted to go to the big city to gain some recognition.

Tired from walking, the farmer was resting for a while under a tree when a scholar came along on horseback with his servant. The farmer had been bored and was pleased to see the two men.

"So you're going to the big city. Let's rest a little and then travel together."

"Yes, let's."

Just then, some thieves suddenly appeared.

"Take out everything you've got! If you don't, we'll kill you all."

"Oh my, we haven't got anything. Spare us!"

The servant was frightened and begged for mercy.

But as for the farmer, far from being scared, he opened his eyes wide and shouted, "Come on then!"

The farmer pulled out the big tree that stood beside him by its roots and swung it around like a stick.

When they saw that, the thieves were terrified and ran away.

하인은 존경스러운 눈빛으로 농부를 보았어요. 우쭐해진 농부는 선비에게 뽐내며 말했어요.

"힘 있는 사람이 약한 사람을 돕는 것은 당연하지요. 선비님은 다치신 데가 없습니까?"

"네, 괜찮습니다. 고맙습니다. 그런데 당신보다 힘센 도둑이었으면 어쩔 뻔했습니까?"

선비의 말에 농부는 기분이 나빠졌어요.

"그게 무슨 소리요? 세상에 나보다 힘이 센 사람이 어디에 있겠어요?"

그러자 선비는 옆에 있는 큰 바위를 손으로 번쩍 들어올렸어요.

"와, 세상에!" 농부는 깜짝 놀랐어요. 그리고 자기도 들어 보려고 했어요. 그렇지만 바위를 도저히 들어올릴 수 없었어요.

"농부 아저씨, 세상은 아주 넓고 힘센 사람도 많답니다. 조금 전에 도둑이 나타났을 때 잘못하면 당신이나 하인이 다칠까 봐 사정을 살피려고 내가 가만히 있었던 것이었지요."

"아, 내가 힘만 믿고 내가 최고라고 생각을 했구나."

농부는 자기의 어리석음을 깨닫고 다시 고향으로 돌아가서 열심히 농사를 지었답니다.

☆ ☆ ☆

Vocabulary

힘이 세다 **himi seda** to be strong, mighty

틀림없다 **teullim eopda** to be certain

칭찬을 듣다 **chingchaneul deutda** to be praised

최고이다 **choegoida** to be supreme, the best

생각이 들다 **saenggagi deulda** to come to mind

큰 도시 **keun dosi** big city

인정을 받다 **injeongeul batda** to receive recognition

밑 **mit** under

말 **mal** horse

선비 **seonbi** scholar

하인 **hain** servant

심심하다 **simsimhada** to be bored

반갑다 **bangapda** to be glad

도둑 **doduk** thief

내놓다 **naenota** to take out

손이 발이 되도록 빌다 **soni bari doedorok bilda** to beg for mercy

겁먹다 **geommeokda** to be afraid

눈을 뜨다 **nuneul tteuda** to open one's eyes

소리치다 **sorichida** to shout

덤비다 **deombida** to come at, attack

뽑다 **ppopda** to pull out, to tear out

지팡이 **jipangi** stick, cane

휘두르다 **hwidureuda** to swing

존경스럽다 **jongyeongseureopda** to be respectful, admiring

The servant looked at the farmer with admiring eyes.

The proud farmer boasted to the scholar, "It's only natural for the strong to help the weak. You're not hurt anywhere, are you, sir?"

"No, I'm all right, thank you. But what would have happened if the thief had been stronger than you?"

The farmer was upset by the scholar's words. "What do you mean? Where in the world is there a stronger man than me?"

The scholar effortlessly lifted up a big rock that was beside him.

"Oh my goodness!" The farmer was amazed. He tried to lift the rock himself, but he couldn't lift it at all.

"Mister Farmer, the world is wide and there are many strong men. When the thieves appeared just now, I was just keeping still and assessing the situation, thinking that if I made a mistake, either you or my servant might get hurt."

"Ah, so I only thought I was the greatest because I was relying on strength alone."

Having realized his foolishness, the farmer went back to his hometown and worked hard at his farming.

☆ ☆ ☆

눈빛 **nunbit** a look
우쭐해지다 **ujjulhaejida** to feel flattered by
뽐내다 **ppomnaeda** to boast
약하다 **yakada** to be weak
돕다 **dopda** to help
당연하다 **dangyeonhada** to be natural
님 **nim** sir, madam
다치신 데 **dachisinde** injured area
어쩔 뻔하다 **eojjeol ppeonhada** what do you expect if . . . , what would happen if . . . ?
무슨 소리요 **museun soriyo** What do you mean?
큰 바위 **keun bawi** big rock
번쩍 들어올리다 **beonjjeok deureoollida** to lift up effortlessly

와, 세상에 **wa, sesange** Wow, oh my goodness!
깜짝 놀라다 **kkamjjak nollada** to be startled
도저히 **dojeohi** at all
아저씨 **ajeossi** middle-aged man, "mister"
넓다 **neolpda** to be broad
다치다 **dachida** to get hurt
사정을 살피다 **sajeongeul salpida** to test the water, assess the situation
힘만 믿다 **himman mitda** to rely only on one's strength
어리석다 **eoriseokda** to be silly
깨닫다 **kkaedatda** to realize

Selected grammar points

- 아/어지다 **"to become," "to turn into"**

  This verb form is used with descriptive verbs to show a change in state, equivalent to "become" or "turn into" in English.

  큰 도시로 가서 인정을 받고 **싶어졌어요**.

  He wanted to go to the big city and gain some recognition.

- 았/었던 **Reminiscence: "used to be," "had been"**

  This expression is used when recalling a past event or state of affairs that has not continued to the present.

  심심했던 농부는 두 사람을 만나서 반가웠어요.

  The farmer had been bored and was pleased to see the two men.

- 기는커녕 **"let alone," "far from"**

  농부는 **겁먹기는커녕** 눈을 크게 뜨고 소리쳤어요.

  As for the farmer, far from being scared, he opened his eyes wide and shouted.

- (으)ㄹ 때 **"when one does X"**

  This verb form is used to indicate the time that an action occurs, not in the sense of "at 10:30 pm" but in the sense of "when I . . . , X happens."

  조금 전에 도둑이 **나타났을 때** 잘못하면 당신이나 하인이 다칠까 봐 사정을 살피려고 내가 가만히 있었던 것이었지요.

  When the thieves appeared just now, I was just keeping still and assessing the situation, thinking that if I made a mistake, either you or my servant might get hurt.

- Verb + (으)ㅁ **Making an action verb or descriptive verb into a noun**

  농부는 자기의 **어리석음**을 깨닫고 다시 고향으로 돌아가서 열심히 농사를 지었답니다.

  Having realized his foolishness, the farmer went back to his hometown and worked hard at his farming.

After reading the story

1. 농부는 어디로 가고 있었어요?
   Where was the farmer going?
2. 선비와 하인을 만났을 때 농부는 무엇을 하고 있었어요?
   What was the farmer doing when he met the scholar and his servant?
3. 도둑이 나타났을 때 하인, 농부, 선비는 각자 어떻게 행동했어요?
   When the thieves appeared, what did the servant, the farmer and the scholar each do?
4. 농부는 그 후에 무엇을 했어요?
   What did the farmer do after that?

Let's talk!

용기와 만용이 어떻게 다를까요? 예를 들어 이야기해 보세요.
What's the difference between bravery and recklessness? Give an example.

Notes on Korean culture

The farmer was both strong and brave. But because he was over-confident in his strength, he acted recklessly without having assessed the situation properly. This story tells us that, no matter how brave and capable we may be, we should not be without humility. The scholar is a strong man, but he also has the wisdom to assess the situation before acting. Koreans believe that truly wise people are those who don't show off their own ability but know how to be humble.

산삼을 지킨 이무기

옛날에 가난한 농부가 가족과 같이 살았어요. 그런데 겨울에 먹을 것이 다 떨어졌어요.

"아버지, 배고파요."

어린 아이들이 배고파서 우는 것을 보고, 농부는 먹을 것을 찾으러 산으로 갔어요. 여기저기 다니다가 벼랑 가운데에 있는 파란 잎을 보았어요. 자세히 보니까 바로 산삼이었어요.

"아니, 이게 뭐야. 진짜 산삼이란 말이야? 하느님 감사합니다. 이제 제 아이들이 배고프지 않게 먹을 수 있게 되었습니다."

농부는 너무나 기뻤어요. 산삼은 인삼보다 훨씬 더 비싸기 때문에 산삼만 캘 수 있으면 가난하지 않게 살 수 있으니까요. 그런데 문제가 있었어요. 산삼이 벼랑에 있어서 도저히 캘 수가 없는 거예요. 농부는 안타까워서 벼랑 위에 그냥 앉아 있었어요.

그때 같은 마을에 사는 이웃 사람이 지나가다가 이 농부를 보게 되었어요.

Guardian of the Ginseng

Long ago, a poor farmer lived with his family. In the winter, all their food ran out.

"Daddy, I'm hungry."

Seeing his children crying from hunger, the farmer went to the hills to look for something to eat. After wandering around here and there, he saw a green leaf in the middle of a cliff. He looked carefully, and yes, it was wild ginseng.

"My goodness, what's this? Is it really wild ginseng? Thank you, God! Now my children will be able to eat and not be hungry."

The farmer was overjoyed, because wild ginseng was much more expensive than ordinary ginseng, so anyone who could dig out wild ginseng would be able to live free from poverty. But there was a problem. The wild ginseng was on a cliff, so there was no way of digging it out at all. Saddened, the farmer just sat down at the top of the cliff.

Just then, a neighbor who lived in the same village was passing by and saw the farmer.

"김 서방, 추운데 왜 그렇게 앉아 있어요?"

"저 벼랑 가운데 산삼이 보이시지요? 그런데 도저히 내려갈 수가 없어서 이렇게 앉아만 있답니다."

이웃 사람이 말했어요.

"아, 그렇네요. 그런데 방법이 하나 생각났어요. 내가 밧줄을 만들어서 벼랑 위에서 잡고 있을 테니까 김 서방이 그걸 타고 내려가 산삼을 캐 오면 어때요?"

그게 좋은 방법인 것 같았어요. 그래서 밧줄을 타고 내려가 산삼을 캐서 바구니에 담았어요. 그리고 바구니를 밧줄에 묶어서 올려 줬어요.

그런데 아무리 기다려도 밧줄이 다시 내려오지 않는 거예요. 이웃 사람이 산삼을 혼자 가지려고 그냥 가 버린 거지요. 농부는 올라갈 수도 없고 내려갈 수도 없었어요.

그때 커다란 뱀 한 마리가 벼랑을 타고 내려오더니 입을 크게 벌렸어요.

"아이고, 이제 나 죽는구나."

그런데 뱀은 이상하게도 농부를 잡아먹지 않았어요. 그 대신 자기 위에 타라는 듯이 몸을 들이댔어요.

농부는 뱀 등에 탔어요. 그러자 뱀이 벼랑 위로 올라갔어요. 그리고 벼랑 위에 농부를 내려놓고는 조용히 숲 속으로 사라졌어요.

이렇게 농부가 뱀 덕분에 살아서 산을 내려오는데, 길가에 산삼을 가지고 먼저 내려간 이웃 사람이 쓰러져 죽어 있는 거예요. 목에는 뱀의 이빨 자국이 있었고요. 나쁜 사람이어서 천벌을 받은 거지요.

농부는 산삼을 팔아 음식을 사서 아이들에게 배부르게 먹여 주었어요. 이웃 사람들에게도 나눠 주었고요. 그리고 남은 돈으로는 땅을 사서 농사를 지으면서 잘 살았대요.

☆ ☆ ☆

"Mr. Cho, it's cold—why are you sitting there like that?"

"You see that wild ginseng in the middle of the cliff? But I can't get down at all, so I'm just sitting here."

"Ah, so I see," said the neighbor. "But I've thought of a way. How about if I make a rope and stand holding it at the top of the cliff, while you go down on the rope to dig out and bring back the wild ginseng?"

That seemed like a good method. So the farmer went down on the rope, dug out the wild ginseng and put it in his basket. Then he tied the basket to the rope and sent it back up.

But although he waited for a long time, the rope didn't come back down again. The neighbor had just gone away, intending to keep the wild ginseng for himself. The farmer could neither go up nor down.

Then a great snake came down the cliff and opened its mouth wide.

"Oh my, now I'm going to die!"

But strangely enough, the snake didn't eat the farmer. Instead, it came up close as if to invite him to ride on its back.

The farmer got on the snake's back. Then the snake went back up the cliff. And after setting the farmer down at the top of the cliff, it disappeared quietly into the woods.

So, thanks to the snake, the farmer was coming down from the hills alive, when beside the path he found the dead body of the neighbor who had come down before him with the wild ginseng. On his neck were the marks of a snake's teeth. He had received his divine punishment for being such a bad man.

The farmer sold the wild ginseng and bought enough food for his children to eat their fill. He even shared it with his neighbors. And with the rest of the money, he bought some land and lived well by farming it.

Vocabulary

산삼 **sansam** wild ginseng

지키다 **jikida** to guard, protect

이무기 **imugi** big snake

먹을 것이 떨어지다 **meogeul geosi tteoreojida** to run out of food

여기저기 **yeogijeogi** here and there

벼랑 **byeorang** cliff

가운데 **gaunde** center, middle

파란 잎 **paran ip** green leaf

자세히 보다 **jasehi boda** to take a close look at, look carefully

훨씬 더 **hwolssin deo** much more

캐다 **kaeda** to dig out

안타깝다 **antakkapda** to be sad

그냥 **geunyang** just

지나가다 **jinagada** to go by

김 서방 **kim seobang** Mr. Kim

거기서 **geogiseo** there

내려가다 **naeryeogada** to go down

밧줄 **batjul** rope

바구니 **baguni** basket

묶다 **mukda** to tie

올려 주다 **ollyeo juda** to lift

커다랗다 **keodaratda** to be huge

그 대신 **geu daesin** instead

들이대다 **deuridaeda** to be close

내려놓다 **naeryeonota** to put down

조용히 **joyonghi** quietly

숲 **sup** forest

사라지다 **sarajida** to disappear

덕분에 **deokbune** thanks to

길가 **gilga** roadside

목 **mok** neck

이빨 자국 **ippal jaguk** teeth marks

천벌을 받다 **cheonbeoreul batda** to receive divine punishment

나누다 **nanuda** to share

Selected grammar points

- 게 되다 **"It comes about that . . . ," "it turns out that . . ."**

  This form expresses a change in a situation as a result (not necessarily intentional) of some other action or circumstance.

  이웃 사람이 지나가다가 이 농부를 보게 되었어요.

  A neighbor who lived in the same village was passing by and [so it turned out that he] saw the farmer.

- 아/어 가다/오다 **"(verb) and bring [take] it"**

  When the verbs of motion are used after the 아/어 form of action verbs, it gives a sense of direction—to buy something and bring it with you, to prepare something and take it with you and so on. Often the best translation is "bring" or "take."

  내가 밧줄을 만들어서 벼랑 위에서 잡고 있을 테니까 김 서방이 그걸 타고 내려가 산삼을 캐 오면 어때요?

  How about if I make a rope and stand holding it at the top of the cliff, while you go down on the rope to dig out and bring back the wild ginseng?

- (으)ㄴ/는/(으)ㄹ 것 같다 **"seems to be"**
  This form expresses conjecture about present, future or past events or states of affairs.
  그게 좋은 **방법인 것 같았어요.**
  That seemed like a good method.
- 는 듯이 **"as if (to say)," "like"**
  자기 위에 **타라는 듯이** 몸을 들이댔어요.
  It came up close as if to invite him to ride on its back.
- 덕분에 **"thanks to"**
  농부가 **뱀 덕분에** 살아서 산을 내려왔어요.
  Thanks to the snake, the farmer came down from the hills alive.

After reading the story
1. 농부는 왜 산에 갔어요?
   Why did the farmer go to the hills?
2. 농부는 왜 산삼을 캘 수 없었어요?
   Why couldn't the farmer dig out the wild ginseng?
3. 이웃 사람이 어떻게 하자고 했어요?
   What did the neighbor suggest they should do?
4. 누가 농부를 벼랑에서 올려 줬어요?
   Who carried the farmer up from the cliff?
5. 이웃 사람은 어떻게 되었어요?
   What happened to the neighbor?

Let's talk!
산삼은 건강에 아주 좋지만 많이 없기 때문에 아주 비쌉니다. 여러분 나라에도 이런 식료품이 있나요?
Wild ginseng is very good for your health, but it's terribly expensive because it's so rare. Is there a similar foodstuff in your country?

Notes on Korean culture
The ginseng grown in Korea is sought after in other countries as well because it has more nutrients than other kinds of ginseng. But wild ginseng, which isn't grown in a field but grows naturally in the mountains, is even more efficacious, and since olden times it has been said that anyone who finds wild ginseng will make a lot of money. In this story, the neighbor coveted the wild ginseng so much that he left the farmer hanging on the cliff and went off by himself to keep all the ginseng, before meeting with divine retribution.

방울 장수

방울 장수가 이 마을 저 마을을 다니며 방울을 팔았어요. 그런데 어느 날 밤에 산 속에서 길을 잃어버렸어요.

"어떡하지? 밤이 깊어지는데 길도 잘 모르겠고, 이러다가 호랑이라도 나타나면 큰일인데 . . ."

방울 장수는 호랑이를 만날까 봐 걱정이 되기 시작했어요. 그런데 저 멀리 어떤 집이 보였어요. 너무 반가워서 문을 두드리니까 할머니가 나와서 말했어요.

"어서 오세요. 밤이 늦었는데 길을 잃으셨나 보네요. 이 근처에는 우리집밖에 없으니 우리집에서 하룻밤 주무시고 내일 가세요."

할머니는 방울 장수에게 맛있는 저녁도 해 주셨어요.

"정말 맛있게 먹었습니다."

"하루종일 방울을 파느라 피곤하시겠구려. 방을 따뜻하게 해 놓았으니 편히 좀 쉬세요."

The Bell Seller

A bell seller went around from village to village selling bells. One night, he lost his way in the hills.

"What shall I do now? The night is wearing on and I don't know the way. If a tiger appears now, I'll be in big trouble."

The bell seller started to worry about meeting a tiger. Then he caught sight of a house in the distance. Overjoyed, he knocked on the door and an old woman came out and spoke to him.

"Welcome! So it's late and you've lost your way. There's no other house but mine around here, so you'd better spend the night in my house and go on in the morning."

The old woman also cooked a tasty dinner for the bell seller.

"That was really delicious."

"You must be tired from selling bells all day. I've warmed the room for you, so have a nice rest."

그러면서 할머니는 빈 그릇을 가지고 일어섰어요. 그런데 방을 나가는 할머니의 뒷모습을 보고 방울 장수는 깜짝 놀랐어요. 할머니의 치마 밑으로 호랑이의 꼬리가 보였거든요.

"아이고, 할머니로 둔갑한 호랑이구나. 큰일났다. 내가 잠이 들면 나를 잡아먹으려고 할 텐데 어떡하지?"

그때 좋은 생각이 났어요. 그래서 할머니한테 말했어요.

"할머니, 제가 파는 이 방울은요, 호랑이를 잡아먹는 신기한 방울이랍니다. 할머니는 혼자 산 속에 사시니까 호랑이 때문에 무서우실 것 같은데 하나 드릴까요?"

할머니는 방울 장수의 말이 끝나기가 무섭게 아무 대답도 하지 않고 방을 나가 버렸어요.

할머니는 방을 나오자마자 호랑이로 변했어요. 그리고 방 앞에서 방울 장수가 잠이 들면 잡아먹으려고 기다렸어요. 그렇지만 피곤해서 잠이 들어 버렸어요.

그것을 보고 방울 장수는 조용히 방을 나왔어요. 그리고 호랑이의 꼬리에 방울을 매달았어요. 그리고 멀리 멀리 도망쳤어요.

호랑이는 잠에서 깨어났어요. 그리고 일어나려고 움직이니까 꼬리에 달린 방울이 크게 울렸어요.

"아이고! 호랑이 잡아먹는 방울이구나!"

호랑이는 무서워서 도망치기 시작했어요. 하지만 호랑이가 달리면 달릴수록 방울은 더 크게 울렸어요. 그것을 보고 산 속 동물들이 재미있게 웃었어요.

☆ ☆ ☆

Vocabulary

방울 **bangul** bell

길을 잃다 **gireul ilta** to get lost

밤이 깊어지다 **bami kipeojida** the night deepens

잘 **jal** well

모르다 **moreuda** not to know

이러다가 **ireodaga** at this rate

멀리 **meolli** far away

문을 두드리다 **muneul dudeurida** to knock on the door

어서 오세요 **eoseo oseyo** welcome, come right in

늦다 **neutda** to be late

편히 **pyeonhi** comfortably

주무시다 **jumusida** [honorific] to sleep

저녁 **jeonyeok** dinner

With that, the old woman picked up the empty bowl and stood up. As she was leaving the room, the bell seller saw her from behind and got a big shock. Below the old woman's skirt he could see a tiger's tail!

"Oh my, it's a tiger that's turned itself into an old woman! This is terrible. It's probably planning to eat me when I fall asleep—what should I do?"

Then he had a good idea. So he spoke to the old woman.

"Ma'am, the bells that I'm selling are magical bells that kill tigers. Since you live alone in the hills, you must be worried about tigers, so shall I give you one?"

No sooner had the bell seller finished speaking than the old woman went out of the room without giving any reply.

As soon as she had left the room, the old woman turned into a tiger. And she waited outside the room to catch and eat the bell seller once he was asleep. But she was tired and fell asleep herself.

On seeing that, the bell seller quietly came out of his room. He hung a bell on the tiger's tail. Then he ran far, far away.

The tiger woke up from her sleep. And when she moved to get up, the bell hanging from her tail rang loudly.

"Oh my! It's the bell that kills tigers!"

Terrified, the tiger began to run away. But the harder she ran, the louder the bell rang. When they saw that, all the other animals in the hills laughed joyfully.

☆ ☆ ☆

뒷모습 **dwinmoseup** appearance from behind

치마 **chima** skirt

둔갑하다 **dungaphada** to change, turn into

신기하다 **singihada** to be amazing, magical

잠이 들다 **jami deulda** to go to sleep

방문 **bangmun** room door

열다 **yeolda** to open

매달다 **maedalda** to hang

도망치다 **domangchida** to run away

잠에서 깨어나다 **jameseo kkaeeonada** to wake from sleep

일어나다 **ireonada** to stand up

움직이다 **umjigida** to move

달리다 **dallida** to be hung

크게 울리다 **keuge ullida** to ring loudly

달리다 **dallida** to run

재미있게 **jaemiitge** joyfully

Selected grammar points

- (으)ㄹ까 봐(서) **"in fear of"**

  방울 장수는 호랑이를 **만날까 봐** 걱정이 되기 시작했어요.

  The bell seller started to worry about meeting a tiger.

- 네요 **Exclamatory sentence ending, or realization, "oh" "I see," "so that's how it is"**

  This ending is used to express surprise or a realization upon learning something through direct experience or when agreeing with something said by someone else.

  밤이 늦었는데 길을 **잃으셨나 보네요**.

  So it's late and you've lost your way.

- 기가 무섭게 **"as soon as," "no sooner . . . than . . . "**

  할머니는 방울 장수의 말이 끝나**기가 무섭게** 아무 대답도 하지 않고 방을 나가 버렸어요.

  No sooner had the bell seller finished speaking than the old woman went out of the room without giving any reply.

After reading the story

1. 방울 장수가 산 속에서 길을 잃었을 때 무엇 때문에 걱정이 되었어요?

   When the bell seller lost his way in the hills, what was he worried about?

2. 방울 장수는 할머니의 뒷모습을 보고 왜 놀랐어요?

   Why was the bell seller shocked when he saw the old woman from behind?

3. 방울 장수는 할머니가 호랑이라는 것을 알고 어떻게 했어요?

   What did the bell seller do when he realized the old woman was a tiger?

Let's talk!

한국에서는 호랑이나 여우가 사람으로 둔갑한다는 이야기가 있는데 여러분 나라에도 비슷한 이야기가 있나요?

In Korea there are various stories about tigers or foxes turning themselves into humans. Are there any stories like that in your country?

Notes on Korean culture

There are times in our lives when we face trouble. In this story, the bell seller lost his way in the middle of the night and was in danger of being eaten by a tiger, but he used his wits to escape. The moral of the story is that no matter what perils we face, if we think calmly and don't panic, a good solution will appear. There's a Korean saying about this: "호랑이에게 물려가도 정신만 차리면 살 수 있다" which means "Even if you're being chased by a tiger, keep your wits about you and you'll survive."

요술 항아리

어느 마을에 가난하지만 부지런한 농부가 살았어요. 농부는 열심히 일을 해서 돈을 모아 같은 마을에 사는 부자의 밭을 샀어요. 좋은 땅은 아니었지만 농부는 자기의 땅을 가지게 되어서 행복했어요. 그래서 매일매일 밭에 나가 열심히 일을 했어요.

어느 날 밭에서 열심히 일을 하던 농부는 땅 속에서 큰 항아리를 발견했어요.

농부는 항아리를 집으로 가지고 왔어요. 그리고 항아리 속에 호미를 넣어 두었어요.

그런데 다음 날 아침, 농부는 깜짝 놀랐어요. 항아리에 호미를 하나 넣어 두었는데 호미가 항아리에 가득 있었거든요.

"어? 이게 어떻게 된 일이지? 혹시 요술 항아리인가?"

농부는 이번에는 항아리에 동전을 하나 넣었어요. 그랬더니 이번에는 동전이 항아리에 가득 차는 거예요.

"와, 정말 요술 항아리구나."

곧 다른 사람들도 요술 항아리에 대해서 알게 되었어요. 농부에게 땅을 팔았던 부자도 그 이야기를 듣고 너무 배가 아팠어요. 그래서 농부를 찾아가서 말했어요. "그 항아리는 내 거니까 나한테 돌려줘."

The Magic Pot

In a certain village lived a poor but diligent farmer. By working hard, the farmer saved some money and bought a field from a rich man who lived in the same village. It wasn't good land, but the farmer was happy to have some land of his own. So every day he went out to the field and worked hard.

One day, while working hard in his field, the farmer discovered a big pot in the ground. He brought the pot home. And into the pot he put a trowel.

The next morning, the farmer got a big surprise. He had only put one trowel in the pot, but now the pot was completely full of trowels.

"Huh? How did this happen? Is it a magic pot?"

This time, the farmer put a coin in the pot. And the pot became completely filled with coins.

"Wow, it really is a magic pot!"

Soon, other people came to know about the magic pot too. The rich man who had sold the land to the farmer also heard the story and was very jealous. So he went to see the farmer and said, "That pot is mine, so give it back."

농부는 기가 막혔어요.

"아니, 그게 무슨 말씀이세요? 이 항아리는 제가 산 밭에서 나왔으니까 당연히 제 거지요."

"난 밭만 판 거지, 항아리는 안 팔았네. 그러니까 항아리는 내 거야."

두 사람은 싸우게 되어서 결국 사또를 찾아가서 물어봤어요.

"이 항아리가 누구 거라고 생각하십니까?"

사또는 요술 항아리를 보자 자기가 가지고 싶어졌어요.

그래서 이렇게 거짓말을 했어요.

"이 항아리는 아주 귀한 것이니까 임금님께 드려야겠다. 그럼 임금님이 큰 상을 주실 테니까 너희는 집에 돌아가서 기다려라."

사또는 혼자 생각했어요.

"이제 난 부자가 되겠구나."

사또는 항아리를 옆에 두고 잠깐 잠이 들었어요.

마침 사또의 아버지가 지나가다가 항아리를 보았어요.

"이게 뭐지? 안에 뭐가 들어 있나?"

사또의 아버지는 궁금해서 항아리 안을 들여다보려고 했는데, 잘못해서 항아리 안에 빠지고 말았어요.

"아이고, 사람 살려."

사또가 깜짝 놀라 일어났어요. 소리는 항아리 안에서 들려오고 있었어요.

"설마 아버지가 항아리에 들어있는 건 아니겠지?"

이렇게 걱정하면서 항아리 속에서 아버지를 꺼냈어요. 그런데 항아리 속에서는 똑같이 생긴 아버지들이 계속해서 나오는 거예요.

"내가 네 아버지다."

"아냐, 내가 네 아버지야."

사또의 아버지는 열 명이 넘었고, 아버지들끼리 자기가 진짜 아버지라고 싸우기 시작했어요.

그러는 통에 항아리는 깨져 버렸고요.

"아이고, 어떡해?"

사또는 후회했지만 너무 늦었어요.

☆ ☆ ☆

The farmer was staggered.

"What? What do you mean? This pot came out of the field that I bought, so it obviously belongs to me."

"I only sold you the field, I didn't sell the pot. Consequently, the pot is mine."

The two men fought over it and eventually they went to see the district magistrate and asked him.

"Who do you think this pot belongs to, sir?"

When the magistrate saw the magic pot, he wanted to have it himself. So he spoke deceitfully:

"As this pot is very valuable, I'd better give it to the king. Then the king will give a big reward, so you two just go home and wait."

The magistrate thought to himself, "Now I'm going to get rich!"

With the pot beside him, the magistrate fell asleep for a while.

Just then, the magistrate's father was passing by when he saw the pot.

"What's this? Is there anything inside?"

Curious, the magistrate's father tried to look inside the pot, but by accident he fell right into it.

"Oh my, someone save me!"

The magistrate woke up in surprise. A sound was coming from inside the pot.

"Surely my father can't be in the pot?"

Concerned, he lifted his father out of the pot. But from inside the pot, identical fathers kept coming out.

"I'm your father."

"No, I'm your father."

There were more than ten of the magistrate's fathers and they started to argue among themselves as to which one was the real father.

While this was going on, the pot broke.

"Oh no, what'll I do?"

The magistrate was sorry, but it was too late.

Vocabulary

요술 **yosul** magic

항아리 **hangari** pot

돈을 모으다 **doneul moeuda** to save money

매일매일 **maeil (maeil)** every day

발견하다 **balgyeonhada** to discover

호미 **homi** trowel, hand-held hoe

가득 **gadeuk** fully

차다 **chada** to be filled

동전 **dongjeon** coin

대해서 **daehaeseo** about

배가 아프다 **baega apeuda** to be jealous

돌려주다 **dollyeojuda** to return

기가 막히다 **giga makida** to be amazed, exasperated

당연히 **dangyeonhi** certainly, obviously

싸우다 **ssauda** to fight

사또 **satto** district magistrate

물어보다 **mureoboda** to ask

거짓말을 하다 **geojinmareul hada** to lie, speak falsely

귀하다 **gwihada** to be valuable

임금님 **imgeumnim** king

큰 상 **keun sang** great reward

너희 **neohui** you all

두다 **duda** to put

들여다보다 **deuryeodaboda** to look in

빠지다 **ppajida** to fall

살리다 **sallida** to save

소리 **sori** sound

들려오다 **deullyeooda** to sound, be heard

설마 **seolma** no way

들어있다 **deureoitda** to be filled with

꺼내다 **kkeonaeda** to pull out, to take out

똑같이 **ttokgachi** exactly the same

생기다 **saenggida** to look like

계속해서 **gyesokhaeseo** continuously

아버지 **abeoji** father

열 **yeol** ten

넘다 **neomda** to exceed

진짜 **jinjja** real

깨지다 **kkaejida** to be broken

후회하다 **huhoehada** to regret, be sorry

Selected grammar points

- 아/어 두다 **"to do something and keep it that way for future use"**

  항아리 속에 호미를 넣어 두었어요.

  He put a trowel into the pot.

- 거든요 **"because"**

  This is added to the end of a sentence to provide a reason.

  농부는 깜짝 놀랐어요. 항아리에 호미를 하나 넣어 두었는데 호미가 항아리에 가득 있었거든요.

  The farmer got a big surprise. He had only put one trowel in the pot, but now the pot was completely full of trowels.

- 에 대해서 **"about," "concerning"**

  다른 사람들도 요술 항아리에 대해서 알게 되었어요.

  Other people came to know about the magic pot too.

- **자 Expressing the ordering of behavior**
  This is used when the situation in the preceding clause is the cause or motivation for some resulting state of affairs stated in the following clause.
  사또는 요술 항아리를 **보자** 자기가 가지고 싶어졌어요.
  When the magistrate saw the magic pot, he wanted to have it himself.
- **끼리 "among themselves," "by themselves"**
  Attached to a human or animal noun, this expression indicates exclusiveness in a group activity or gathering.
  아버지들**끼리** 자기가 진짜 아버지라고 싸우기 시작했어요.
  They started to argue among themselves as to which one was the real father.

After reading the story

1 농부는 요술 항아리를 어디에서 발견했어요?
   Where did the farmer find the magic pot?
2. 왜 부자는 요술 항아리가 자기 것이라고 했어요?
   Why did the rich man say the magic pot was his?
3. 사또는 항아리가 자기 것이라고 주장하는 두 사람에게 뭐라고 말했어요?
   What did the district magistrate say to the two men who were both insisting that the pot was theirs?
4. 사또는 항아리 속에서 무엇을 꺼냈어요?
   What did the magistrate take out of the pot?
5. 결국 항아리는 어떻게 되었어요?
   What happened to the pot in the end?

Let's talk!

여러분은 이 경우에 항아리를 누가 가져야 된다고 생각합니까?
In this case, who do you think should have the pot?

Notes on Korean culture

From the Goryeo dynasty (918–1392) to the Joseon era (1392–1910), Korea's central government sent magistrates (사또 **satto**) to be in charge of provincial areas. A post lasted for five years and among magistrates there were some who worked tirelessly for the local people and had monuments erected to them after they left. But there were also greedy and selfish magistrates like the one that appears in this story. Consequently, the Joseon dynasty established a system of secret inspectors. At the special command of the king, an inspector would go around disguised as a beggar, finding out about the living conditions and grievances of the people. They would then reveal their true identity to reward good governance and punish corruption. In old stories, a secret inspector often arrives to punish a bad magistrate. Through these stories, people must have felt a sense of justice and catharsis.

의좋은 형제

옛날 옛날 어느 마을에 형과 동생이 살았어요. 형과 동생은 같이 열심히 농사를 지었지요.

그러던 어느 날 동생이 결혼을 해서 가까운 곳으로 이사를 갔어요. 형은 동생에게 재산을 똑같이 나누어 주었지요.

봄이 되었어요. 형은 형의 논에서, 동생은 동생의 논에서 열심히 일을 했어요. 또 서로 왔다 갔다 하면서 도와 주기도 했지요.

"수고했다. 이제 농사가 잘 되겠지."

"그럼요, 형님. 열심히 했으니까 올해에도 잘 될 거예요."

여름이 되었어요. 형은 형의 밭에서, 동생은 동생의 밭에서 열심히 풀을 뽑았어요. 또 서로 왔다 갔다 하면서 도와 주기도 했어요.

"콩밭이 깨끗해졌구나."

"네, 형님, 올해에도 농사가 잘 될 거예요."

가을이 되었어요. 논과 밭은 잘 익은 곡식으로 가득찼어요.

"하늘이 도와 주셔서 올해도 농사가 잘되었구나."

"네, 그렇네요, 정말 감사한 일이지요."

드디어 잘 익은 벼를 다 베었어요. 벼를 묶어 볏단을 쌓아올렸어요.

"영차, 영차."

하늘 높이 볏단이 쌓였어요. 형님네 볏가리와 동생네 볏가리의 높이가 똑같아요.

Good Brothers

Long, long ago, two brothers lived in a certain village. The elder brother and the younger brother worked hard together at their farming.

One day, the younger brother got married and moved to a nearby place. The elder brother shared all their property with him equally.

Spring came. The elder brother worked hard in his rice paddy and the younger brother in his. They also went back and forth to help each other.

"You've worked hard. Now the farm work will turn out well."

"Yes, brother. Since we've worked so hard, it should go well again this year."

Summer came. The elder brother worked hard weeding his field and the younger brother his. They also went back and forth to help each other.

"I see the pea patch is clear."

"Yes, brother, the farm work should go well this year too."

Autumn came. The rice paddies and fields were full of well-ripened grain.

"With Heaven's help, the farm work has gone well again this year."

"Yes, indeed, it's really something to be thankful for."

At last, they harvested all the well-ripened rice. They bound the rice stalks together and stacked up the sheaves of rice.

"Yo-ho, yo-ho!"

The stacks of rice rose high as the sky. The height of the two brothers' rice stacks was exactly the same.

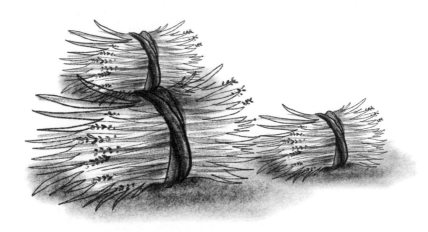

형이 말했어요. "아우야, 너는 이제 막 결혼을 했으니 곡식이 나보다 더 필요할 것 같구나. 그러니 우리 볏단을 더 가지고 가."

동생이 대답했어요. "아닙니다. 형님. 저도 이것으로 충분합니다. 형님이야말로 식구가 많으니 제 볏단을 가지고 가세요."

형이 대답했어요. "그럼, 안되지. 우리도 이만하면 충분해."

밤에 동생이 곰곰이 생각했어요.

"아무래도 형님 네는 식구가 많으니 우리 것을 조금 더 드려야지."

동생은 조용히 일어나 자기 볏단을 좀 가져다가 형님 네 볏가리에 올려놓았어요.

형도 곰곰이 생각했어요.

"아무래도 동생은 새로 결혼을 했으니 나보다 더 필요하겠지. 우리 것을 조금 나눠 줘야겠다."

형도 조용히 일어나 자기 볏단을 좀 가져다가 동생네 볏가리에 올려놓았어요.

그 다음날

"어? 이상하다, 그대로네? 왜 하나도 줄어들지 않았지? 오늘 다시 갖다 줘야지."

형이 이렇게 생각하고 있을 때 동생도 생각했어요.

"어 . . . 이상하다, 어젯밤에 분명히 형님한테 갖다 드렸는데 왜 줄어들지 않았을까? 오늘 다시 갖다 드려야지."

다시 밤이 되었어요. 동생이 볏단을 가지고 형님 네로 갔어요. 형님도 볏단을 가지고 동생 네로 갔어요. 두 사람은 중간에서 딱 마주쳤어요.

"이게 누구냐?"

"아이고 형님."

"그랬었구나."

"그랬었군요."

"형님, 고맙습니다."

"동생아, 나도 고맙다."

형제는 볏단을 놓고 서로를 부둥켜 안았습니다.

"우리 언제까지나 이렇게 살아가자."

"그래요, 형님."

달님이 환하게 웃으며 두 사람을 내려다봤어요.

☆ ☆ ☆

The elder brother said, "Oh, but you've just gotten married, so you'll need more grain than me. Take some of my rice."

The younger brother answered, "No, brother, this much is enough for me. It's you who have more family members, so take some of my rice."

"No, that won't do," said the elder brother. "This much is enough for us too."

That night, the younger brother thought it over carefully.

"However you look at it, big brother has more family members, so I should give him some of my rice."

The younger brother quietly got up, took one of his sheaves of rice and put it on his brother's stack.

The elder brother thought it over too.

"Whatever he says, little brother is newly married so he needs more than me. I'd better share some of our rice with him."

The elder brother also got up quietly, took one of his sheaves of rice and put it on his brother's stack.

The next day, the elder brother thought, "Huh? This is strange, it's just as before. Why isn't my stack any smaller? I'd better give him some more tonight."

Meanwhile, the younger brother was thinking, "Huh? This is strange, I definitely gave a rice sheaf to my brother last night, so why isn't my stack any smaller? I'd better give him another one tonight."

Night fell again. The younger brother took a rice sheaf and set off for his elder brother's place. Meanwhile, the elder brother also took a rice sheaf and set off for his younger brother's place. They bumped into each other on the way.

"Who is that?"

"Oh, brother!"

"So that's what happened!"

"Ah, that's what happened!"

"Thank you, brother."

"Thank you too, brother."

The two brothers put their sheaves of rice down and embraced each other.

"Let's always live like this."

"Yes, brother."

The moon looked down at the two men with a bright smile.

☆ ☆ ☆

Vocabulary

의좋다 **uijota** to be on good terms
가깝다 **gakkapda** to be nearby
이사를 가다 **isareul gada** to move (house)
재산 **jaesan** property
똑같이 **ttokgachi** evenly, equally
나누어 주다 **nanueo juda** to allot, share
논 **non** rice paddy
왔다 갔다 하다 **whatta gatta hada** to keep coming and going
수고하다 **sugohada** to work hard
여름 **yeoreum** summer
풀을 뽑다 **pureul ppopda** to pull up weeds
콩밭 **kongbat** pea patch
깨끗하다 **kkaekkeuthada** to be clean
익다 **ikda** to ripen
올해 **olhae** this year
감사하다 **gamsahada** to thank
드디어 **deudieo** finally, at last
벼 **byeo** unhusked rice
볏단 **byeotdan** sheaf of unhusked rice
쌓아올리다 **ssaaollida** to stack up
영차 **yeongcha** Yo-ho!
쌓이다 **ssaida** to be piled up
볏가리 **byeotgari** stack of rice straw
형님네 **hyeongnimne** older brother's
동생네 **dongsaengne** younger brother's
높이 **nopi** height

똑같다 **ttotgatda** to be exactly the same
막 **mak** just
필요하다 **piryohada** to need
충분하다 **chungbunhada** to be enough
식구 **sikgu** family member
이만하다 **imanhada** to be this much
곰곰이 **gomgomi** carefully, thoughtfully
올려 놓다 **ollyeo nota** to put on
새로 **saero** newly
그대로 **geudaero** as it is
줄어들다 **jureodeulda** to decrease
갖다주다 **gatda juda** to deliver
어젯밤 **eojetbam** last night
분명히 **bunmyeonghi** surely
갖다 드리다 **gatda deurida** [humble] to deliver
중간 **junggan** the middle
딱 마주치다 **ttak majuchida** to just bump into
누구 **nugu** who
부둥켜 안다 **budeungkyeo anda** to hold in one's arms, embrace
언제까지나 **eonjekkajina** as long as one likes
달님 **dalnim** the moon
환하다 **hwanhada** to be bright
내려다보다 **naeryeodaboda** to look down

Selected grammar points

- (으)ㄹ 거예요 **Future tense "will," "is going to"**
  This pattern is formed by adding (으)ㄹ 거예요 to the stems of verbs. ㄹ 거예요 is used when the verb stem ends in ㄹ or a vowel. 을 거예요 is used when the verb stem ends in a consonant.

  열심히 했으니까 올해에도 잘 될 거예요.
  Since we've worked so hard, it should go well again this year.

- (이)야말로 **"indeed," "exactly," "the very," "it is X that . . ."**
  This form is used to emphasize the preceding noun, which is the best among other possible choices.
  형님이야말로 식구가 많으니 제 볏단을 가져가세요.
  It's you who have more family members, so take some of my rice.
- 아/어 놓다 **"to do something and keep it that way"**
  This is used when preparation is done before performing an action, and the resulting state is maintained.
  몰래 일어나 자기 볏단을 좀 가져다가 형님 네 볏가리에 **올려 놓았어요**.
  He quietly got up, took one of his sheaves of rice and put it on his brother's stack.
- 구나/군요 **"I see (that)," "indeed"**
  Used to express surprise or wonder upon learning something new either by direct observation or experience or by hearing about it from someone else.
  아, 그랬었군요.
  Ah, that's what happened!

After reading the story

1. 형은 왜 동생이 자기보다 곡식이 더 많이 필요할 거라고 생각했어요?
   Why did the elder brother think that the younger brother would need more grain than himself?
2. 동생은 왜 형이 자기보다 곡식이 더 많이 필요할 거라고 생각했어요?
   Why did the younger brother think that the elder brother would need more grain than himself?
3. 왜 낫가리가 줄어들지 않았어요?
   Why didn't the rice stacks get any smaller?
4. 동생은 밤에 누구와 마주쳤어요?
   Who did the younger brother bump into at night?

Let's talk!

이렇게 서로를 배려하는 따뜻한 이야기를 알면 이야기해 보세요.
Do you know any heartwarming stories about people caring for each other like this?

Notes on Korean culture

Koreans have always had a strong sense of community. That's why they don't say "my house" or "my family" but rather "our house" and "our family." Married women even say "our husband" rather than "my husband." This reflects their desire to live in a community where people help each other. This story expresses the principle that doing good to others is really doing good to yourself. If we value others like ourselves, we should be able to feel that we are not alone and live our lives a little more warmly and happily.

방귀쟁이 며느리

어느 집에 아들이 결혼해서 며느리가 들어왔습니다. 그런데 건강하던 며느리는 시집오고 난 뒤부터 얼굴이 노래지고 건강이 안 좋아졌습니다. 시어머니는 걱정이 되어서 며느리한테 물어봤습니다.

　"너는 왜 시집오고 난 뒤부터 얼굴색이 점점 나빠지니? 무슨 걱정이 있니?"

　며느리가 대답했습니다.

　"네, 어머니. 있어요. 그런데 너무 부끄러워서 말씀을 못 드리겠어요."

　시어머니가 말했습니다.

　"나한테 부끄러울 일이 뭐가 있어? 다 괜찮으니까 솔직히 말해 봐."

　그러니까 며느리가 이렇게 말했습니다.

　"그럼, 말씀드릴게요. 저는 원래 방귀를 많이 뀌었어요. 그런데 시집온 뒤부터는 부끄러워서 편하게 방귀를 못 뀌는 바람에 병이 난 것 같아요."

　시어머니는 그것이 우스웠지만 불쌍하다는 생각도 들었습니다.

　"괜찮으니까 걱정 말고 마음대로 방귀를 뀌어도 돼."

　"정말 그래도 될까요?"

The Farting Daughter-in-Law

In a certain household, the son got married and the daughter-in-law moved in. But although she was previously healthy, from the time she got married the daughter-in-law's face grew yellow and her health grew worse. The mother-in-law was worried and asked her, "Why has your complexion grown gradually worse since you got married? Is there something you're worried about?"

"Yes, mother, there is," the daughter-in-law replied. "But I'm too shy to tell you."

"What is there to be shy about with me?" said the mother-in-law. "Everything's all right: just tell me openly."

So the daughter-in-law explained.

"All right, I'll tell you. I always used to fart a lot. But since I got married, I've been too shy to fart comfortably. I think that's why I'm ill."

The mother-in-law thought that was funny, but she also felt sorry for her.

"It's all right, you can fart as much as you like and don't worry about it."

"Can I really?"

"Of course—who doesn't fart? It's OK."

"그럼, 방귀 안 뀌는 사람이 어디 있니? 괜찮아."

"그렇지만 제 방귀는 보통 방귀가 아니에요."

"그래도 괜찮으니 마음 놓고 뀌어라."

그제서야 며느리는 안도의 한숨을 쉬었습니다. 그리고 가족들 모두를 불러 달라고 말했습니다. 가족들이 모이자 가족들에게 말했습니다.

"제가 이제 방귀를 뀌겠습니다. 아버님은 문고리를 잡으세요. 어머니는 솥뚜껑을 누르고 계시고, 서방님은 기둥을 붙잡고 계세요."

가족들이 그렇게 하니까 며느리가 방귀를 천둥같이 뀌었습니다. 문이 날아갔습니다. 문고리를 잡고 있던 시아버지는 마당에 떨어졌습니다. 솥뚜껑이 솟아올랐습니다. 솥뚜껑을 누르고 있던 시어머니도 같이 날아올랐다가 떨어졌습니다. 기둥도 흔들흔들거렸습니다. 남편도 기둥과 같이 뱅글뱅글 돌았습니다.

이렇게 방귀를 뀌니까 며느리는 속이 시원해서 얼굴이 환해졌습니다. 그런데 다른 식구들은 모두 다 걱정이 되었습니다. 앞으로 방귀를 뀔 때마다 큰 일이 날 것 같기 때문입니다.

"아이고, 안 되겠다. 네가 우리집에서 같이 살면 우리가 죽겠다."

그래서 시아버지와 시어머니는 며느리를 친정으로 돌려보내기로 했습니다.

시아버지와 남편이 며느리를 친정으로 데리고 가는 길이었습니다. 힘들어서 잠깐 감나무 아래에서 쉬기로 했어요. 그런데 하루 종일 걸어서 배가 고팠습니다. 위를 보니까 맛있는 감이 주렁주렁 열려 있었습니다. 먹고 싶었지만 너무 높이 있어서 따 먹을 수가 없었습니다. 시아버지가 말했습니다.

"에고, 배가 고프구나. 저 감이라도 먹을 수 있으면 좋을 텐데 . . ."

그것을 듣고 며느리가 말했습니다.

"두 분은 잠깐만 저기에 가서 피해 계세요."

그리고는 감나무에다 방귀를 뀌었습니다. 그랬더니 천둥 치는 소리가 나면서 바람이 불었습니다. 그 바람 때문에 감이 우르르 떨어졌습니다. 세 사람은 떨어진 감을 맛있게 먹었습니다. 그리고 자루에 가득 담았습니다.

시아버지가 말했습니다.

"우리 며느리 방귀가 쓸모없는 방귀가 아니구나. 얘야, 어서 집으로 돌아가자."

그래서 며느리를 다시 집으로 데리고 와서 행복하게 잘 살았습니다.

☆ ☆ ☆

"But my farts are no ordinary farts."

"It doesn't matter, just fart and don't worry."

At that, the daughter-in-law heaved a sigh of relief. She asked her mother-in-law to call all the family together. When they were all gathered, she spoke to them.

"I am now going to fart. Father, hold onto the door handle. Mother, press down on the cauldron lid and Husband, hold onto the pillar."

The family members all did as she said and the daughter-in-law let fly a fart like thunder. The door flew open, and the father-in-law, who was holding onto the door handle, fell out into the yard. The cauldron lid flew up, and the mother-in-law, who was holding it down, flew up with it and then fell down. The pillar shook and the husband spun around it.

Having let out such a fart, the daughter-in-law felt fresh inside and her face grew brighter. But the other family members were all worried that there would be trouble like this every time she farted.

"Oh no, this will never do. If you live with us, we'll die."

So the father-in-law and the mother-in-law decided to send the daughter-in-law back to her parental home.

When the husband and father-in-law were taking her back to her parents, they got tired and decided to rest for a while under a persimmon tree. Having walked all day, they were hungry. They looked up and saw lots of delicious persimmons hanging. They wanted to eat them, but the fruit was too high to pick.

"Oh dear, I'm so hungry," said the father-in-law. "I wish I could eat some of those persimmons . . ."

On hearing that, the daughter-in-law said, "You two escape over there for a moment."

Then she farted at the persimmon tree. With a sound like thunder, the wind rose. Because of the wind, the persimmons fell down. The three of them ate some of the delicious fallen persimmons and completely filled their bags with the rest.

The father-in-law spoke.

"Our daughter-in-law's farts are no useless farts. Young lady, let's go home now."

They took the daughter-in-law back home and they all lived together happily.

Vocabulary

방귀쟁이 **banggwijaengi** farting person
아들 **adeul** son
들어오다 **deureooda** to come in, to join
건강하다 **geonganghada** to be healthy
시집오다 **sijiboda** (for a woman) to marry
노래지다 **noraejida** to turn yellow
건강 **geongang** health
시어머니 **sieomeoni** mother-in-law
얼굴색 **eolgulsaek** complexion
점점 **jeomjeom** gradually
솔직히 **soljiki** openly
원래 **wollae** originally, before
방귀를 뀌다 **banggwireul kkwida** to fart
편하게 **pyeonhage** comfortably
병이 나다 **byeongi nada** to get ill
우습다 **useupda** to be funny
불쌍하다 **bulssanghada** to feel sorry for
마음대로 **maeumdaero** as you please
보통 **botong** ordinary
마음 놓고 **maeum noko** without worrying
안도 **ando** relief
한숨을 쉬다 **hansumeul swida** to heave a sigh
모이다 **moida** to gather
문고리 **mungori** door handle
잡다 **japda** to hold
솥뚜껑 **sotttukkeong** cauldron lid
누르다 **nureuda** to press
서방님 **seobangnim** husband
기둥 **gidung** pillar, column
붙잡다 **butjapda** to hold
천둥 **cheondung** thunder
날아가다 **naragada** to be blown
솟아오르다 **sosaoreuda** to rise high
흔들흔들거리다 **heundeulheundeulgeorida** to shake
뱅글뱅글 돌다 **banggeulbanggeul dolda** to turn round and round
시원하다 **siwonhada** to feel fresh
앞으로 **apeuro** from now on
친정 **chinjeong** married woman's parents' home
돌려보내다 **dullyeobonaeda** to send back
데리고 가다 **derigo gada** to take (a person)
힘들다 **himdeulda** to be hard
감나무 **gamnamu** persimmon tree
주렁주렁 열리다 **jureong jureong yeollida** to hang in clusters
따다 **ttada** to pick
피하다 **pihada** to escape, to avoid
바람이 불다 **barami bulda** the wind rises
우르르 **ureureu** loud sound
쓸모없다 **sseulmo eopda** no use

Selected grammar points

- **는 바람에 "as a result": giving an unexpected reason for a consequence**
  This is used when an event or situation in the first statement leads to a result in the following statement which is mostly negative.
  편하게 방귀를 **못 뀌는 바람에** 병이 난 것 같아요
  I've been too shy to fart comfortably. I think that's why I'm ill.

- 아/어도 되다 **"may," "be allowed to"**

  This is used to ask, give or deny permission to do something.

  마음대로 방귀를 **뀌어도 돼**.

  You can fart as much as you like.

- 았/었다가 **"but then"**

  This indicates that after the completion of an event, the opposite event happens.

  솥뚜껑을 누르고 있던 시어머니도 같이 **날아올랐다가** 떨어졌습니다.

  The mother-in-law, who was holding the cauldron lid down, flew up with it and then fell down.

- 기로 하다 **"to decide to"**

  This is used to give the meaning "decide to do something."

  시아버지와 시어머니는 며느리를 친정으로 **돌려보내기로 했습니다**.

  The father-in-law and the mother-in-law decided to send the daughter-in-law back to her parental home.

After reading the story

1. 며느리가 병이 난 이유는 무엇이었습니까?

    Why did the daughter-in-law become ill?

2. 며느리가 방귀를 뀔 때 시아버지는 무엇을 붙잡고 있었습니까?

    What did the father-in-law hold onto when the daughter-in-law farted?

3. 며느리를 친정으로 돌려 보내려고 한 이유는 무엇입니까?

    Why were they going to send the daughter-in-law back to her parental home?

4. 왜 며느리를 다시 집으로 데리고 돌아왔습니까?

    Why did they bring the daughter-in-law back home?

Let's talk!

여러분도 부끄러워서 하지 못한 일이 있으면 이야기해 보세요.

Has shyness ever prevented you from doing something that you wanted to?

Notes on Korean culture

Things have changed today, but in Korea in the past, when a son got married he went on living in his parents' house. So when a woman got married, she had to live with her mother-in-law and she had to be careful of her behavior. The funny story of the daughter-in-law who fell ill from being unable to fart comfortably is probably meant to tell of the troubles of daughters-in-law who had to live so carefully.

피리 부는 목동과 선녀

옛날에 한 목동이 살고 있었어요. 이 목동은 피리를 아주 잘 불었어요. 목동의 피리 소리는 누구든지 들으면 눈물을 흘릴 정도로 너무 아름다웠어요.

하늘나라에 사는 옥황상제에게는 일곱 명의 딸이 있었는데, 막내 선녀가 그 피리 소리를 들었어요.

"아, 세상에는 이렇게 아름답고 슬픈 소리가 있구나."

아래를 내려다 보니 연못가에서 목동이 피리를 부는 것이 보였어요. 선녀는 세상에 내려가고 싶어졌어요. 그런데 아버지가 아시면 분명히 화를 크게 내실 것 같았어요 그래서 몰래 자기의 몸을 금붕어로 바꿔 세상으로 내려와 연못 속에 살면서 피리 소리를 들었어요. 며칠 동안 그렇게 피리 소리를 듣다 보니 선녀는 목동을 만나 이야기를 하고 싶어졌어요.

"내일은 물 밖으로 나가서 말을 해 봐야지."

선녀는 그렇게 하려고 했지만 막상 목동이 나타나면 부끄러워서 그렇게 할 수 없었어요.

"내일은 꼭 나가 봐야지."

The Shepherd Boy and the Fairy

Long ago there lived a shepherd boy. This shepherd boy was very good at playing on a pipe. The sound of his piping was so beautiful that anyone who heard it would weep.

The Great Jade Emperor who lived in Heaven had seven fairy daughters. The youngest fairy heard the shepherd boy's piping.

"Ah, so on Earth there is such a beautiful and sad sound as this!"

Looking down, she saw the shepherd boy playing his pipe beside a pond. The fairy wanted to go down to Earth. But if her father knew, he would certainly get very angry. So the fairy secretly turned herself into a goldfish, went down to Earth and lived in the pond, listening to the piping.

After listening like this for a few days, the fairy wanted to meet the shepherd boy and talk to him.

"Tomorrow I must leave the water and speak."

그렇지만 그 다음날도 용기가 나지 않았어요. 이렇게 며칠을 망설이다가 드디어 용기를 내어 선녀의 모습이 되어 물 밖으로 나갔어요. 그리고 목동 앞으로 가서 절을 했어요.

목동은 갑자기 아름다운 선녀가 나타나자 깜짝 놀랐어요.

"아니, 아가씨는 누구십니까? 왜 여기에 계십니까?"

"놀라지 마세요. 이제부터 제가 누구인지 다 말씀 드릴게요."

선녀는 그동안 있었던 일에 대해 다 이야기해 주었어요. 목동은 한편으로는 놀라기도 하고 또 한편으로는 기쁘기도 했어요. 곧 사랑에 빠진 두 사람은 결혼을 해서 행복하게 살았어요.

그런데 하늘나라는 선녀가 없어진 것을 알게 되어 발칵 뒤집혔어요. 하늘나라를 샅샅이 다 살펴보았지만 선녀는 어디에도 없었어요.

"선녀가 하늘나라에 없는 것을 보니까 틀림없이 땅나라에 내려간 것 같다. 빨리 땅으로 내려가서 선녀를 데리고 와라."

사신은 땅으로 내려와서 선녀를 찾아냈어요.

"선녀님, 여기 계셨군요. 옥황상제님이 찾으시니 빨리 하늘나라로 올라가셔야 합니다."

하지만 선녀는 고개를 흔들었어요.

"제가 원해서 땅으로 내려왔고 이제는 결혼까지 했는데 어떻게 하늘나라로 다시 올라갈 수가 있겠어요. 저는 절대로 올라가지 않을 거예요."

사신은 할 수 없이 혼자 하늘나라로 올라가서 옥황상제에게 말씀드렸어요.

"선녀는 목동과 결혼해서 살고 있는데, 하늘나라로 돌아오지 않겠다고 합니다."

"아니, 땅에서 천한 목동과 결혼을 해? 안되겠다. 힘이 센 장군이 내려가서 얼른 선녀를 잡아 오너라."

화가 난 옥황상제가 명령했어요. 명령을 받은 장군은 땅으로 내려갔어요. 그리고 강제로 선녀를 말에 태워서 하늘로 돌아왔어요. 옥황상제는 선녀가 다시 땅나라로 내려가지 못하도록 동굴 속에 가두어 버렸어요.

Although the fairy intended to do that, when the shepherd boy actually appeared she grew shy and couldn't do it.

"Tomorrow I must definitely leave the water."

But the next day, too, she didn't have the courage. After hesitating like this for several days, she finally plucked up courage, changed back into a fairy and left the water. She went up to the shepherd boy and bowed.

When this beautiful fairy suddenly appeared, the shepherd boy was startled.

"What? Who are you, Miss? Why are you here?"

"Don't be shocked. I'll tell you all about who I am now."

The fairy told him everything that had happened up to then. On the one hand, the shepherd boy was amazed and on the other hand, he was delighted. The two soon fell in love, got married and lived happily together.

Meanwhile, in Heaven, there was great uproar when it became known that the fairy was missing. They searched all over Heaven, but the fairy was nowhere to be found.

"As the fairy is not in Heaven, she must certainly have gone down to Earth. Go quickly down to Earth and bring her back."

An envoy went down to Earth and found the fairy.

"Miss Fairy, so this is where you've been. The Great Jade Emperor is looking for you, so you must go quickly up to Heaven."

But the fairy shook her head.

"I came down to Earth because I wanted to, and now I'm married, so how can I go back up to Heaven? I'm absolutely not going up."

The envoy had no choice but to go up to Heaven alone and tell the Great Jade Emperor.

"The fairy is married to a shepherd boy and says she will not come back to Heaven."

"What? She's married to a lowly shepherd boy on Earth? That's no good. Let a strong general go down and drag her back right now," the angry Emperor commanded.

The general who received the order went down to Earth. He forcibly set the fairy on his horse and brought her back to Heaven. To prevent her from going down to Earth again, the Great Jade Emperor imprisoned her in a cave.

한편, 땅에서는 목동이 선녀를 애타게 찾으며 눈물을 흘리며 피리를 불고 있었어요. 그 소리를 듣고 너무나 마음이 아파진 선녀는 언니들에게 도와 달라고 부탁했어요. 언니들은 동생이 너무 슬퍼하는 것을 보고 동굴 문을 열어 주었어요. 그렇게 해서 선녀는 땅으로 다시 내려와서 목동을 다시 만날 수 있었어요.

그런데 하늘나라 옥황상제는 선녀가 도망 간 것을 알고 너무나 화가 났어요.

"아버지의 말을 듣지 않고 아버지를 속이는 선녀를 금붕어로 만들어라. 그리고 다시는 원래 모습으로 돌아오지 못하도록 해라."

이렇게 해서 선녀는 다시 금붕어가 되어 연못에서 살게 되었어요. 또 다시 아내를 잃어버린 목동은 날마다 슬프게 피리를 불었어요. 금붕어가 된 선녀는 목동이 피리를 부는 연못가에 있었음에도 불구하고 목동에게 말 한마디 할 수 없었어요.

목동은 슬프게 살다가 세상을 떠났어요. 하지만 금붕어가 된 선녀는 죽지도 못하고 날마다 눈물을 흘리면서 연못 속에서 살았대요.

☆ ☆ ☆

Vocabulary

피리 **piri** pipe (instrument)
불다 **bulda** to blow
목동 **mokdong** shepherd boy
선녀 **seonnyeo** fairy
연못가 **yeonmotga** by a pond
누구든지 **nugudeunji** whoever
아름답다 **areumdapda** to be beautiful
슬프다 **seulpeuda** to be sad
모두 다 **modu da** all, everyone
눈물을 흘리다 **nunmureul heullida** to shed tears
하늘나라 **haneulnara** Heaven
옥황상제 **okhwangsangje** the Great Jade Emperor
일곱 **ilgop** seven
딸 **ttal** daughter

막내 **mangnae** the youngest
화를 내다 **hwareul naeda** to get angry
금붕어 **geumbungeo** goldfish
바꾸다 **bakkuda** to change
막상 **maksang** actually
용기가 나다 **yonggiga nada** to have the courage
망설이다 **mangseorida** to hesitate
아가씨 **agassi** young lady
한편으로는 **hanpyeoneuroneun** on the one hand
사랑에 빠지다 **sarange ppajida** to fall in love
행복하게 **haengbokage** happily
발칵 뒤집히다 **balkak dwijipida** to be topsy-turvy, in uproar

Meanwhile, on Earth, the shepherd boy was anxiously searching for the fairy, playing his pipe with tears in his eyes. When she heard the sound, the fairy's heart felt as if it was breaking and she begged her sisters to help her. When the sisters saw how sad she was, they opened the door of her cave. In that way, the fairy was able to go down to Earth again and meet the shepherd boy.

When the Great Jade Emperor found out that the fairy had run away, he was terribly angry.

"The fairy has disobeyed and deceived her father. Turn her into a goldfish. And don't let her change back to her original form again."

With that, the fairy became a goldfish again and came to live in the pond. The shepherd boy, having lost his wife, played his pipe sadly every day. Although the fairy who had become a goldfish was in the pond where the shepherd boy was piping, she couldn't speak a single word to him.

After living sadly for a while, the shepherd boy departed from this life. But the fairy who had become a goldfish was unable to die and went on living in the pond, weeping every day.

☆ ☆ ☆

샅샅이 **satsachi** thoroughly
땅나라 **ttangnara** the land
데리고 오다 **derigo oda** to bring (a person)
사신 **sasin** envoy
고개를 흔들다 **gogaereul heundeulda** to shake one's head
원하다 **wonhada** to want
천하다 **cheonhada** to be humble, lowly
장군 **janggun** general (military role)
잡아오다 **jabaoda** to capture and bring
명령하다 **myeongryeonghada** to command
강제로 **gangjero** forcibly
말에 태우다 **mare taeuda** to set on a horse

동굴 **donggul** cave
가두다 **gaduda** to shut up, imprison
한편 **hanpyeon** meanwhile
애타게 **aetage** anxiously
마음이 아프다 **maeumi apeuda** one's heart aches
문 **mun** door
속이다 **sogida** to deceive
모습 **moseup** appearance
아내 **anae** wife
날마다 **nalmada** every day
말 한마디 **mal hanmadi** a word
세상을 떠나다 **sesangeul tteonada** to depart from this life

Selected grammar points

- **(으)ㄹ 정도로 "to the extent of"**

  This expression is used to describe a certain degree with a specific example.

  목동의 피리 소리는 누구든지 들으면 **눈물을 흘릴 정도로** 너무 아름다웠어요.

  The sound of the sheperd boy's piping was so beautiful that anyone who heard it would weep.

- **다 보니(까) "while doing something, one realizes . . ."**

  아래를 내려다 보니 연못가에서 목동이 피리를 부는 것이 보였어요.

  Looking down, she saw the shepherd boy playing his pipe beside a pond.

- **아/어 달라고 하다 "to ask somebody to do something"**

  This form is used when the original speaker of a quoted sentence asks for an action to be done for him/her.

  선녀는 언니들에게 **도와 달라고** 부탁했어요.

  The fairy begged her sisters to help her.

- **에도 불구하고 "despite", "although"**

  금붕어가 된 선녀는 목동이 피리를 부는 연못가에 **있었음에도 불구하고** 목동에게 말 한마디 할 수 없었어요.

  Although the fairy, who had become a goldfish, was in the pond where the shepherd boy was piping, she couldn't speak a single word to him.

After reading the story

1. 목동은 무엇을 잘했어요?

   What was the shepherd boy good at?

2. 선녀는 땅으로 내려온 후에 처음 며칠 동안 어디에서 살았어요?

   Where did the fairy live for the first few days after going down to Earth?

3. 선녀가 없어진 것을 알고 옥황상제는 어떻게 했어요?

   What did the Great Jade Emperor do when he found out the fairy was missing?

4. 옥황상제는 선녀가 다시 땅으로 내려가시 못하도록 어떻게 했어요?

   How did the Great Jade Emperor prevent the fairy from going down to Earth again?

5. 선녀는 왜 죽을 수가 없었어요?

   Why couldn't the fairy die?

Let's talk!

위의 이야기처럼 이루어지지 못한 슬픈 사랑 이야기를 소개해 보세요.

Tell a story of unfulfilled love like the one above.

Notes on Korean culture

Stories of unfulfillable love, like *Romeo and Juliet* seem to be found everywhere. In Korea, too, parents used to decide whom their children would marry. Of course, today, times have changed and it's far more common for people to choose their own marriage partners, although even then it's considered important to get the parents' approval. Once people have fallen in love, they are not easily separated, even by their parents.

요술 거울

옛날 옛날에 사이 좋은 부부가 있었어요. 어느 날 남편이 일 때문에 장에 가게 됐어요.

"부인, 내일 장에 가는데 필요한 게 있어요?"

"그럼 머리빗 하나만 사다가 주세요."

"머리빗?"

아내는 남편이 머리빗이라는 단어를 잊어버릴까 봐서 걱정이 됐어요. 그래서 하늘의 초승달을 가리키면서 말했어요.

"여보, 저 달처럼 생긴 걸 사다가 주세요."

남편은 장에 도착해서 이것저것을 샀어요. "아내가 부탁한 물건이 뭐였지? 아, 달처럼 생긴 걸 사 오라고 했지."

남편은 길에서 여러 가지 물건을 팔고 있는 상인에게 말했어요.

"혹시 달처럼 생긴 물건이 있으면 하나 주세요."

"아, 거울이요? 여기 있습니다."

남편은 집에 도착해서 아내에게 장에서 사온 물건을 주면서 말했어요. "부인이 부탁한 물건 사 왔어요."

"머리빗을 사 왔어요? 고마워요." 아내는 신이 나서 남편이 주는 거울을 받았어요. 이리저리 거울을 살펴보다가 깜짝 놀라서 말했어요. "에구머니나!"

"부인, 왜 그래요?"

"아니, 장에서 머리빗을 사 오라고 했는데 왜 젊은 여자를 데리고 왔어요?" 그러자 남편이 말했어요.

The Magic Mirror

Long, long ago, there lived a married couple who got along well. One day, the husband had to go to the market on business.

"Dear, I'm going to the market tomorrow. Is there anything you need?"

"Just buy me a comb."

"A comb?"

The wife became worried that her husband would forget the word *comb*. So she pointed to the crescent moon in the sky and said, "Dear, buy me a thing shaped like that moon."

The husband arrived at the market and bought various things. "What did my wife ask for? Oh yes, she asked me to buy a thing shaped like the moon."

The husband asked a merchant who was selling various things on the street.

"If you have a thing shaped like the moon, give me one, please."

"Oh, a mirror? Here it is."

When he got home, the husband gave his wife the thing that he had bought at the market. "I've bought the thing you asked for," he said.

"You've bought me a comb? Thank you!" The wife excitedly took the mirror that her husband gave her. She examined the mirror this way and that and said in surprise, "Oh my God!"

"What's the matter, dear?"

"I asked you to buy me a comb at the market—why have you brought a young woman back with you?"

"내가 젊은 여자를 데리고 왔다니요? 도대체 그게 무슨 소리예요?"

아내는 울면서 방에서 나오는 시어머니에게 달려갔어요. 그리고 시어머니에게 거울을 주면서 말했어요.

"어머니, 이 사람이 장에서 젊은 여자를 데리고 왔어요. 이제 저는 어떡해요."

시어머니는 거울을 찬찬히 살펴본 후 말했어요.

"여기 젊은 여자가 어디에 있니? 늙은 여자밖에 없는데."

"늙은 여자라니요? 어머니, 잘 보세요. 여기 분명히 젊은 여자가 있잖아요."

"늙은 여자밖에 없는데 왜 자꾸 젊은 여자가 있다고 그래."

아내와 시어머니의 말소리는 점점 더 커졌어요.

"내가 재수 없는 물건을 사왔군. 이 물건을 버려야겠어."

남편은 다투고 있는 시어머니와 아내 몰래 거울을 들고 밖으로 나왔어요. 그때 마침 밖에서 놀고 있던 아들이 남편을 보고 달려왔어요.

"아버지, 들고 계신 게 뭐예요?"

"재수 없는 물건이라서 버릴 거다."

아들은 거울 속의 남자 아이를 보고 놀라서 말했어요.

"아버지, 이 남자 아이는 누구예요?"

"뭐라고? 남자 아이?"

자세히 보니까 거울 속의 남자 아이는 아들과 손에 든 것과 똑같은 떡을 손에 들고 있었어요. 이것을 본 아들은 화가 나서 소리쳤어요.

"너, 내 떡 언제 훔쳤어? 그 떡 내놔!"

아들은 계속 소리쳤지만 거울 속의 아이는 계속 떡을 손에 들고 있었어요. 그러자 아들은 더 화가 나서 말했어요.

"내 떡 내놓으라니까!"

결국 아들은 화를 참지 못하고 주먹으로 남편이 들고 있던 거울을 쾅 쳤어요. 그 바람에 남편은 거울을 떨어뜨렸고 거울은 산산조각이 났어요.

이 소리를 듣고 시어머니와 아내가 달려왔어요. 모두들 가만히 서서 조심스럽게 깨진 거울을 살펴봤어요. 거울을 열심히 살펴봤지만 젊은 여자도, 늙은 여자도, 손에 떡을 든 남자 아이도 모두 사라지고 없었어요.

☆ ☆ ☆

The husband said, "You say I've brought a young woman? What on earth do you mean?"

The wife ran crying to her mother-in-law, who was just coming out of her room. Giving the mirror to her mother-in-law, she said, "Mother, this man has brought a young woman from the market. What am I to do now?"

The mother-in-law slowly examined the mirror and said, "Where's the young woman here? There's only an old woman."

"An old woman? Mother, look carefully. There's clearly a young woman here."

"There's only an old woman—why do you keep saying there's a young woman?" The voices of the wife and mother-in-law gradually grew louder.

"I see I've bought an unlucky object," thought the husband. "I'd better throw it away."

Unobserved by the quarrelling wife and mother-in-law, the husband took the mirror and went outside. Then his son, who had been playing outside, saw him and came running up. "Daddy, what's that thing you're holding?"

"It's an unlucky object, so I'm going to throw it away."

His son was surprised to see a boy in the mirror.

"Daddy," he said, "who's this boy?"

"What did you say? A boy?"

On close inspection, the son noticed that the boy in the mirror was holding in his hand a rice cake just like the one he was holding himself. When he saw that, the son was angry. "You!" he shouted. "When did you steal my rice cake? Give it back!"

The son went on shouting, but the boy in the mirror went on holding the rice cake in his hand. Then the son grew even angrier and shouted, "I said give me my rice cake!"

Finally, the son was unable to contain his anger and with his fist he hit the mirror that the husband was holding. As a result, the husband dropped the mirror and it shattered in pieces.

Hearing that sound, the wife and mother-in-law came running. They all stood still and carefully examined the broken mirror. They looked at it very closely, but the young woman, the old woman and the boy holding the rice cake had all disappeared.

☆ ☆ ☆

Vocabulary

거울 **geoul** mirror

사이가 좋다 **saiga jota** to be on good terms

부부 **bubu** married couple

장 **jang** market

부인, 여보 **buin, yeobo** darling, dear

머리빗 **meoribit** comb

단어 **daneo** word

잊어버리다 **ijeobeorida** to forget

초승달 **choseungdal** crescent moon

가리키다 **garikida** to point

알겠다 **algetda** I got it

도착하다 **dochathada** to arrive

이것저것 **igeotjeogeot** this and that

부탁하다 **butakhada** to request

여러 가지 **yeoreo gaji** various

상인 **sangin** merchant

이리저리 **irijeori** this way and that

에구머니나 **egumeonina** Oh my God!

젊다 **jeomda** to be young

여자 **yeoja** woman

달려가다, 달려오다 **dallyeogada, dallyeooda** to dash

어머니 **eomeoni** mother

찬찬히 **chanchanhi** thoroughly

자꾸 **jakku** repeatedly

커지다 **keojida** to grow loud

재수 **jaesu** luck

버리다 **beorida** to throw away

남자 아이 **namja ai** boy

손 **son** hand

떡 **tteok** rice cake

훔치다 **humchida** to steal

화를 참다 **hwareul chamda** to suppress one's anger

주먹 **jumeok** fist

쾅 치다 **kwang chida** to bang, hit

그 바람에 **geu barame** consequently

산산조각이 나다 **sansanjogagi nada** to be smashed to pieces

조심스럽게 **josimseureopge** carefully

Selected grammar points

- 밖에 **"only," "[nothing] but"**

  This form expresses the only thing or option available, with no possibility of anything else and in Korean it is always followed by a negative form.

  늙은 여자밖에 없는데요.

  There's only an old woman.

- 다니요? **"Really?" "I can't believe . . ."**

  This is used to indicate a surprise, an exclamation or a feeling of disbelief about a certain fact that the speaker actually heard or observed. It uses different conjugations based on sentence types. Basically, add 니요 to the indirect quotation form.

  늙은 여자라니요?

  An old woman?

- 잖아요 "as you know," "clearly," "don't forget that . . ."
  This ending is attached to an action verb, a descriptive verb or a "noun+이다,"
  reminding the listener of a fact that they already know.
  여기 분명히 젊은 여자가 있잖아요.
  There's clearly a young woman here.

After reading the story

1. 이내는 남편에게 장에서 무엇을 사다가 달라고 부탁했어요?
   What did the wife ask her husband to buy her at the market?
2. 남편은 장에서 아내에게 무엇을 사다가 줬어요? 왜 그 물건을 샀어요?
   What did the husband buy for his wife at the market? Why did he buy that?
3. 남편이 아내에게 장에서 사온 물건을 줬을 때 아내는 왜 깜짝 놀랐어요?
   Why was the wife surprised when her husband gave her the thing he had bought at
   the market?
4. 왜 아내와 시어머니가 다투었어요?
   Why did the wife and mother-in-law argue?
5. 아들이 왜 남편이 장에서 사온 물건을 쾅 쳤어요?
   Why did the son hit the thing that the husband had bought at the market?

Let's talk!

어떤 물건이든지 한 가지를 가질 수 있다면 무엇을 가지고 싶어요? 그 이유는
무엇이에요? 친구들과 이야기해 보세요.

If you could have any one object, what would you like to have? What's the reason?
Discuss this with your friends.

Notes on Korean culture

In the old days, making a mirror was a very difficult task. For that reason, in Korea, a
mirror was not just considered a tool for reflecting someone's appearance, but as an object with special significance. Mirrors were used by shamans as fortune-telling devices
and by kings as symbols of their sovereignty. In old stories, mirrors also appear as love
tokens that enable lovers to recognize each other after being separated for a long time.

천 냥짜리 아버지

옛날 어느 마을에 젊은 부부가 살고 있었어요. 부부는 가난해도 행복했지만 부모님이 모두 일찍 돌아가신 것이 늘 아쉬웠어요.

"여보, 우리도 부모님이 계시면 얼마나 좋을까요?"

"그러게요. 나도 부모님을 모시고 사는 사람들을 보면 여간 부러운 게 아니에요."

그러던 어느 날 장에 간 남편은 한 가게 주인에게서 이상한 이야기를 듣게 됐어요.

"그 소문 들었어요?"

"무슨 소문이요?"

"아, 글쎄, 돈 천 냥에 아버지를 판다는 사람이 있대요."

"정말이에요?"

"정말이고말고요. 저기 벽에 글이 써 있으니까 확인해 보세요."

남편이 가게 주인이 알려준 곳에 가 봤더니 거기에는 진짜 아버지를 천 냥에 판다는 방이 붙어 있었어요. 남편은 집에 돌아오자마자 아내에게 그 이야기를 해줬어요. 아내는 남편의 이야기를 듣고 너무 놀라서 한참을 멍하게 있었어요. 그러다가 갑자기 무릎을 탁 치면서 남편에게 말했어요. "여보, 좋은 생각이 났어요."

"좋은 생각? 그게 뭔데요?"

"우리가 그 아버지를 사서 모시는 게 어때요?"

Father for Sale

Long ago in a certain village, lived a young married couple. Though poor, they were happy, but they always felt sorry that their parents had died at an early age.

"My dear, wouldn't it be wonderful if our parents were here?"

"Yes. Whenever I see people living with their parents, I feel so jealous."

Then one day, when the husband went to the market, he heard a strange story from one of the shopkeepers.

"Have you heard the rumor?"

"What rumor?"

"Ah, well, they say there's a man who is selling his father for a thousand nyang in cash."

"Is it true?"

"Sure it's true. It's written on that wall over there—see for yourself."

The husband went to the place that the shopkeeper indicated and there indeed he saw a notice about selling a father for one thousand nyang. As soon as he got home, the husband told this story to his wife. She was so surprised at hearing his story that for a while she was quite stupefied. Then she suddenly slapped her leg and said to her husband, "Dear, I've got a good idea."

"A good idea? What is it?"

"How about if we buy that father and look after him?"

"그러면 좋겠지만 우리한테 돈 천 냥이 없잖아요."

"돈은 빌릴 수 있을 거예요. 우리가 모시지 않으면 그 아버지가 고생하실 테니까 우리가 사서 모셔요"

"알겠어요. 그럼 그렇게 합시다."

다음 날부터 젊은 부부는 여기저기 돈을 구하러 다녔어요. 하지만 아무도 천 냥을 빌려주지 않았어요.

"여보, 이제 어떡하지요?"

"할수 없지요. 그냥 집으로 돌아가는 수밖에." 젊은 부부는 실망한 채 집으로 발길을 돌렸어요. 그런데 저 앞에 집이 하나 있었어요. 젊은 부부는 혹시나 하는 마음에 그 집에 들어가 봤어요. 거기에는 할머니 한 분이 계셨어요.

"할머니, 죄송하지만 돈 천 냥만 빌려주시겠어요?"

"돈 천 냥을 무엇에 쓰려고 그래요?"

"돈 천 냥에 아버지를 판다는 사람이 있어서 저희가 그 아버지를 사서 모시려고 해요. 돈은 나중에 꼭 갚도록 하겠습니다."

할머니는 남편의 이야기를 듣고서 젊은 부부에게 돈 천 냥을 빌려줬어요. 젊은 부부는 기쁜 마음으로 돈 천 냥을 가지고 아버지를 판다는 집을 찾아갔어요. 아버지를 팔 정도라서 그 집이 아주 가난할 거라고 생각했는데 그 집은 꽤 잘 사는 집이었어요. 젊은 부부는 이런 집에서 아버지를 팔려고 하는 게 이상하다고 생각하면서 주인을 찾았어요. 그러자 집 안에서 점잖아 보이는 노인이 나왔어요.

"무슨 일로 오셨습니까?"

"아버지를 판다는 소문을 듣고 왔는데요. 여기가 그 집이 맞나요?"

"맞습니다. 그런데 돈 천 냥은 가지고 왔습니까?"

"네. 여기 있습니다."

노인은 돈을 받으면서 젊은 부부에게 물었어요. "그런데 늙은 노인을 사서 뭘 하려고 합니까?"

그러자 남편이 대답했어요. "저희는 부모님이 모두 일찍 돌아가셔서 평생 부모님을 모시는 것이 소원이었습니다. 그래서 비록 남의 아버지이시지만 모시고 싶습니다. 저희 형편이 넉넉한 것은 아니지만 그래도 정성을 다해서 모실 것입니다."

남편의 말이 끝나자 노인은 남편의 손을 꼭 잡고 말했어요.

"내가 바로 그 아버지입니다. 나는 돈은 많지만 자식이 없어서 양자를 얻으려고 했습니다. 그런데 내 재산만 보고 양자가 되고 싶어 하는 사람들이

"That would be nice, but we haven't got a thousand nyang in cash."

"We should be able to borrow the money. If we don't buy him, that father might have a hard time, so let's buy him and look after him."

"OK, then let's do that."

From the next day, the young couple went here and there to raise money. But no one would lend them a thousand nyang.

"What can we do now, dear?"

"There's nothing we can do but just go back home." Disappointed, the young couple turned their steps toward home. But just in front of them there was a house. Just on the off-chance, the young couple went into the house. Inside was an old woman.

"Grandmother, I'm sorry but will you lend us one thousand nyang in cash?"

"What do you want to use the thousand nyang for?"

"There's a man who is selling his father for a thousand nyang and we want to buy that father and look after him. We'll be sure to pay the money back later."

On hearing the husband's story, the old woman lent them the money. Happy, the young couple took the thousand nyang to the house where the father was for sale. They had thought that it must be a very poor household to be driven to selling the father, but the house was actually quite prosperous. Thinking it strange that the occupants of such a house should be selling their father, they looked for the owner. Just then, a dignified-looking elderly man came out of the house.

"What brings you here?"

"We heard a rumor that there's a father for sale. Is this the right house?"

"That's right. Did you bring a thousand nyang in cash?"

"Yes, here it is."

The old man took the money and asked the young couple, "But what do you want to do when you've bought the old man?"

The husband answered, "All our parents passed away early and all our life we've wished that we could look after them. So even if it's someone else's father, we want to look after him. We're not very well off, but we'll look after him with all our heart."

As soon as the husband finished speaking, the elderly man firmly took his hand.

"I am none other than that father," he said. "I have plenty of money but no children, and I wanted to adopt a son. But there are some people who would want to become my adopted son just because of my property, and that's why I

있어서 그런 거짓 글을 써서 붙인 것입니다. 드디어 내가 바라던 아들을
찾아서 나도 소원을 풀었습니다!"

각자 서로의 소원을 풀게 해 준 젊은 부부와 노인은 그후로 한 집에서
행복하게 살았대요.

☆ ☆ ☆

Vocabulary

천 **cheon** thousand

냥 **nyang** unit of old Korean coinage

짜리 **jjari** value

부모님 **bumonim** parents

돌아가시다 **doragasida** [honorific] to
pass away

부럽다 **bureopda** to envy

가게 **gage** shop, store

주인 **juin** owner

소문 **somun** rumor, hearsay

글쎄 **geulsse** well

벽 **byeok** wall

확인하다 **hwaginhada** to check

멍하다 **meonghada** to stupefy

무릎을 탁 치다 **mureubeul tak chida**
to smack or slap one's leg

생각이 나다 **saenggagi nada** to come
into one's mind, have an idea

구하다 **guhada** to obtain

발길을 돌리다 **balgireul dollida** to turn
one's steps

분 **bun** [honorific] counter for people

죄송하다 **joesonghada** to be sorry

나중에 **najunge** later

꽤 **kkwae** quite

점잖다 **jeomjanta** to be gentle, dignified

노인 **noin** elderly person

소원 **sowon** wish, hope

비록 **birok** although, even if

형편 **hyeongpyeon** conditions

넉넉하다 **neongneokada** to be well-to-
do

정성을 다하다 **jeongseongeul
dahada** to do one's best

자식 **jasik** sons and daughters

양자 **yangja** adopted child

얻다 **eutda** to get, to gain

거짓 **geojit** to be fake

바라다 **barada** to wish, to desire

소원을 풀다 **sowoneul pulda** to realize
one's wish

각자 **gatja** each

Selected grammar points

■ 여간 -게 아니다 "**very**," "**uncommonly**"

As in the English expression "no ordinary X," the grammatically negative form actually expressive a strong positive affirmation of the meaning.

나도 부모님을 모시고 사는 사람들을 보면 **여간 부러운 게 아니에요**.

Whenever I see people living with their parents, I feel so jealous.

wrote that false advertisement. At last I've found the son that I wanted, and my wish has come true too!"

Having made each other's wish come true, the young couple and the elderly man then lived happily together in one house.

☆ ☆ ☆

- 아/어 보다 **"to try [doing something]"**
  This form expresses trying out or experiencing an action.
  젊은 부부는 혹시나 하는 마음에 그 집에 **들어가 봤어요**.
  Just on the off-chance, the young couple went into the house.
- 도록 하다 **"make sure you do something"**
  돈은 나중에 꼭 **갚도록 하겠습니다**.
  We'll be sure to pay the money back later.

After reading the story

1. 젊은 부부의 소원은 무엇이었어요?
   What was the young couple's wish?
2. 남편은 장에서 무슨 소문을 들었어요?
   What rumor did the husband hear at the market?
3. 젊은 부부는 왜 돈을 구하러 다녔어요?
   Why did the young couple go around to raise money?
4. 노인은 왜 거짓 글을 써서 붙였어요?
   Why had the elderly man written a false advertisement?

Let's talk!

여러분은 이루고 싶은 소원이 있어요? 그 소원을 이루기 위해서 어떤 노력을 하고 있어요?

Do you have a wish that you want to fulfil? What are you doing to make it come true?

Notes on Korean culture

In the past, Koreans attached great importance to sons. The father was the head of the family and the son was his successor, so the family line would be carried on through the son. A daughter could not be a successor, so in families that had only daughters, or no children at all, it was common to adopt a son. Because a son was a necessity for continuing the family line, a wife who failed to give birth to a son could even be punished like a criminal. Today, when sons and daughters are both prized, it's hard to imagine, isn't it?

지네 처녀와 지렁이

옛날에 한 남자가 살았어요. 이 남자의 집이 너무 가난해서 가족들은 밥을 굶기 일쑤였어요.

"내일이 설날인데 떡국은커녕 밥을 지을 쌀조차 없네. 우리 아이들도 다른 집 아이들처럼 새 옷을 입고 세배를 다닐 수 있다면 얼마나 좋을까?"

남자는 설날 전날에도 아내와 여섯 명의 아이들이 굶고 있는 걸 봐야 하는 게 너무 괴로웠어요.

"이렇게는 더이상 못 살겠네. 차라리 내가 죽는 게 낫겠어."

남자는 죽으려고 새끼줄을 가지고 산에 올라갔어요. 산을 오르다가 소나무를 발견하고 그 나무에 새끼줄을 매었어요. 그런데 멀리서 발소리가 들렸어요.

"사람이 올라오는 모양이군. 지금은 안 되겠어."

The Centipede Woman and the Worm

Long ago there lived a man. This man's household was so poor that the family often had nothing to eat.

"Tomorrow is New Year's Day and we've got no rice to cook, let alone rice-cake soup. How nice it would be if our children could do their New Year's bow in new clothes like other people's children!"

The man was deeply distressed to see his wife and six children starving even on New Year's Eve.

"I can't live like this any more. It will be better if I die."

The man took a straw rope and went up a hill to hang himself. On the hill, he found a pine tree and tied the rope to it. But then he heard some footsteps in the distance.

"It looks like someone is coming up. I can't do it now."

남자는 소나무 위에 숨어서 사람이 지나갈 때까지 기다리기로 했어요. 그런데 사람은 소나무쪽으로 걸어왔어요. 남자가 자세히 보니까 그 사람은 한복을 곱게 입은 여자였어요. 여자는 떡시루를 소나무 아래에 내려놓고서는 뭔가를 중얼거리며 빌었어요. 그리고 갑자기 말했어요.

"나무 위에 계신 거 압니다. 거기 그렇게 계시지 말고 내려오셔서 떡 좀 드세요."

남자는 할 수 없이 나무 아래로 내려왔어요. 배가 너무 고팠던 남자는 여자가 가지고 온 떡을 허겁지겁 먹기 시작했어요. 남자가 떡을 다 먹자 여자는 남자에게 물었어요.

"왜 죽으려고 하셨습니까?"

남자는 자신의 이야기를 여자에게 했어요. 여자는 남자의 이야기를 다 듣고 남자를 자신의 집으로 데리고 가서 돈을 주면서 말했어요.

"이 돈으로 쌀과 옷을 사 가지고 집으로 돌아가셔서 가족과 설날을 보내세요. 그리고 혹시 집에 가시다가 상복을 입은 사람을 만나시면 그 사람이 하는 말을 절대로 들으시면 안 됩니다."

남자는 집으로 가는 길에 정말로 여자가 말한 대로 상복을 입은 사람을 만나게 됐어요. 그 사람은 남자에게 다가와서 말했어요.

"당신, 여자에게서 돈을 받아서 집으로 가고 있지요? 그 여자는 사람이 아니라 지네입니다. 빨리 그 여자 집으로 다시 가서 그 여자가 지네인 것을 확인한 후에 "지네다!"라고 소리치세요. 지네를 보고도 소리치지 않으면 당신이 죽을 것입니다."

남자는 누구의 말을 들어야 할지 몰라서 너무 고민이 됐지만 가족이 생각나서 쌀과 옷을 사 가지고 집으로 갔어요. 남자는 아내와 아이들이 배부르게 먹고 새옷을 입고 즐거워하는 모습을 보니까 기분이 아주 좋았어요. 그런데 상복을 입은 사람이 한 말이 계속 생각났어요.

"그 여자가 진짜 지네일까?"

남자는 사실을 확인하려고 여자의 집으로 갔어요. 여자의 집에 몰래 들어가서 방 문구멍으로 안을 들여다보니까 거기에는 큰 지네 한 마리가 있었어요.

"어떡하지? 내가 "지네다!"라고 소리치면 지네가 죽게 되지만 안 그러면 내가 죽게 될 텐데. 하지만 도움을 받았으니까 지네를 죽게 할 수는 없지. 차라리 내가 죽자."

The man decided to hide in the tree and wait until the person had passed by. But the person walked toward the tree. The man looked closely and saw that it was a woman in a beautiful hanbok dress.

The woman put a pot of rice cakes down below the tree and muttered something in prayer. Then she suddenly spoke. "I know you are in the tree. Don't stay there like that—come down and have some rice cakes."

Having no choice, the man came down from the tree. He had been desperately hungry and he began hurriedly eating the rice cakes the woman had brought.

When he had eaten all the rice cakes, the woman asked him, "Why did you want to die?"

The man told her his story. When she had heard the whole story, she took the man back to her own house and gave him some money.

"With this money," she said, "buy some rice and clothes, take them home and spend New Year's Day with your family. And if, on your way home, you meet a man in mourning clothes, you must absolutely not listen to what he says."

On his way home, the man did indeed meet a man in mourning clothes, as the woman had said.

That man came up to him and said, "You, you're going home after receiving some money from a woman, aren't you? That woman is not a human—she's a centipede. Go quickly back to her house and see for yourself that she's a centipede, then shout 'Centipede!' If you don't shout after seeing the centipede, you'll die."

The man was terribly worried, not knowing who to believe, but, thinking of his family, he bought some rice and clothes and took them home. When he saw his wife and children eating their fill and enjoying themselves in their new clothes, he felt very happy. But he still kept thinking of what the man in mourning clothes had said.

"Is that woman really a centipede?"

To find out the truth, the man went to the woman's house. He secretly went into the house and looked in through the keyhole of a door and there indeed was a big centipede.

"What should I do? If I shout 'Centipede!' the centipede will die, but if I don't, I'll die. But as I've received its help, I can't kill the centipede. I'd rather die myself."

남자는 아무 말도 안 하고 집밖으로 나왔어요. 그런데 남자는 죽지 않고 살아 있었어요. 자신이 죽지 않은 것이 이상해서 다시 여자의 집으로 가서 문을 두드리니까 여자가 나왔어요. 남자는 여자에게 지금까지의 일을 다 이야기했어요. 그러자 여자가 말했어요.

"사실 저는 선녀입니다. 그런데 죄를 지어서 이곳에 오게 됐습니다. 그 죄 때문에 제가 사람이 볼 때는 여자의 모습이지만 사람이 보지 않을 때는 지네의 모습이 된 것입니다. 저는 백 사람의 목숨을 살려야만 다시 하늘로 돌아갈 수 있는데 당신이 제가 백 번째로 살린 사람이었습니다. 상복을 입은 남자는 사실 지렁이입니다. 그 지렁이는 백 사람의 목숨을 죽여야만 하늘로 돌아갈 수 있습니다. 만약 저를 보고 "지네다!"라고 소리쳤다면 당신은 죽고 지렁이가 하늘로 올라갔을 것입니다."

여자의 말이 끝나자마자 갑자기 여자도 집도 바람과 함께 사라져 버렸어요. 집으로 가는 길에 남자는 다리를 지나갔는데 거기에는 큰 지렁이 한 마리가 죽어 있었어요.

☆ ☆ ☆

Vocabulary

지네 **jine** centipede

처녀 **cheonyeo** unmarried woman

지렁이 **jireongi** earthworm

굶다 **gumda** to starve, have nothing to eat

설날 **seollal** New Year's Day (lunar)

떡국 **tteotguk** rice-cake soup

밥을 짓다 **babeul jitda** to cook rice

새 **sae** new

세배 **sebae** New Year's bow

전날 **jeonnal** the previous day

여섯 **yeoseot** six

아이들 **aideul** children

괴롭다 **goeropda** to be distressed

낫다 **natda** to be better

새끼줄 **saekkijul** straw rope

산을 오르다 **saneul oreuda** to climb a hill

소나무 **sonamu** pine tree

매다 **maeda** to tie

발소리 **balsori** footstep

숨다 **sumda** to hide

한복 **hanbok** Korean traditional clothes

곱게 **gopge** finely

The man came out of the house without saying a word. Yet he didn't die, but was still alive. Thinking it strange that he didn't die, he went back to the woman's house and knocked on the door and the woman came out.

The man told her everything that had happened up until then.

Then the woman said, "Actually I'm a fairy. But I had to come here after committing a sin. Because of my sin, when people see me I take on the form of a woman, but when people don't see me I have the shape of a centipede. Only after saving the lives of a hundred people can I go back to the Other World, and you were the hundredth person that I saved. The man in the mourning clothes is actually a worm. That worm can only go back to the Other World after killing a hundred people. If you had shouted 'Centipede!' when you saw me, you would have died and the worm would have gone to the Other World."

As soon as she had finished speaking, the woman and the house suddenly vanished with the wind. On his way home, the man crossed a bridge where he saw a big worm lying dead.

☆ ☆ ☆

떡시루 **tteoksiru** rice cake pot
중얼거리다 **jungeolgeorida** to mutter
빌다 **bilda** to pray
허겁지겁 **heogeopjigeop** hurriedly
보내다 **bonaeda** to spend time
상복 **sangbok** mourning dress
다가오다 **dagaoda** to come closer
고민이 되다 **gomini doeda** to worry
즐거워하다 **jeulgeowohada** to be
　delighted, enjoy oneself
사실 **sasil** fact, truth
안 **an** inside

도움 **doum** help
차라리 **charari** rather
아무 말도 안 하다 **amu maldo an
　hada** to say nothing
살아 있다 **sara itda** to keep alive
죄를 짓다 **joereul jitda** to commit a sin
백 **baek** hundred
목숨을 살리다 **moksumeul sallida** to
　spare a life
백 번째 **baek beonjjae** the 100th
다리 **dari** bridge
하늘 **haneul** Heaven, the Other World

Selected grammar points

- **기 일쑤이다 Expressing habits and attitude**

  This is mainly used in a negative sense to express that an undesirable action occurs repeatedly.

  이 남자의 집이 너무 가난해서 가족들은 밥을 **굶기 일쑤였어요**.

  This man's household was so poor that the family often had nothing to eat.

- **조차 "even," "let alone"**

  This particle is used to express "not only others but also the main thing."

  내일이 설날인데 떡국은커녕 밥을 지을 **쌀조차** 없네.

  Tomorrow is New Year's Day and we've got no rice to cook, let alone rice cake soup.

- **는 모양이다 "I guess . . . (judging from)"**

  This expression is used when attempting to infer or guess the circumstances of a particular situation after directly seeing it or hearing about it.

  사람이 **올라오는 모양이군**.

  It looks like someone is coming up.

- **지 말고 (으)세요 "don't do X (but) do Y (instead)"**

  거기 그렇게 **계시지 말고** 내려오셔서 떡 좀 드세요.

  Don't stay there like that—come down and have some rice cakes.

- **는 길에 "while," "on the way"**

  This form is generally only used with verbs indicating physical movement, such as 가다, 오다 and 나가다.

  남자는 집으로 **가는 길에** 정말로 여자가 말한 대로 상복을 입은 사람을 만나게 됐어요.

  On his way home, the man did indeed meet a man in mourning clothes, as the woman had said.

After reading the story

1. 남자는 왜 죽으려고 했어요?
   Why did the man want to die?

2. 산에 간 남자는 왜 죽지 않고 다시 가족에게 돌아갔어요?
   After going up the hill, why did the man not die but go back to his family?

3. 여자는 왜 지네의 모습을 하게 됐어요?
   Why did the woman take on the form of a centipede?

4. 상복을 입은 사람은 무엇이 변한 것이었어요?
   What was it that had turned into a man in mourning clothes?

5. 여자는 왜 남자를 살려줬어요?
   Why did the woman save the man?

Let's talk!

여러분의 나라에서는 설날을 어떻게 보내세요? 설날에 먹는 음식이나 설날에 하는 일에 대해서 이야기해 보세요.

How do you celebrate New Year's Day in your country? Talk about any special things you do or foods that you eat at New Year.

Notes on Korean culture

The first day of the first month of the lunar calendar is called 설날 **Seollal** in Korea. On Seollal morning, it's the tradition to dress in nice Korean clothing and bow deeply to your elders. Also, people always eat rice-cake soup, made by taking a long rope of rice cake that symbolizes long life, cutting it into round slices and boiling it with meat and vegetables. There's an interesting saying associated with rice-cake soup: "When you eat a bowl of rice-cake soup, you grow a year older." Children who want to grow up quickly might eat two or three bowls of rice-cake soup, but when they get older, they might not feel like eating it so much!

아들을 구한 금덩이

옛날 옛날 깊은 산골 마을에 한 아이가 살고 있었어요. 아이의 집은 너무 가난해서 밥을 먹는 날보다 못 먹는 날이 더 많았어요. 그러던 어느 날 아이가 부모님께 말했어요. "이제 저도 열 살이 됐으니까 집을 나가서 돈을 벌겠습니다."

그 말을 듣고 어머니께서 말씀하셨어요. "아이고, 네가 뭘 해서 돈을 벌어오겠다고 그러니?"

"아버지, 어머니 걱정하지 마세요. 꼭 돈을 많이 벌어서 돌아오겠습니다." 아이는 부모님께 인사를 드리고 집을 떠났어요.

집을 나와서 걸은 지 며칠 후 아이는 사람들이 금을 캐고 있는 것을 보게 됐어요. 아이는 금광 주인에게 자기도 금을 캐는 일을 하게 해 달라고 부탁했어요. 주인은 아이가 일하는 사람들과 함께 지내면서 일을 할 수 있게 해 줬어요. 아이는 날마다 열심히 일했어요. 하지만 금을 캐는 일은 쉽지 않았어요. 하루 종일 흙 속을 열심히 찾아도 금을 못 찾는 날이 많았어요.

힘든 것도 꾹 참고 일한 지 오 년이 지나자 아이는 이제 집에 가도 되겠다고 생각했어요. 아이는 주인에게 집에 가고 싶다고 말했어요. 그러자 주인은 보자기에 싼 금덩이를 주면서 말했어요.

"알겠다. 이건 네가 지난 오 년 동안 일한 값이다. 잘 가지고 가거라."

How a Gold Nugget Saved a Life

Long, long ago, a boy lived in a village deep in the mountains. The boy's family was so poor that they went hungry more often than not. One day the boy said to his parents, "I'm ten years old now, so I'll go out and earn some money."

When his mother heard that, she said, "Oh my, what will you do to make money?"

"Father, Mother, don't worry. I'll be sure to bring lots of money back." The boy said goodbye to his parents and left the house.

After leaving the house and walking for a few days, the boy saw some people digging for gold. He asked the gold mine owner to let him dig for gold too. The owner let him work and live with the other people who worked for him. The boy worked hard every day. But digging for gold wasn't easy. Although he searched hard in the soil all day, there were many days when he didn't find any gold.

When he had endured all these hardships and worked for five years, the boy thought it would be all right to go home now. He told the owner that he wanted to go home.

The owner gave him a gold nugget wrapped in a cloth and said, "OK. This is the value of your work over the last five years. Take it with you."

아이는 금덩이를 안고서 신이 나 가지고 집으로 향했어요.

집으로 가다가 보니까 어느덧 밤이 돼서 아이는 주막집에서 하룻밤을 잤어요. 그리고 다음 날 해가 뜨기가 무섭게 다시 집으로 향했어요. 그런데 길을 걷다가 어젯밤에 머물렀던 주막집에 금덩이를 두고 온 것을 알게 됐어요. "아이고, 큰일났다. 빨리 주막집에 가서 금덩이를 가지고 와야겠다."

아이가 떠난 후 주막집 주인은 방에 들어갔다가 금덩이를 보고 깜짝 놀랐어요. "이 방 손님이 금덩이를 두고 갔나 보네. 주인이 이걸 찾으러 오면 못 봤다고 할까?"

얼마 후 아이가 주막집에 도착해서 주인에게 말했어요. "혹시 방에서 금덩이를 못 보셨나요? 제가 오 년 동안 금광에서 힘들게 일한 값으로 받은 것이에요. 그게 있어야 부모님을 호강시켜 드릴 수 있어요."

주인은 자기가 잠시 나쁜 생각을 했던 것을 반성하고는 아이에게 금을 돌려줬어요. 아이는 금덩이를 가슴에 꼭 안고서 다시 집으로 향했어요. 그렇게 한참을 걸어서 강 옆을 지나갈 때 무슨 소리가 들렸어요.

"사람 살려 주세요!" 아이가 주위를 둘러보니까 한 어린 아이가 강에 빠져서 허우적대고 있었어요.

"나는 수영을 못하는데 어떡하지?" 강 주위로 사람들이 모여들었어요. 하지만 다들 그저 쳐다만 볼 뿐 아무도 강에 빠진 어린 아이를 구하려고 하지 않았어요. 아이는 너무 답답했어요. 이대로 두면 어린 아이가 죽을 것 같았어요. 아이는 가슴에 꼭 안고 있던 금덩이를 꺼내서 말했어요.

"저 아이를 살리시는 분께 이 금덩이를 드리겠습니다!"

그러자 한 나그네가 강으로 뛰어들어서 어린 아이를 구해 냈어요. 아이는 그 나그네에게 금덩이를 주었어요.

아이는 강에서 구해 낸 어린 아이가 알려주는 곳으로 그 어린 아이를 업고 갔어요. 그런데 그 어린 아이가 알려준 곳은 바로 자기가 어제 머물렀던 주막집이었어요. 사실 강에 빠졌던 어린 아이는 주막집 주인의 하나밖에 없는 아들이었어요.

주막집 주인이 놀라서 소리쳤어요. "아이고, 이게 도대체 무슨 일이야?"

주막집 주인은 자신의 아들이 아이 덕분에 살았다는 이야기를 듣고서 아이에게 많은 돈을 주었어요.

집으로 돌아간 아이는 주막집 주인이 준 돈으로 부모님과 함께 오래오래 행복하게 살았대요.

☆ ☆ ☆

Clutching the gold nugget, the boy excitedly set off for home. On his way home, he found that it was already dark and he spent the night at a tavern. The next day, when the sun had barely risen, he headed for home again.

As he was walking, the boy realized that he had left the gold nugget at the tavern where he stayed last night. "Oh my, this is serious," he thought. "I'd better go quickly back to the tavern and fetch my gold nugget."

After the boy had left the tavern, the owner had gone into the room and been surprised to see the gold nugget. "The guest from this room seems to have left a gold nugget. If he comes looking for it, shall I say I haven't seen it?"

Later, the boy arrived at the tavern and said to the owner, "Did you see a gold nugget in my room? I got it as my payment for working hard in a gold mine for five years. If I just have that, I'll be able to make my parents' life comfortable."

The owner reconsidered the bad thoughts he had been thinking for a while and gave the gold nugget back to the boy. Holding the gold nugget tightly to his chest, the boy set off for home once more. After walking like that for a while, he passed a river bank and heard a sound.

"Someone save me!" Looking around, the boy saw that a small child had fallen in the river and was floundering in the water.

"I can't swim—what should I do?" he thought. People came gathering by the river, but they all just watched and no one tried to save the child that had fallen in the water. The boy felt very frustrated. If he left things like this, the child would probably drown. He took out the gold nugget that he had been clasping to his chest and said, "I will give this gold nugget to whoever saves that child!"

At that, a traveler jumped into the river and saved the child. The boy gave the gold nugget to the traveler. The boy then carried the child who had been saved from the river on his back to a place the child directed him to. But the place the child took him was no other than the tavern where he had stayed last night. In fact, the child that had fallen into the river was the only son of the owner of the tavern.

The tavern owner cried out in surprise. "Oh my, what on earth happened?"

When the tavern owner heard how his son had survived thanks to the boy, he gave the boy a great deal of money. When the boy got home, he lived happily for a long, long time with his parents on the money the tavern owner had given him.

Vocabulary

구하다 **guhada** to save

금덩이 **geumdeongi** gold nugget

깊다 **gipda** to be deep

산골 **sangol** mountainous district

인사하다 **insahada** to greet

떠나다 **tteonada** to leave

금을 캐다 **geumeul kaeda** to dig for gold

금광 **geumgwang** gold mine

함께 **hamkke** together

지내다 **jinaeda** to live

쉽다 **swipda** to be easy

년 **nyeon** year

지나다 **jinada** to pass, to go by

보자기 **bojagi** wrapping cloth

싸다 **ssada** to wrap

값 **gap** price, value

향하다 **hyanghada** to head for, set off for

어느덧 **eoneudeot** already

주막집 **jumakjip** tavern

하룻밤 **harutbam** one night

해 **hae** the sun

뜨다 **tteuda** to rise

머무르다 **meomureuda** to stay

두고 오다 **dugo oda** to leave
   (something)

손님 **sonnim** guest

얼마 후 **eolma hu** after a while

호강시키다 **hogangsikida** to let
   somebody live in comfort

반성하다 **banseonghada** to reflect,
   reconsider

가슴에 꼭 안다 **gaseume kkok anda**
   to hold (something) tight to one's chest

주위 **juwi** around

둘러보다 **dulleoboda** to take a look

어리다 **eorida** to be young, little

허우적대다 **heoujeokdaeda** to flounder

수영하다 **suyeonghada** to swim

모여들다 **moyeodeulda** to gather

그저 **geujeo** only, just

쳐다보다 **chyeodaboda** to look at,
   to watch

답답하다 **dapdaphada** to feel
   uncomfortable, frustrated

이대로 두다 **idaero duda** to leave
   (something) as it is

하나 **hana** one

오래오래 **oraeorae** for a long time

Selected grammar points

■ 아/어 가지고 **"so," "because"**

This is used to express the reason for something. It's typically used in informal conversation between friends and family members.

아이는 금덩이를 안고서 **신이 나 가지고** 집으로 향했어요.

Clutching the gold nugget, the boy excitedly set off for home.

■ (으)ㄹ 뿐이다 **"only," "just"**

다들 그저 쳐다민 **볼 뿐** 아무도 강에 빠진 어린 아이를 구히려고 하지 않았어요.

They all just watched and no one tried to save the little child that had fallen in the water.

■ 아/어 내다 **"to do something to the very end"**

This is used to express that although a certain task/action is troublesome or difficult, one completes the action to the very end.

한 나그네가 강으로 뛰어들어서 아이를 **구해 냈어요.**

A traveler jumped into the river and saved the child.

After reading the story

1. 아이는 열 살이 됐을 때 왜 집을 나가겠다고 했어요?

   When the boy was ten years old, why did he say he would leave the house?

2. 아이는 오 년 동안 무슨 일을 했어요?

   What kind of work did the boy do for five years?

3. 아이가 주막집에 무엇을 두고 왔어요?

   What did the boy leave at the tavern?

4. 강에 빠진 어린 아이를 구하기 위해서 아이가 무엇을 했어요?

   What did the boy do to save the child that had fallen in the river?

5. 강에 빠진 어린 아이는 누구였어요?

   Who was the child that fell in the river?

Let's talk!

나쁜 일이 좋은 일이 된 경험에 대해서 이야기해 보세요.

Talk about a time when a bad event turned into a good one.

Notes on Korean culture

Since ancient times, Koreans have used gold and regarded it as precious. Korea's long history of goldsmithing can be traced through articles made of gold such as rings and necklaces that are thousands of years old as well as relics like clothing ornaments, knives and golden Buddha statues. But gold has not always been welcomed in Korean history. In the Joseon era, when Confucianism was the official state ideology and individual greed was frowned upon, gold was considered a thing to be avoided.

달을 산 사또

옛날 어느 마을에 새 사또가 오게 됐어요. 이 사또는 백성들에게는 관심이 없고 술을 마시고 노는 것만 좋아했어요. 사또는 마을에 온 첫날부터 매일 사람들을 불러서 잔치를 벌였어요.

그렇게 일은 전혀 하지 않고 놀기만 한 지 며칠이 지난 어느 날 사또는 하늘을 보면서 말했어요.

"내가 이 마을에 온 지 벌써 오 일째인데 왜 아직도 달이 안 뜨는 것이냐?"

그러자 마침 잔치에 오신 스님이 말했어요.

"사또, 지금 달이 어떻게 뜨겠습니까?" 스님은 지금이 월초라서 달이 뜨기에는 이르다는 의미로 이런 말을 한 것이었어요. 그런데 사또는 스님의 말을 이해하지 못하고 화를 내면서 말했어요.

"지금 나 때문에 달이 안 뜬다는 것이냐?"

스님은 사또의 말을 듣고 생각했어요. '이 사또는 달이 어떻게 뜨고 지는지조차 모르는 바보로군. 술 마시고 놀 줄만 알지 백성들에게는 관심도 없는 이 사또를 혼 좀 내줘야지.'

스님은 사또에게 말했어요. "사또의 정성이 부족해서 달이 안 뜨는 것이지요. 부처님께 공양을 하지 않는 한 달은 뜨지 않을 것입니다."

The Magistrate Who Bought the Moon

Once, a new district magistrate came to a certain village. He had no interest in the people; he only liked drinking and taking it easy. From the first day that he arrived, he held banquets every day to which he invited many people.

One day, when he had been amusing himself like this and not doing a stroke of work for several days, the magistrate looked at the sky. "It's already the fifth day since I came to this village," he said. "Why has the moon still not risen?"

A monk who had come to the banquet replied.

"Magistrate, how can the moon rise now?" The monk meant that it was now the beginning of the month and too early for the moon to rise. But the magistrate didn't understand him and became angry.

"You mean the moon doesn't rise now because of me?" he demanded.

Hearing this, the monk thought, "This magistrate is a fool who doesn't even know how the moon rises and falls. He only knows how to drink and amuse himself, and has no interest in the people. I'd better teach him a lesson."

The monk spoke to the magistrate.

"The moon doesn't rise because you're lacking in devotion. So long as you haven't made an offering to Buddha, the moon won't rise."

스님의 말을 듣고 사또가 말했어요.

"그래? 내가 얼마를 공양하면 달이 뜰 것이냐?"

"돈 쉰 냥을 부처님께 공양하시면 달이 뜰 것입니다."

사또는 다음 날 바로 절로 돈 쉰 냥을 보냈어요. 그리고 며칠 뒤 사또가 잔치를 하다가 하늘을 보니까 정말 스님이 말한 대로 하늘에 달이 떠 있었어요. 그 달은 눈썹처럼 생긴 초승달이었어요.

"달이 뜨기는 했지만 너무 작고 밝지도 않아서 별로 마음에 들지 않는구나. 더 큰 달을 볼 수 있었으면 좋겠다."

그러자 스님이 말했어요.

"저 달은 돈 쉰 냥짜리 달입니다. 돈을 더 많이 공양하시면 달은 더 커지는 법입니다."

스님의 말을 듣고 사또가 물었어요.

"그렇군. 그럼 얼마를 공양하면 큰 달을 볼 수 있느냐?"

"돈 백 냥을 공양하시면 큰 달을 보실 수 있을 것입니다."

사또는 다음 날 날이 밝기가 무섭게 절로 돈 백냥을 보냈어요. 그로부터 오 일 후 사또가 잔치를 하다가 하늘을 보니까 정말 지난번보다 달이 커져 있었어요. 하지만 사또는 이 달도 마음에 들지 않았어요.

"달이 커지기는 했지만 반만 둥근 모양인 것이 마음에 들지 않는구나. 둥근 달을 볼 수 있었으면 좋겠다"

그러자 스님이 말했어요.

"사또께서 백 냥을 공양하셨으니까 그렇지요."

사또는 스님에게 물었어요.

"둥글고 큰 달을 보려면 얼마를 공양해야 하느냐?"

그러자 스님이 대답했어요.

"돈 천 냥을 공양하시면 둥글고 큰 달을 보실 수 있을 겁니다."

다음 날 사또는 절로 돈 천 냥을 또 보냈어요. 일주일쯤 지난 어느 날 사또가 잔치를 하다가 하늘을 보니까 둥글고 큰 보름달이 떠 있었어요. 사또는 기뻐하면서 말했어요.

"오늘 드디어 마음에 드는 달이 떴구나. 달이 돈을 먹는 만큼 커지는 것을 이제라도 알게 돼서 참 다행이다."

☆ ☆ ☆

On hearing the monk's words, the magistrate said, "Really? How much do I need to offer for the moon to rise?"

"If you offer fifty nyang to Buddha, the moon will rise."

The very next day, the magistrate sent fifty nyang in cash to the temple. And a few days later, when he was holding a banquet, he looked at the sky and there, just as the monk had said, the moon had risen. It was a crescent moon, shaped like an eyebrow.

"The moon has risen all right, but I don't like it much—it's too small and not very bright. I wish I could see a bigger moon."

The monk replied, "That moon is a fifty nyang moon. If you donate more money, the moon is sure to grow bigger."

On hearing this, the magistrate replied, "I see. Then how much do I have to donate to see a big moon?"

"If you donate one hundred nyang, you'll be able to see a big moon."

The next day, as soon as it was light, the magistrate sent one hundred nyang to the temple. Five days later, when the magistrate was holding a banquet, he looked at the sky and indeed the moon was bigger than before. But the magistrate didn't like this moon either.

"The moon is bigger all right, but I don't like the way it's shaped like only half a circle. I wish I could see a round moon."

"It's that way because you only donated a hundred nyang," said the monk.

The magistrate asked the monk, "If I want to see a big round moon, how much do I have to donate?"

The monk replied, "If you donate one thousand nyang, you'll be able to see a big round moon."

The next day, the magistrate sent another thousand nyang to the temple. One day about a week later, when he was holding a banquet, he looked at the sky and there indeed a big round full moon had risen. The magistrate was pleased.

"Today at last a moon that I like has risen," he said. "It's a good thing I now know that the moon gets bigger the more money it gets."

Vocabulary

백성 **baekseong** the people

관심 **gwansim** interest

첫날 **cheonnal** the first day

사람들을 부르다 **saramdeureul
bureuda** to invite people

잔치 **janchi** feast, banquet

벌이다 **beorida** to throw

전혀 **jeonhyeo** not at all

벌써 **beolsseo** already

오 일째 **o iljjae** the fifth day

월초 **wolcho** the beginning of a month

이르다 **ireuda** to be early

이해하다 **ihaehada** to understand

바보 **babo** fool

혼을 내다 **honeul naeda** to scold,
punish

정성 **jeongseong** sincerity

공양을 하다 **gongyangeul hada** to offer
to Buddha

절 **jeol** temple

쉰 **swin** fifty

눈썹 **nunsseop** eyebrow

마음에 들다 **maeume deulda** to like

커지다 **keojida** to grow bigger

오일 **oil** five days

지난번 **jinanbeon** the last time

반 **ban** half

둥글다 **dunggeulda** to be round

모양 **moyang** shape

일주일쯤 **iljuiljjeum** about one week

보름달 **boreumdal** full moon

다행이다 **dahaengida** to be a relief,
to be lucky

Selected grammar points

- 는 한 **"so long as"**

  This is used to indicate that the preceding clause forms the premise or condition for the content in the following clause.

  부처님께 공양을 하지 **않는 한** 달은 뜨지 않을 것입니다.

  So long as you haven't made an offering to Buddha, the moon won't rise.

- (으)ㄴ/는 대로 **"just as," "true to"**

  This is used to signify "in the same pattern as the previous action or condition."

  정말 스님이 **말한 대로** 하늘에 달이 떠 있었어요.

  Just as the monk had said, the moon had risen.

- (으)면 좋겠다 **"I wish/hope that . . ."**

  This form expresses a person's wish or hope about something yet to be realized.

  더 큰 달을 볼 수 **있었으면 좋겠다.**

  I wish I could see a bigger moon.

- (으)ㄴ/는 법이다 **"it's bound to . . ." "it's certain that . . ."**

  This is used to indicate that some action or state of affairs is already decided to be a certain way or that it's only natural that it will become so.

  돈을 더 많이 공양하시면 달은 더 커지는 **법입니다.**

  If you donate more money, the moon is sure to grow bigger.

- 는 만큼 **"as much as," "to the extent that"**

  This is used to indicate that an action/state is similar or equal to another.

  달이 돈을 **먹는 만큼** 커지는 것을 이제라도 알게 돼서 참 다행이다.

  It's a good thing I now know that the moon gets bigger the more money it gets.

After reading the story

1. 새 사또는 어떤 사또예요?

   What kind of person was the new district magistrate?

2. 새 사또가 좋아하는 것은 뭐예요?

   What did the new magistrate like to do?

3. 스님이 말한 달이 커지게 하는 방법이 뭐예요?

   What did the monk say was the way to make the moon get bigger?

4. 사또는 어떤 달을 보고 싶어 했어요?

   What kind of moon did the magistrate want to see?

Let's talk!

사또가 스님이 자신을 속인 사실을 알게 된다면 이후의 이야기가 어떻게 될 것 같아요?

각자 이야기를 만들어서 친구들이 만든 이야기와 비교해 보세요.

What do you think will happen next if the magistrate realizes that he has been tricked?

Make up your own story and then compare it with those of your friends.

Notes on Korean culture

Traditionally, the moon has great importance in Korea. In the agricultural society of the past, the size of the moon was the most precise means of knowing the changes of the seasons. Korea's main holiday, Chuseok, was timed to coincide with the first full moon of the year, so Koreans have traditionally associated bright moonlight with festivals, singing and dancing.

여우 동생

옛날 옛날에 세 명의 아들을 둔 부부가 있었어요. 이 부부는 딸을 가지는 것이 소원이었어요. 부부는 매일 뒷산 동굴에 가서 산신령님께 빌었어요.

"신령님, 제발 딸 하나만 갖게 해 주세요."

부부는 신령님께 매일 열심히 빌었어요. 그런데 사실 이 동굴에는 꼬리가 아홉 개 달린 천 년 묵은 여우가 살고 있었어요. 부부가 소원 비는 것을 동굴 속에서 몰래 엿듣던 여우는 어느 날 생각했어요.

"저 부부의 딸이 돼서 마음대로 사람과 짐승을 잡아먹어야지."

일 년 후 부부에게 드디어 딸이 태어났어요. 두 사람은 바라던 대로 예쁜 딸을 얻게 돼서 너무 행복했어요. 부부는 귀한 딸을 온갖 정성을 다해서 키웠어요.

그런데 딸이 여덟 살이 됐을 때 집에 이상한 일이 생기기 시작했어요. 매일 가축들이 한 마리씩 죽는 것이었어요.

"그저께는 소가 죽더니 오늘은 말이 죽었네. 첫째야, 오늘 밤에 네가 가축 우리를 좀 지키거라."

"네, 아버지."

Fox Sister

Long, long ago, there lived a couple with three sons. This couple wanted to have a daughter. Every day they went to a cave in the hills at the back of their house and prayed to the mountain spirit.

"Dear Spirit, please let us have a daughter."

The couple prayed hard to the spirit every day. But it happened that in this cave lived a thousand-year-old fox with nine tails. The fox secretly eavesdropped on the couple's prayers from inside the cave and one day she had an idea.

"If I become this couple's daughter, I'll be able to eat people and animals to my heart's content."

A year later, the couple at last gave birth to a daughter. They were very happy to have acquired a pretty daughter just as they had wished. The couple raised their precious daughter with every loving care. But when she was eight, a strange thing started to happen in the household. Every day one of their animals died.

"The day before yesterday a cow died and today a horse has died. First son, tonight you go out and guard the livestock pen."

"Yes, Father."

그날 밤에 첫째 아들은 숨어서 가축 우리를 지켰어요. 졸음이 오는 것을 꾹 참고 우리를 지켜보고 있는데 누군가 살금살금 우리로 들어왔어요. 첫째 아들은 우리 안으로 들어온 사람의 얼굴을 보고 깜짝 놀랐어요. 그 사람은 바로 여동생이었어요. 여동생은 소에게 다가가서 간을 빼서 맛있게 먹었어요. 그러자 소가 쓰러져서 죽었어요.

다음 날 첫째 아들은 아버지에게 어젯밤에 본 것을 말했어요. 그러자 아버지가 화가 나서 말했어요.

"도대체 그게 무슨 소리냐? 네가 여동생이 질투가 나서 거짓말을 하는구나."

그날 밤 아버지는 둘째 아들더러 가축 우리를 지키라고 했어요. 둘째 아들은 졸린 눈을 비비면서 열심히 우리를 지키다가 여동생이 소의 간을 빼서 먹는 것을 보게 됐어요. 둘째는 다음 날 아버지에게 자기가 본 것을 말했어요.

"너도 여동생이 미워서 거짓말을 하는구나."

둘째 아들이 아버지에게 사실을 말했건만 아버지는 화를 냈어요.

아버지는 그날 밤은 셋째 아들더러 가축 우리를 지키라고 했어요. 셋째 아들은 열심히 우리를 지키다가 잠이 들어서 아침에 일어났어요. 다음 날 아버지가 셋째 아들에게 어젯밤에 뭘 봤냐고 묻자 소가 갑자기 쓰러져서 죽었다고 거짓말을 했어요. 그러자 아버지가 말했어요.

"첫째와 둘째가 한 말이 역시 거짓말이었군!"

아버지는 화가 나서 첫째 아들과 둘째 아들을 내쫓았어요. 형제는 집을 나와서 산속 깊은 곳에 있는 절로 들어가서 살았어요.

형제는 몇 년이 지나자 부모님이 보고 싶어졌어요. 형제가 스님께 집에 가고 싶다고 하자 스님은 병 세 개를 주면서 급한 일이 생기면 쓰라고 했어요.

형제가 집에 가니까 집은 폐허가 돼 있었어요. 집으로 들어가자 여동생이 울면서 뛰어나왔어요.

"오빠들, 드디어 오셨군요. 오빠들이 집을 나간 사이에 마을에 전염병이 돌아서 부모님과 셋째 오빠가 돌아가시고 말았어요. 참, 배 고프시지요? 제가 밥을 차려 올 테니까 잠깐만 계세요."

형제는 방을 나가는 여동생의 뒷모습을 보고 깜짝 놀랐어요. 치마 밑으로 꼬리 아홉 개가 나와 있었어요. 첫째가 여동생을 향해서 소리쳤어요.

"이 여우야! 너 그동안 사람인 척하면서 사람과 짐승을 잡아먹었지?"

그러자 여동생은 여우로 변했어요.

That night, the first son hid while watching over the livestock pen. Firmly suppressing his sleepiness, he was watching over the pen when someone stealthily crept into it. When he saw the face of the person who had crept into the pen, the first son was amazed. It was none other than his sister! She went up to a cow, took out its liver and ate it with relish. Then the cow fell down and died.

Next day, the first son told his father what he'd seen. His father grew angry. "What are you talking about? You must be lying because you're jealous of your sister."

That night, the father told his second son to guard the livestock pen. The second son dutifully watched over the pen while rubbing his sleepy eyes and saw his sister taking out a cow's liver and eating it. The next day, the second son told his father what he had seen.

"You too are lying out of hate for your sister!"

The second son had only told his father the truth, but the father was angry.

That night, the father told his third son to guard the livestock pen. The third son diligently watched over the pen but then fell asleep and woke up in the morning. When his father asked him what he had seen last night, he lied that a cow had suddenly fallen down and died.

His father said, "Then the first and second sons were lying, right enough!"

Incensed, the father turned his first and second sons out of the house. The brothers left the house and went to live in a temple deep in the mountains.

A few years passed and the brothers came to miss their parents. They told the monk they wanted to go home. The monk gave them three bottles, telling the brothers to use them in an emergency. When the brothers got home, their house was in ruins. As they went in, their sister came running out to them in tears.

"Brothers, at last you've come! Since you left home, a plague has spread to the village, and mother and father and our third brother have all passed away. Well, you must be hungry? I'll bring some food, so just wait a little."

When the brothers saw their sister from behind as she was leaving the room, they got quite a shock. Below her skirt, nine tails were hanging down!

The first son shouted at his sister, "You, fox! You've been eating people and animals while pretending to be human, haven't you?"

Then the sister turned into a fox.

"잘도 알아냈구나. 이젠 너희를 잡아먹어야겠다."

여우가 형제에게 달려들려고 하자 형제는 스님이 주신 병 중에서 하얀 병을 여우에게 던졌어요. 그러자 큰 가시덤불이 생겼어요.

"그렇게 해 봤자 결국 너희는 나한테 잡힐거야!"

여우는 피를 흘리며 가시덤불을 뚫고 나와서 계속 형제를 쫓아갔어요. 여우가 점점 가까워지자 형제는 여우에게 파란 병을 던졌어요. 그러자 갑자기 큰 강이 생겼어요. 여우는 강을 헤엄쳐서 겨우 밖으로 빠져나와 다시 형제를 쫓아갔어요. 어느새 여우는 형제 바로 뒤까지 따라왔어요. 형제가 여우에게 마지막으로 남은 빨간 병을 던지자 큰 불이 났어요. 불길이 점점 커져서 여우는 불에 타 죽고 말았어요.

형제는 집 앞에 부모님과 동생의 무덤을 만들어 주고는 다시 절로 들어가서 평생 살았대요.

☆ ☆ ☆

Vocabulary

여우 **yeou** fox

세 (셋) **se (set)** three

아들을 두다 **adeureul duda** to have sons

뒷산 **dwitsan** hill at the back of one's house

신령 **sillyeong** god, spirit

제발 **jebal** please

아홉 **ahop** nine

개 **gae** counter for non-animate objects

천 년 묵다 **cheon nyeon mukda** to be a thousand years old

엿듣다 **yeotdeutda** to eavesdrop

일 **il** one

예쁘다 **yeppeuda** to be pretty

온갖 **ongat** all, every

여덟 **yeodeol** eight

가축 **gachuk** livestock

씩 **ssik** each

그저께 **geujeokke** the day before yesterday

첫째 **cheotjjae** the first

우리 **uri** pen

졸음이 오다 **joreumi oda** to feel sleepy

지켜보다 **jikyeoboda** to watch

살금살금 **salgeumsalgeum** quietly

여동생 **yeodongsaeng** younger sister

간 **gan** liver

빼다 **ppaeda** to take out

질투가 나다 **jiltuga nada** to be jealous

둘째 **duljjae** the second

졸리다 **jollida** to be sleepy

눈을 비비다 **nuneul bibida** to rub one's eyes

"So you've found out. Now I'd better eat you two!"

Just as the fox was about to attack the brothers, they threw one of the white bottles the monk had given them at the fox. Suddenly a big thornbush appeared.

"Even if you do that, you'll still be caught by me in the end!"

The fox ran bleeding through the thornbush and went on chasing the brothers.

As the fox came gradually closer, the brothers threw the blue bottle at her. Suddenly a big river appeared. The fox swam across the river and came out to chase the brothers again. Soon, the fox was following right behind the brothers. The brothers threw their last remaining bottle—a red one—at the fox, and a big fire broke out. As the flames grew higher, the fox was finally burned to death.

The brothers made tombs for their parents and younger brother and went back to the temple, where they lived for the rest of their lives.

밉다 **mipda** to dislike, hate
셋째 **setjjae** the third
역시 **yeoksi** as expected
내쫓다 **naejjotda** to kick out
보고 싶다 **bogo sipda** to miss
병 **byeong** bottle
급하다 **geuphada** to be urgent
폐허 **pyeheo** ruin
뛰어나오다 **ttwieonaoda** to run out
오빠 **oppa** older brother
전염병이 돌다 **jeonyeombyeongi dolda** to spread (of a plague)
밥을 차리다 **babeul charida** to get a meal ready
알아내다 **aranaeda** to find out

달려들다 **dallyeodeulda** to attack
가시덤불 **gasideombul** thornbush
생기다 **saenggida** to be formed
뚫다 **ttulta** to push through
쫓아가다 **jjochagada** to chase
파랗다 **pajata** to be blue
헤엄치다 **heeomchida** to swim
겨우 **gyeou** barely
빠져나오다 **ppajyeonaoda** to escape
어느새 **eoneusae** already
마지막으로 **majimageuro** lastly
불이 나다 **buri nada** a fire breaks out
불길 **bulgil** flame
타 죽다 **ta jukda** to be burned to death
무덤 **mudeom** grave

Selected grammar points

■ 더러 **"to (a person)"**

This is similar to 한테/에게 , but used in indirect speech.

아버지는 둘째 아들더러 가축 우리를 지키라고 했어요.

The father told his second son to guard the livestock pen.

■ 건만 **"despite," "but"**

This is used when the situation in the following clause runs counter to what you might expect based on the information in the preceding clause.

아버지에게 사실을 **말했건만** 아버지는 화를 냈어요.

The second son had only told his father the truth, but the father was angry.

■ (으)ㄴ/는 사이에 **"while," "during the time that," "when"**

This indicates that an action occurs concurrently with another; it can be translated as "while . . . ing." It is referring to a moment within a period of time, not the entire length of time.

오빠들이 집을 **나간 사이에** 동네에 전염병이 돌아서 부모님과 셋째 오빠가 돌아가시고 말았어요.

Since you left home, a plague has spread to the village, and mother and father and our third brother have all passed away.

■ (으)ㄴ 척하다 **"pretend to," "act like"**

너 그동안 **사람인 척하면서** 사람과 짐승을 잡아먹었지?

You've been eating people and animals while pretending to be human, haven't you?

■ 아/어 봤자 **"even if . . . it's no use"**

Mainly combined with a verb, this indicates that any attempt is of no use.

그렇게 **해 봤자** 결국 너희는 나한테 잡힐거야!

Even if you do that, you'll still be caught by me in the end!

After reading the story

1. 부부는 뒷산 동굴에 가서 무슨 소원을 빌었어요?
   What did the couple pray for at the cave in the hills behind their house?
2. 동굴에 누가 살고 있었어요?
   Who was living in the cave?
3. 아버지는 왜 첫째 아들과 둘째 아들을 내쫓았어요?
   Why did the father turn his first and second sons out of the house?
4. 여동생은 무엇이 변한 것이있어요?
   What was it that had turned into the younger sister?
5. 첫째 아들과 둘째 아들은 어떻게 여동생을 만나고도 목숨을 구할 수 있었어요?
   How did the first and second sons save their lives even after meeting their sister?

Let's talk!

여러분은 형제 자매가 있어요? 자신의 형제 자매에 대해서 이야기해 보세요.
Do you have any brothers or sisters? Talk about them.

Notes on Korean culture

A fox with nine tails is called a 구미호 **gumiho**. In traditional folktales, a gumiho that has lived for over a thousand years is depicted as a being with special powers. Historically the number nine has special significance. In Korea, three is traditionally considered a number that brings good fortune, and, because it's equal to three times three, nine is thought to bear even more positive energy. But something that's very good can also bring high levels of danger, so the number nine was considered both an auspicious number and a number to be handled with care.

콩쥐와 팥쥐

옛날 어느 마을에 사이좋은 부부가 살고 있었어요. 결혼한 지 이십 년이 됐건만 부부에게는 아이가 없었어요.

"우리에게도 아이가 생기게 해 주세요."

매일 열심히 빈 끝에 부부는 드디어 딸을 낳게 됐고 그 딸의 이름을 "콩쥐"라고 지었어요. 그런데 콩쥐가 태어나고 백 일이 됐을 때 콩쥐 어머니가 돌아가시고 말았어요.

아버지는 혼자서 열심히 콩쥐를 키웠지만 콩쥐가 엄마가 없어서 고생을 하는 것 같아서 늘 마음이 안 좋았어요. 마음씨 착한 콩쥐는 아버지가 외로울까 봐서 걱정했어요.

"콩쥐에게 엄마가 있으면 콩쥐가 덜 힘들겠지?"

그러던 어느 날 아버지는 새어머니를 맞았어요. 새어머니에게는 전에 결혼해서 낳은 팥쥐라는 딸이 있었어요. 새어머니와 팥쥐는 콩쥐의 아버지가 있을 때는 콩쥐에게 잘해주는 척했지만 콩쥐의 아버지가 집을 비울라치면 콩쥐를 못살게 굴고 괴롭히기 일쑤였어요. 그리고 얼마 후 콩쥐의 아버지마저 병으로 돌아가셨어요. 콩쥐의 아버지가 돌아가시자 새어머니와 팥쥐는 기다렸다는 듯이 콩쥐를 더 못살게 굴었어요. 새어머니가 콩쥐에게 일을 더 많이 시키는 통에 콩쥐는 하루 종일 쉬지도 못하고 일해야 했을 뿐더러 새어머니가 밥도 주지 않아서 굶을 때도 있었어요.

Kongji and Patji

Long ago in a certain village, there lived a loving couple. Although they had been married for twenty years, they didn't have any children.

Every day they fervently prayed, "Please let us have a child," until at last they had a daughter, whom they named Kongji. But just a hundred days after Kongji's birth, her mother passed away.

The father worked hard to raise Kongji by himself, but he always felt sad to see that Kongji was struggling without a mother. Meanwhile Kongji was worried that her father might be lonely.

"Things wouldn't be so hard for Kongji if she had a mother," her father thought to himself.

Then one day he took a new wife. Kongji's new mother had a daughter named Patji from a previous marriage. When Kongji's father was around, the stepmother and Patji pretended to be nice to her, but whenever he went out, they treated her harshly and bullied her.

Some time later, Kongji's father himself passed away from illness. As soon as he was dead, the stepmother and Patji grew even more mean to Kongji, as if they had been waiting for this. Not only did Kongji have to work all day without rest because her stepmother gave her so much to do, but sometimes she even went without meals because her stepmother didn't give her any food.

어느 날 새어머니는 콩쥐와 팥쥐를 불렀어요. 그리고 콩쥐에게는 나무 호미를 주고 팥쥐에게는 쇠 호미를 주면서 말했어요. "너희도 이제 농사 일을 할 줄 알아야지. 콩쥐는 돌밭을 매고 팥쥐는 모래밭을 매어라. 밭을 다 매야 저녁을 먹을 수 있을 거야."

콩쥐는 열심히 밭을 맸어요. 그런데 밭을 매기 시작한 지 얼마 되지 않아서 나무 호미가 돌에 부딪혀서 부러지고 말았어요. 콩쥐는 어떻게 해야 할지 몰라서 그 자리에 주저앉아서 울었어요. 그때 검은 소가 나타나서 콩쥐에게 말했어요. "콩쥐 아가씨, 밭을 제가 맬 테니까 걱정하지 마세요."

검은 소는 순식간에 밭을 매고 사라졌어요. 콩쥐는 서둘러서 집으로 돌아갔어요. 집에 돌아가니까 새어머니와 팥쥐가 저녁을 먹고 있었어요.

"어머니, 밭을 다 맸어요."

"뭐라고? 하지만 팥쥐보다 훨씬 늦게 왔으니까 오늘 네가 먹을 저녁은 없어." 콩쥐는 또 저녁을 굶어야 했어요.

며칠 후 새어머니는 콩쥐를 불러서 이렇게 말했어요. "나는 팥쥐와 나갔다가 올 테니까 우리가 돌아올 때까지 이 독에 물을 가득 채워 놓아라."

집에 혼자 남은 콩쥐는 열심히 물을 길어다가 독에 부었어요. 그런데 아무리 독에 물을 부어도 독이 차지 않았어요. 하도 이상해서 콩쥐가 독 안을 살펴보니까 독의 밑바닥이 깨져 있었어요. "밑바닥이 깨진 독에 물을 부어봤자 가득 채울 수 있을 턱이 없어. 이제 어떻게 하지?"

콩쥐는 새어머니에게 혼날 것이 여간 걱정이 되지 않아서 울기 시작했어요. 그런데 그때 두꺼비가 나타나서 말했어요. "콩쥐 아가씨, 울지 마세요. 제가 독 안으로 들어가서 깨진 곳을 막을게요."

두꺼비가 독의 깨진 곳을 막아 준 덕분에 콩쥐는 독에 물을 가득 채울 수 있었어요. 집에 돌아온 새어머니는 독에 물이 가득 찬 것을 보고 깜짝 놀랐어요.

"밑바닥이 깨진 독에 어떻게 물을 가득 채웠지?"

얼마 후 마을에 큰 잔치가 열렸어요. 새어머니는 팥쥐와 함께 집을 나서면서 콩쥐에게 말했어요. "콩쥐야, 마당에 있는 벼를 다 찧고 옷감을 다 짜면 잔치에 와도 좋다."

콩쥐는 마당에 산처럼 쌓여 있는 벼를 보자 눈물이 났어요.

"이렇게 많은 벼를 언제 다 찧지?"

그런데 그때 참새들이 날아들어서는 벼의 껍질을 까기 시작했어요. 그러자 순식간에 벼는 하얀 쌀로 바뀌었어요.

콩쥐가 쌀을 모두 독에 담자 이번에는 콩쥐 앞에 선녀가 나타났어요. 선녀는 콩쥐에게 예쁜 한복과 꽃신을 주면서 말했어요. "옷감은 제가 짤

One day the stepmother called Kongji and Patji. She gave Kongji a wooden hoe and Patji a metal hoe and said, "You two need to learn farm work now. Kongji, clear the stony field and Patji, clear the sandy field. Only when you've cleared the whole field do you get your dinner."

Kongji hoed the field diligently, but not long after she had started, her wooden hoe struck a stone and broke. Not knowing what to do, Kongji just flopped down on the spot and cried. Then a black ox appeared and said to her, "Miss Kongji, don't worry, I'll clear the field for you."

The black ox cleared the field in a moment and disappeared. Kongji hurried home. When she got there, her stepmother and Patji were having dinner.

"Mother, I've finished clearing the field."

"What? But you came much later than Patji, so there's no dinner for you today." So Kongji had to go without her dinner again.

A few days later, the stepmother called Kongji and said, "I'm going out with Patji and before we come back, you must completely fill this pot with water."

At home by herself, Kongji busily kept bringing water and pouring it into the pot. But no matter how much water she poured in, the pot didn't get full. It was very strange, so Kongji looked inside the pot. The bottom of the pot was broken.

"If I pour water into a pot with a broken bottom, it's never going to get full. What should I do now?" Worried about being scolded by her stepmother she started to cry. Then a toad appeared and said, "Don't cry, Miss Kongji. I'll go inside and block the broken part."

Thanks to the toad blocking the broken part of the pot, Kongji could fill the pot right to the top. When her stepmother came home, she was surprised to see the pot completely full.

"How did she fill a pot with a broken bottom?" she wondered.

Later, a big banquet was being held in the village. As she was leaving the house with Patji, the stepmother said, "Kongji, when you've husked all the rice kernels in the yard and woven all the cloth, you can come to the banquet."

When Kongji saw the rice kernels piled up like a mountain in the yard, her eyes filled with tears. "When will I finish husking all this rice?"

But then some sparrows flew in and started pecking the husks off the rice. Soon the rice kernels were transformed into pure white rice.

As soon as Kongji had put all the rice into a pot, a fairy appeared before her. The fairy gave Kongji a pretty dress and a pair of beautifully decorated shoes

테니까 콩쥐 아가씨는 어서 잔치에 갈 준비를 하세요."

콩쥐는 서둘러서 잔치가 열리는 곳으로 향했어요. 그런데 개울물을 건너다가 꽃신 한 짝을 개울물에 빠뜨리고 말았어요.

"내 꽃신!"

콩쥐는 꽃신을 잃어버려서 슬펐지만 잔치에 늦을까 봐서 그냥 갔어요.

그때 마침 마을 원님이 그곳을 지나가고 있었어요. 하인은 개울물을 따라서 내려온 꽃신을 주워서 원님에게 가지고 갔어요.

"꽃신의 주인을 찾아서 그 꽃신을 돌려주어야겠다."

원님과 하인은 온 마을을 돌아다니면서 꽃신의 주인을 찾아내려고 애를 썼지만 꽃신의 주인은 나타나지 않았어요. 마지막으로 콩쥐의 집에 도착해서 하인이 말했어요.

"혹시 이 집에 이 꽃신의 주인이 있습니까?"

"제가 그 꽃신의 주인이에요."

팥쥐는 이렇게 말하면서 하인에게서 꽃신을 빼앗아다가 신었어요. 하지만 팥쥐의 발은 너무 커서 꽃신을 신을래야 신을 수가 없었어요. 이때 콩쥐가 말했어요.

"제가 그 꽃신을 신어 봐도 될까요?"

콩쥐가 꽃신을 신어 보니까 꽃신이 콩쥐의 발에 딱 맞았어요. 이것을 보고 원님이 말했어요.

"꽃신의 주인도 꽃신만큼 아름답군."

원님은 콩쥐에게 반해서 그 자리에서 청혼을 했어요. 콩쥐는 원님과 결혼해서 오래오래 행복하게 살았대요.

☆ ☆ ☆

Vocabulary

이십 **isip** twenty
아이 **ai** child
낳다 **nata** to give birth to
이름을 짓다 **ireumeul jitda** to name
마음씨 **maeumssi** temper, personality
외롭다 **oeropda** to be lonely
덜 **deol** less
새어머니 **saeeomeoni** stepmother
맞다 **matda** to take
잘해주다 **jalhaejuda** to be nice
비우다 **biuda** to empty

못살게 굴다 **motsalge gulda** to act harshly
괴롭히다 **goeropida** to bully
끼니 **kkini** meal
부르다 **bureuda** to call
쇠 **soe** iron
돌밭 **dolbat** stone field
모래밭 **moraebat** sandy field
밭을 매다 **bateul maeda** to weed a field
부딪히다 **budichida** to be bumped into
부러지다 **bureojida** to be broken

and said, "I'll weave the cloth, so you hurry and get ready to go to the banquet."

Kongji rushed off toward the place where the banquet was being held. But as she was crossing a stream, one of her beautiful shoes fell into the water.

"My shoe!"

Kongji was sad to have lost her shoe, but she didn't want to be late for the banquet, so she went on her way.

Just at the right time, the county magistrate was passing by. His servant picked up the shoe that had fallen in the water and brought it to the magistrate.

"We'd better find the owner of this shoe and give it back."

The magistrate and his servant went round the whole village trying to find the owner of the shoe, to no avail. Finally they came to Kongji's house.

"Is the owner of this shoe in this house by any chance?" asked the servant.

"I'm the owner of that shoe!" cried Patji.

She grabbed the shoe from the servant and tried to put it on. But Patji's feet were too big and she couldn't get the shoe on no matter how she tried.

Then Kongji spoke. "May I try that shoe on?"

When Kongji put the shoe on, it was just right for her foot.

On seeing that, the magistrate said, "The owner of the shoe is as beautiful as the shoe itself."

The magistrate fell in love with Kongji and proposed to her on the spot. Kongji married him and they lived happily for a long, long time.

☆ ☆ ☆

자리 **jari** seat, spot
주저앉다 **jujeoanda** to flop
순식간에 **sunsikgane** in an instant
서둘러(서) **seodulleo(seo)** in a hurry
독 **dok** pot
채우다 **chaeuda** to fill
물을 긷다 **mureul gitda** to carry water
붓다 **butda** to pour
밑바닥 **mitbadak** bottom
혼나다 **honnada** to be scolded
두꺼비 **dukkeobi** toad
막다 **makda** to block

잔치가 열리다 **janchiga yeollida** a feast is held
집을 나서다 **jibeul naseoda** to leave home
찧다 **jjitda** to pound
옷감을 짜다 **otgameul jjada** to weave cloth
참새 **chamsae** sparrow
날아들다 **naradeulda** to fly into
까다 **kkada** to shell
꽃신 **kkotsin** beautifully decorated shoes

준비하다 **junbihada** to prepare
개울물 **gaeulmul** stream water
한 짝 **han jjak** one of a pair
빠뜨리다 **ppatteurida** to drop
원님 **wonnim** a county magistrate
따라서 **ttaraseo** along
온 **on** entire
돌아다니다 **doradanida** to go around

애를 쓰다 **aereul sseuda** to make an
 effort
빼앗다 **ppaeatda** to take away
신다 **sinda** to wear (shoes)
발 **bal** foot
딱 맞다 **ttak matda** to fit perfectly
만큼 **mankeum** as . . . as
반하다 **banhada** to fall in love
청혼하다 **cheonghonhada** to propose

Selected grammar points

- (으)ㄴ 끝에 **"after (a long and hard effort)"**
  This is used to indicate that a result wasn't obtained until after a long period of time
  or a difficult process.
  매일 열심히 **빈 끝에** 부부는 드디어 딸을 낳게 되었어요.
  Every day they fervently prayed, until at last they had a daughter.

- (으)ㄹ라치면 **"every time," "whenever you try to do something"**
  This is used to indicate that the situation in the following clause occurs whenever the
  subject carries out the action stated in the preceding clause.
  아버지가 집을 **비울라치면** 콩쥐를 못살게 굴고 괴롭히기 일쑤였어요.
  Whenever the father went out, they treated Kongji harshly and bullied her.

- 는 통에 **"due to (a negative or unpleasant reason)," "because"**
  새어머니가 콩쥐에게 일을 더 많이 **시키는 통에** 콩쥐는 하루 종일 쉬지도 못했어요.
  Kongji had to work all day without rest because her stepmother gave her so much
  to do.

- (으)ㄹ뿐더러 **"not only . . . but also . . ."**
  새어머니가 콩쥐에게 일을 더 많이 시키는 통에 콩쥐는 하루 종일 쉬지도 못하고
  일해야 **했을 뿐더러** 새어머니가 밥도 주지 않아서 굶을 때도 있었어요.
  Not only did Kongji have to work all day without rest because her stepmother gave
  her so much to do, but sometimes she even went without meals because her stepmother didn't give her any food.

- (으)ㄹ 턱이 없다 **"there is no reason that . . . ," "it's not possible that . . ."**
  밑바닥이 깨진 독에 물을 부어봤자 가득 채울 수 있을 **턱이 없어.**
  If I pour water into a pot with a broken bottom, it's never going to get full.

- (으)ㄹ래야 (으)ㄹ 수가 없다 **"intended to . . . but couldn't"**
  팥쥐의 발은 너무 커서 꽃신을 **신을래야 신을 수가 없었어요.**
  Patji's feet were too big and she couldn't get the shoe on no matter how she tried.

After reading the story

1. 콩쥐의 새어머니는 어떤 사람이에요?
   What kind of person was Kongji's stepmother?
2. 콩쥐는 호미가 부러졌는데 어떻게 밭을 맬 수 있었어요?
   How was Kongji able to clear the field after her hoe broke?
3. 콩쥐는 어떻게 깨진 독에 물을 채울 수 있었어요?
   How was Kongji able to fill the broken pot with water?
4. 콩쥐가 개울물에 무엇을 빠뜨렸어요?
   What did Kongji drop in the stream?
5. 콩쥐는 어떻게 자신의 잃어버린 꽃신을 다시 찾을 수 있었어요?
   How did Kongji get her lost shoe back?

Let's talk!

여러분의 나라에 "콩쥐와 팥쥐" 같은 이야기가 있어요? "콩쥐와 팥쥐"가 여러분이 알고 있는 이야기와 무엇이 같고 다른지 이야기해 보세요.

Is there a story like *Kongji and Patji* in your country? Discuss the similarities and differences between this story and a story that you know.

Notes on Korean culture

The toad is a creature that appears frequently in Korean folktales. From olden times in Korea, the toad has been considered wise and auspicious. Like the toad that appears in this story, the toads in Korean folktales are often depicted as creatures that sacrifice themselves for human beings and bring them good fortune. When children play at building houses out of soil, the song they sing is about a toad, too. As they build the house, they sing to the toad: "We'll give you an old house, so give us a new one." The toad still seems to be considered a self-sacrificing creature today.

솥 안에 넣어 둔 돈

옛날 옛날에 선비가 살았어요. 이 선비는 똑똑할 뿐만 아니라 성품도 훌륭해서 사람들에게 존경을 받았어요. 하지만 돈이나 재산을 모으는 것에 전혀 관심을 가지지 않은 나머지 늘 가난했어요.

선비의 아내는 가난한 살림 때문에 언제나 걱정이 많았어요.

"여보, 불을 피울 나무도 먹을 것도 다 떨어졌어요."

"그래도 이 추운 날씨에 잘 곳이 있으니 얼마나 다행입니까? 우리보다도 더 힘들게 사는 백성도 많은데 참아야지요."

하지만 아내는 선비처럼 아무것도 안 하고 그냥 참고 있을 수가 없었어요. 그래서 돈이 필요할 때마다 집에 있는 물건을 팔았어요. 그런데 이제는 집에 있는 물건도 다 팔아서 더이상 팔 것조차 없었어요.

그러던 어느 날 선비의 집에 도둑이 들었어요. 도둑은 방에 몰래 들어가서 훔쳐갈 물건을 찾았어요. 그런데 방에는 가구는커녕 옷조차 없었어요.

"왜 방에 아무것도 없지?"

The Money in the Cauldron

Long, long ago, there lived a scholar. This scholar was not only intelligent, but had an excellent character and was respected by everyone. But he had absolutely no interest in acquiring money or property, and as a result he was always poor.

The scholar's wife was very worried about their lack of housekeeping money.

"My dear, we've run out of both food and firewood."

"Still, how lucky we are to have somewhere to sleep in this cold weather. There are many people who live a harder life than ours, so we should just endure it."

But the wife could not just endure it and do nothing like her husband. So whenever she needed money she sold something in the house. But now she had sold everything in the house and there was nothing left to sell.

One day, a burglar broke into the scholar's house. The burglar went secretly into a room, looking for something to steal. But in the room there were not even any clothes, let alone furniture.

"Why is there nothing in this room?" he thought.

도둑은 부엌으로 가 봤어요. 그런데 부엌에서도 돈이 될 만한 물건을 찾을 수는 없었어요. 부엌에는 큰 솥 하나밖에 없었어요.

"그냥 돌아갈 수는 없으니 이 솥이라도 훔쳐가야겠군."

도둑은 솥을 훔쳐가려고 뚜껑을 열었어요. 그런데 솥 안에는 물만 가득 들어 있었어요.

"이 집 사람들은 설마 물을 밥 대신 먹은 건가? 자세히 보니 요리를 한 흔적도 없고 이 추운 날씨에 불도 안 피우고 사는 것 같군. 참 나. 내가 도둑질하러 들어간 수많은 집 중에서 이 집이 제일 가난한 것 같네."

도둑은 이 집에 사는 사람들이 안됐다는 생각이 들었어요.

"내가 아무리 도둑이기로서니 여기에서는 도저히 뭘 훔쳐갈 수는 없겠어. 다른 집에서 훔친 돈을 이 집에 두고 가야겠군. 이 돈으로 당분간 밥은 먹을 수 있겠지."

도둑은 솥 안에 돈 주머니를 넣고 뚜껑을 닫은 후 조용히 집을 나갔어요.

다음 날 아침에 선비의 아내가 부엌에 들어왔어요. 고픈 배를 물로 채우려고 솥 뚜껑을 열었어요. 그런데 솥 안에 주머니가 있었어요.

"왜 주머니가 여기 들어있지?"

선비의 아내는 솥에서 주머니를 꺼내 열어 봤어요. 주머니 안에는 돈이 들어 있었어요. 아내는 돈 주머니를 들고 선비에게 가서 말했어요.

"여보, 제가 솥 뚜껑을 열어 보니까 돈이 있었어요. 이 돈이면 쌀도 사고 나무도 살 수 있을 거예요."

그러자 선비가 말했어요.

"지금 도대체 무슨 말을 하는 겁니까? 어떻게 남의 돈을 쓸 수 있다는 말입니까? 그 돈의 주인이 지금 잃어버린 돈 때문에 곤란한 상황에 처해 있을지도 모르니까 빨리 주인에게 돈이 여기 있다고 알려줘야겠습니다."

선비는 자기 집 부엌에 돈을 두고 간 사람은 돈을 찾아 가라고 글을 써서 대문에 붙여 놓았어요.

며칠 뒤 도둑은 우연히 선비의 집 앞을 지나게 됐어요. 도둑은 선비가 붙여 놓은 글을 보고 너무 황당했어요.

"도대체 이 집 주인은 어떤 사람이길래 이렇게 욕심이 없는 거야? 궁금해서 참을 수가 없네."

도둑은 선비의 집 앞에서 큰소리로 말했어요.

"계십니까?"

그러자 선비가 문을 열고 나왔어요.

"돈의 주인이시지요? 자, 두고 가신 돈 여기 있습니다."

The burglar went into the kitchen. But he couldn't find anything worth money in the kitchen either. There was nothing there but a big cauldron.

"I can't just go back empty-handed—I'd better steal this cauldron at least."

To steal the cauldron, the burglar took the lid off. The inside of the cauldron was just completely filled with water.

"Do the people in this house eat water instead of rice?" he thought. "When I look closer, there are no traces of cooking and it looks like these people are living without lighting a fire even in this cold weather. Well, really! Of all the many houses I've burgled, this house must be the poorest."

The burglar began to feel sorry for the people living in this house.

"I may be a burglar, but there's no way I can steal anything from here. I'd better just leave some money here that I stole from another house. With this money they should be able to eat for a while."

The burglar put a purse full of coins inside the cauldron, closed the lid and quietly left the house. The next morning, the scholar's wife went into the kitchen. Intending to fill up her hungry stomach with water, she opened the cauldron lid. And inside the cauldron was a purse.

"Why is there a purse in here?" she wondered.

The scholar's wife took the purse out of the cauldron and opened it. Inside the purse was money. She took the purse and went to her husband.

"Dear, I just opened the cauldron lid and there was money inside. With this money we can buy both rice and firewood."

"What on earth do you mean?" said the scholar. "How can we spend someone else's money? The owner of that money might be in a tight spot because of the lost money. We should quickly let the owner know that the money is here."

The scholar wrote a notice that the person who had left some money in his kitchen should come and get their money and attached it to the front gate.

A few days later, the burglar happened to be passing the scholar's house. When he saw the notice that the scholar had written, he was amazed.

"What kind of man must the owner of this house be, that he has no greed at all? I'm so curious I can't stand it."

In front of the scholar's house, the burglar shouted, "Is anybody home?"

The scholar opened the door and came out.

"You must be the owner of the money? Well, here is the money that you left."

제대로 먹지 못해서 얼굴이 핼쑥한 선비를 보자 도둑은 갑자기 눈물이 났어요. 도둑은 무릎을 꿇고 선비에게 말했어요.

"선비님, 부디 저를 용서해주세요. 그 돈은 제가 다른 집에서 훔친 돈입니다. 저는 평생 남의 물건을 훔친 도둑입니다. 그 돈은 선비님 댁에 도둑질을 하러 왔다가 제가 두고 나온 것입니다."

그러자 선비가 도둑을 일으키면서 말했어요.

"이러지 마세요. 제가 뭐라고 이러십니까?"

그러자 도둑이 말했어요.

"선비님은 지금까지 제가 만난 그 누구보다도 훌륭한 성품을 지닌 분이십니다. 선비님을 뵙고 나서 제가 그동안 얼마나 잘못된 인생을 살아왔는지 알게 됐습니다. 앞으로는 저도 다른 사람에게 부끄럽지 않은 인생을 살고 싶습니다. 선비님, 그렇게 살려면 제가 어떻게 해야 할까요?"

"다른 사람의 물건에 욕심을 내는 것은 옳지 않은 일임에는 틀림없지요. 지금부터라도 도둑질을 하지 않고 올바르게 사시겠다니 정말 다행입니다. 앞으로는 다른 사람에게 도움을 주는 삶을 사셨으면 좋겠습니다."

그러자 도둑이 말했어요.

"네. 알겠습니다. 앞으로는 절대로 도둑질을 하지 않고 착하게 살겠습니다."

도둑은 그때부터 정말 착한 사람이 돼서 어려운 사람들을 도우면서 살았어요. 그리고 선비와 도둑은 이 일을 계기로 서로의 가장 좋은 친구가 됐어요.

☆ ☆ ☆

When he saw the scholar, whose face was pale from not eating properly, the burglar suddenly burst into tears. He went down on his knees and said to the scholar, "Sir, please forgive me. That money is money that I stole from another house. I'm a burglar who's been stealing other people's property all my life. I left that money in your house after breaking in to steal things."

Then the scholar raised the burglar up and said, "Don't act like this. Who am I, that you should kneel to me?"

The burglar replied, "Sir, you have the most excellent character of anyone I've ever met. Through meeting you, I've come to know what a bad life I've been living all this time. From now on, I too want to live a life that I needn't be ashamed of. Sir, what do I have to do to live like that?"

"It's certainly not right to covet other people's possessions. I'm so glad that you are going to give up burgling and live honestly from now on. I hope in future you'll live a life of helping others."

"Yes, I understand," said the burglar. "In future I will not steal at all but live a good life."

From that time on, the burglar really did become a good man and spent his life helping people in difficulties. And through this incident, the scholar and the burglar became best friends.

Vocabulary

성품 **seongpum** personality, character

관심을 가지다 **kwansimeul gajida** to be interested

살림 **sallim** housekeeping

날씨 **nalssi** weather

도둑이 들다 **dodugi deulda** a burglar breaks into a house

훔쳐가다, 도둑질하다 **humchyeogada, dodukjilhada** to steal

흔적 **heunjeok** trace, mark

수많은 **sumaneun** lots of

안되다 **andoeda** to feel sorry for

두고 가다 **dugo gada** to leave (something)

당분간 **dangbungan** for some time

주머니 **jumeoni** pocket, purse

닫다 **datda** to close

곤란하다, 어렵다 **gollanhada, eoryeopda** to be difficult

상황 **sanghwang** situation

처하다 **cheohada** to face

대문 **daemun** front gate

우연히 **uyeoni** by chance

황당하다 **hwangdanghada** to find something absurd, be amazed

제대로 **jedaero** properly

핼쑥하다 **haelssukada** to be thin and pale

무릎을 꿇다 **mureupeul kkulta** to kneel

부디 **budi** please

용서하다 **yongseohada** to forgive

일으키다 **ireukida** to raise

지니다 **jinida** to have

뵙다 **boepda** [humble] to meet

잘못되다 **jalmotdoeda** to be wrong

욕심을 내다 **yeoksimeul naeda** to be greedy, covet

옳다, 올바르다 **olta, olbareuda** to be right

삶 **sam** life

계기 **gyegi** chance, opportunity, occasion

Selected grammar points

- 뿐만 아니라 **"not only . . . but also . . ."**

  이 선비는 똑똑할 뿐만 아니라 성품도 훌륭해서 사람들에게 존경을 받았어요.

  This scholar was not only intelligent, but had an excellent character and was respected by everyone.

- (으)ㄴ 나머지 **"so . . . that"**

  This is used when the following clause is the result of an event which has gone too far in the preceding one.

  재산을 모으는 것에 전혀 관심을 가지지 않은 나머지 늘 가난했어요.

  He had absolutely no interest in acquiring money or property, and as a result he was always poor.

- (으)ㄹ 만하다 **"worth," "worthy"**

  돈이 될 만한 물건을 찾을 수는 없었어요.

  He couldn't find anything worth money.

- 대신(에) **"instead of"**

  이 집 사람들은 설마 물을 밥 대신 먹은 건가?

  Do the people in this house eat water instead of rice?

- 기로서니 **"regardless of," "while"**
  This structure, often used with 아무리, expresses that even though the speaker accepts the situation in the first clause, it is insufficient as a reason for the second clause.
  내가 **아무리 도둑이기로서니** 이 집에서는 도저히 뭘 훔쳐갈 수는 없겠어.
  I may be a burglar, but there's no way I can steal anything from this house.

- 길래 **"what/how . . . that"**
  Attaching 길래 to an action/descriptive verb indicates that the clause before 길래 gives the reason or explanation for the situation stated after 길래. If the sentence begins with a question word, it expresses amazement at the situation and how remarkable the explanation must be.
  도대체 이 집 주인은 **어떤 사람이길래** 이렇게 욕심이 없는 거야?
  What kind of man must the owner of this house be, that he has no greed at all?

- 고 나서 **"do X and then do Y"**
  This form is used to indicate that one action only begins after another has finished.
  선비님을 **뵙고 나서** 제가 그동안 얼마나 잘못된 인생을 살아왔는지 알게 됐습니다.
  Through meeting you, I've come to know what a bad life I've been living all this time.

After reading the story

1. 선비는 어떤 사람이었어요?
   What kind of man was the scholar?
2. 선비의 아내는 왜 걱정이 많았어요?
   Why did the scholar's wife have many worries?
3. 도둑이 선비의 집에 무엇을 두고 갔어요?
   What did the burglar leave in the scholar's house?
4. 도둑은 왜 선비가 쓴 글을 보고 황당해했어요?
   Why was the burglar amazed when he saw what the scholar had written?
5. 선비를 만난 후 도둑은 어떻게 바뀌었어요?
   How did the burglar change after meeting the scholar?

Let's talk!

다른 사람에게 영향을 받아서 자신의 생각이나 행동을 바꾼 경험에 대해서 이야기해
보세요.
Talk about a time you changed your ideas or behavior because of someone's influence.

Notes on Korean culture

A scholar who studies Confucian philosophy is commonly called a 선비 **seonbi**. But in a broader sense, the word seonbi refers to a scholarly person with an admirable character. The most important qualities in a seonbi are concern for other people and a pure, incorruptible spirit. The true seonbi attached so much importance to maintaining their own principles that they would not even refuse death to do the right thing.

바리공주

옛날 옛날 어느 나라에 임금님이 있었어요. 임금님에게는 한 가지 걱정이 있었어요. 그것은 딸만 여섯 명 있고 왕위를 물려 줄 아들이 없는 것이었어요. 그런데 왕비가 임신을 하게 됐어요.

"이번에는 꼭 아들이 태어나게 해 주세요."

임금님은 매일 열심히 빌었어요. 하지만 이번에도 아들이 아니라 또 딸이 태어났어요. 임금님은 너무 화가 나서 일곱째 딸을 바닷가에 버리라고 했어요.

바다 근처에 살고 있던 늙은 부부는 집 근처에서 아기를 발견했어요. 부부는 아이가 없어서 늘 아이를 가지는 것이 소원이었어요.

"여보, 부처님께서 이 아이를 우리에게 보내셨나 봐요."

"그러게요. 부처님께서 드디어 우리 소원을 들어주셨네요."

늙은 부부는 아기에게 버려진 공주라는 의미의 "바리공주"라는 이름을 지어줬어요.

십오 년의 세월이 흘렀어요.

Princess Bari and the Giant

Long, long ago, there was a king of a certain country. The king had just one concern. He had six daughters but no son to inherit the crown.

Then the queen became pregnant.

"This time please let a son be born."

The king prayed fervently every day. But this time, too, a daughter was born and not a son. The king was so angry that he gave the order for his seventh daughter to be abandoned by the sea.

An old couple who lived by the sea found the child near their house. This couple had no children of their own and had always wanted a child.

"My dear, I think Buddha has sent this child to us."

"Yes. Buddha has finally granted our wish."

The old couple named the child Bari Gongju, which means "discarded princess."

Fifteen years passed.

임금님과 왕비님이 병에 걸려서 나라가 온통 걱정과 근심에 빠졌어요. 약이란 약은 다 써 봐도 임금님과 왕비님의 병은 나아지지 않았어요. 어느 날 유명한 의원이 궁궐을 찾아와서 말했어요.

"이 병은 삼신산의 약수를 마셔야 나을 수 있습니다. 그런데 그 약수는 반드시 공주님들께서 직접 구해 오셔야 합니다."

임금님은 여섯 명의 공주들을 불러서 물었어요.

"누가 삼신산에 가서 약수를 구해 오겠느냐?"

여섯 명의 공주들은 각자 이런 저런 이유를 대면서 삼신산에 갈 수 없다고 핑계를 대고는 임금님이 계신 방을 나갔어요. 사실 삼신산은 죽음까지 각오하고 올라가야 할 정도로 험하기로 유명한 산이었어요.

"자식이 여섯이나 있어도 다 의미없구나."

임금님은 갑자기 바다에 버린 일곱 째 딸이 생각났어요.

"그래, 나한테 딸이 하나 더 있었지. 그 딸을 찾아야겠어."

임금님은 신하에게 일곱 째 공주를 찾아오라고 했어요. 신하들은 바다 근처를 샅샅이 찾아서 바리공주를 찾아내서는 궁궐로 데리고 왔어요. 임금님은 바리공주에게 물었어요.

"그래, 너는 삼신산에 가서 약수를 구해 올 수 있겠느냐?"

그러자 바리공주가 대답했어요.

"저를 낳아주신 부모님을 살릴 수 있는 유일한 방법인데 당연히 그렇게 해야지요."

바리공주는 혼자 삼신산으로 떠났어요. 삼신산으로 가는 것은 여간 어려운 일이 아니었어요.

삼신산에 가다가 태풍을 만나서 죽을 뻔하기도 하고 산짐승에게 몇 번이나 잡아먹힐 위기에 처하기도 했어요. 또 삼신산에 가려면 나무가 다 썩어서 금방이라도 무너질 듯한 다리도 건너야 했고 불이 활활 타는 문도 지나가야 했어요.

바리공주는 수많은 죽을 고비를 넘긴 끝에 겨우 약수가 있는 곳에 도착했어요. 그런데 무섭게 생긴 거인이 약수를 지키고 있어서 바리공주는 약수를 가지고 갈 수가 없었어요.

"제 부모님을 살리기 위해서 그 약수를 꼭 가지고 가야 해요. 제발 약수를 가지고 가게 해 주세요."

The king and queen fell ill and the country was entirely immersed in worry and concern. They tried all kinds of medicine, but the king and queen didn't get better.

One day a famous doctor came to the palace.

"This illness can only be cured by drinking the spring water from Three God Mountain," he said. "And the spring water must be brought by the princesses in person."

The king summoned the six princesses and asked them, "Who will go to Three God Mountain and bring the spring water?"

The six daughters all made excuses, each giving some reason why they couldn't go to Three God Mountain, then left the room that the king was in. Indeed, Three God Mountain was famous for being so rugged that it could only be climbed by those who were willing to sacrifice their lives.

"I have six children, but it's all to no avail."

Then the king suddenly thought of his seventh daughter that had been abandoned by the sea.

"Oh yes, I had another daughter too. We'd better look for her."

The king ordered his ministers to find and bring his seventh daughter to him. The ministers went to the seaside and searched hard until they found Princess Bari and brought her to the palace.

The king asked Princess Bari, "Can you go to Three God Mountain and bring back some spring water?"

Princess Bari replied, "As it's the only way to save the parents who gave me life, of course I must do it."

Princess Bari set off alone for Three God Mountain. Getting there was a very arduous task. On her way to the mountain she almost died in a typhoon, and several times she was at risk of being eaten by wild animals. To reach Three God Mountain, she had to cross a rotten wooden bridge that seemed as if it would collapse at any moment and she also had to go through a burning gate.

After surviving many life-threatening dangers, Princess Bari finally arrived at the place where the medicinal spring was. But a scary-looking giant was guarding the spring and Princess Bari couldn't collect any spring water.

"I must take some spring water to save my parents. Please let me take some spring water."

바리공주의 말을 듣고 거인이 말했어요. "만약 네가 세 가지 일을 다해 낸다면 약수를 가지고 가게 해 주겠다."

"그 세 가지 일이 무엇입니까?"

"첫째, 삼 년 동안 매일 이 독으로 물을 길어야 한다. 그리고 둘째, 불씨가 없는 불에 불을 붙여야 한다. 그리고 마지막으로 나와 일곱 명의 자식을 낳아야 한다. 이것들을 할 수 있겠느냐?"

"제 부모님을 살릴 수 있는 일이라면 못할 것이 없습니다. 그럼 무슨 일부터 하면 되겠습니까?"

바리공주는 거인의 마음이 바뀔세라 당장 일을 시작하기로 했어요. 거인이 시킨 일을 하는 것이 너무 힘들었지만 바리공주는 꾹 참고 열심히 일했어요.

세월이 한참 흘러 바리공주는 일곱 째 아들을 낳았어요. 해야 할 일을 모두 마친 바리공주는 거인에게 말했어요.

"시키신 일을 모두 다 마쳤으니 이제 약수를 주세요."

바리공주는 일곱 명의 아들을 데리고 궁궐로 갔어요. 그런데 궁궐에 도착하니까 신하들이 모두 상복을 입고 울고 있었어요. 바리공주를 본 신하가 뛰어나오면서 말했어요.

"아이고, 공주님, 살아 계셨군요. 임금님과 왕비님께서는 방금 전에 돌아가시고 말았습니다."

바리공주는 자리에 주저앉아 울면서 말했어요.

"두 분을 살리기 위해서 온갖 어려움에도 불구하고 약수를 구해 왔는데 이미 돌아가셨다니 . . ."

그러자 일곱 명의 아들들이 다가와 바리공주를 위로했어요.

"어머니, 울지 마세요."

그렇게 한참을 울다가 바리공주가 말했어요.

"어차피 쓸모 없어진 이 약수를 그냥 버리느니 차라리 두 분이 드시게 해 드려야겠어요."

바리공주는 약수를 꺼내서 임금님과 왕비님의 입에 넣어 주었어요.

"아버님, 어머님. 너무 늦게 온 저를 용서해 주세요. 그리고 부디 좋은 곳으로 가시기를 바랍니다."

On hearing Princess Bari's words, the giant said, "I'll let you take some spring water if you do three things."

"What three things are they?"

"First, you must fetch water in this pot every day for three years. Second, you must light a fire without kindling. And last, you must have seven children with me. Can you do all these things?"

"If it can save my parents, there's nothing I can't do. So, which task should I do first?"

Afraid that the giant might change his mind, Princess Bari decided to start the work right away. It was very hard to complete the tasks that the giant had commanded, but Princess Bari endured it all and worked tirelessly.

A considerable time later, Princess Bari gave birth to the seventh son. Having completed everything she had to do, she spoke to the giant.

"I've finished everything you told me to do, so now please give me some spring water."

Princess Bari took her seven sons and went back to the palace. But when they got there, all the ministers were wearing mourning clothes and weeping.

A minister who caught sight of Princess Bari came running out and said, "Oh my, Princess, so you were alive! The king and queen passed away just now."

Princess Bari squatted down on the spot and wept.

"I brought some spring water to save them despite all kinds of difficulties, but they have already passed away . . ."

Princess Bari's seven sons came up to console her.

"Mother, don't cry."

After crying like that for a while, Princess Bari spoke. "Rather than just throw away this useless spring water, I should let my parents drink it."

Princess Bari took out the spring water and put it to the lips of the king and queen.

"Father, mother, forgive me for being too late. I pray that you will go to a good place."

바리공주는 이렇게 말하고 일곱 명의 아들들과 함께 자리를 떠났어요. 그런데 바리공주가 자리를 떠나기가 무섭게 임금님과 왕비님 주위로 이상한 연기가 피어올라서 두 사람의 얼굴을 감쌌어요. 그러자 창백했던 임금님과 왕비의 얼굴이 점점 붉어지더니 다시 숨을 쉬기 시작했어요. 그리고 눈을 뜨고는 천천히 몸을 일으켰어요. 이것을 본 신하가 소리쳤어요.

"임금님과 왕비님께서 다시 살아나셨습니다!"

이 소리를 듣고 바리공주는 안으로 뛰어들어갔어요. 거기에는 정말 다시 살아난 임금과 왕비가 서 있었어요.

"아버님, 어머니. 진짜 다시 살아나신 겁니까?"

그러자 임금이 대답했어요.

"바리공주야. 네 덕분에 우리가 다시 살았구나. 정말 고맙다."

세월이 많이 흘러 바리공주는 죽은 사람의 혼이 좋은 곳으로 갈 수 있게 안내하는 신이 되었고 일곱 명의 아들은 하늘의 북두칠성이 되었다고 해요.

☆ ☆ ☆

Vocabulary

공주 **gongju** princess

한 가지 **han gaji** one kind

왕위를 물려주다 **wangwireul mullyeojuda** to hand over the throne

왕비 **wangbi** queen

임신을 하다 **imsineul hada** to be pregnant

근처 **geuncheo** neighborhood

소원을 들어주다 **sowoneul deureojuda** to grant wishes

십오 **sibo** fifteen

세월 **sewol** time

흐르다 **heureuda** to pass

병에 걸리다 **byeonge geollida** to get ill

온통 **ontong** entirely

걱정 **geokjeong** worry

근심 **geunsim** concern

약 **yak** medicine

유명하다 **yumyeonghada** to be famous, to be popular

의원 **uiwon** doctor

궁궐 **gunggwol** palace

약수 **yaksu** mineral water, spring water

직접 **jikjeop** in person

이런 저런 **ireon jeoreon** this and that, one kind and another

이유를 대다 **iyureul daeda** to give a reason

핑계를 대다 **pinggyereul daeda** to make an excuse

죽음을 각오하다 **jugeumeul gagohada** to prepare for death

험하다 **heomhada** to be rugged

의미없다 **uimieopda** to be meaningless

신하 **sinha** minister, government officer

유일하다 **yuilhada** to be sole

태풍 **taepung** typhoon

산짐승 **sanjimseoung** mountain animal

몇 번 **myeot beon** several times

After saying this, Princess Bari left the place with her seven sons. No sooner had she left the spot than a strange smoke rose around the king and queen and surrounded their faces. Then the pale faces of the king and queen grew gradually redder and they began to breathe again. They opened their eyes and slowly raised their bodies.

A minister shouted, "The king and queen have come back to life!"

When she heard this, Princess Bari went running in. There indeed stood the king and queen, alive again.

"Father, mother, have you really come back to life?"

"Princess Bari, thanks to you we live again. I truly thank you," said the king.

Long after that, they say that Princess Bari became a spirit guiding the souls of the deceased to a good place, while her seven sons became the stars of the Big Dipper in Heaven.

☆ ☆ ☆

잡아먹히다 **jabameokida** to be hunted and preyed on

위기 **wigi** crisis

썩다 **sseokda** to rot

금방이라도 **geumbangirado** at any moment

무너지다 **muneojida** to collapse

건너다 **geonneoda** to cross

불이 활활 타다 **buri hwalhwal tada** to blaze

죽을 고비를 넘기다 **jugeul gobireul neomgida** to survive dangers

거인 **geoin** giant

삼 **sam** three

불씨 **bulssi** kindling (for a fire)

불을 붙이다 **bureul buchida** to light a fire

바뀌다 **bakkwida** to be changed

당장 **dangjang** immediately

시키다 **sikida** to make somebody do

마치다 **machida** to complete

방금 전에 **banggeum jeone** just now

어려움 **eoryeoum** difficulty

이미 **imi** already

위로하다 **wirohada** to console

어차피 **eochapi** anyway

입 **ip** mouth

연기가 피어오르다 **yeongiga pieooreuda** smoke rises

감싸다 **gamssada** to cover

창백하다 **changbaekada** to be pale

붉다 **bukda** to be red

숨을 쉬다 **sumeul swida** to breathe

천천히 **cheoncheonhi** slowly

살아나다 **saranada** to revive

혼 **hon** soul, spirit

안내하다 **annaehada** to guide

신 **sin** god

북두칠성 **bukduchilseong** the Big Dipper

Selected grammar points

- **(으)ㄹ 듯하다 "seems"**

  금방이라도 무너질 듯한 다리도 건너야 했어요.

  She had to cross a bridge that seemed as if it would collapse at any moment.

- **(으)ㄹ 뻔하다 "almost," "nearly"**

  This expression indicates one's relief that a past event almost happened but did not.

  바리공주는 산에 가다가 태풍을 만나서 **죽을 뻔하기도** 했어요.

  On her way to the mountain, she almost died in a typhoon.

- **기 위해서 "in order to"**

  제 부모님을 살리기 위해서 그 약수를 꼭 가져가야 해요.

  I must take some spring water to save my parents.

- **(느)ㄴ다면 "if"**

  This is used to express a condition or to talk about a hypothetical situation.

  만약 네가 세 가지 일을 다 **해낸다면** 약수를 가져가게 해 주겠다.

  I'll let you take some spring water if you do three things.

- **(으)ㄹ세라 "afraid that"**

  This is used when the speaker is afraid that the event in preceding clause will happen.

  바리공주는 거인의 마음이 **바뀔세라** 당장 일을 시작하기로 했어요.

  Afraid that the giant might change his mind, Princess Bari decided to start the work right away.

After reading the story

1. 임금님의 한 가지 걱정은 무엇이었어요?
   What was the one concern of the king?
2. "바리공주"의 의미가 뭐예요?
   What does "Bari Gongju" mean?
3. 왜 여섯 명의 공주들은 삼신산에 가려고 하지 않았어요?
   Why didn't the six princesses want to go to Three God Mountain?
4. 임금님은 왜 버린 일곱째 딸을 찾고 싶어 했어요?
   Why did the king want to find his discarded seventh daughter?
5. 바리공주는 어떻게 약수를 얻었어요?
   How did Princess Bari get the spring water?

Let's talk!

자신이 바리공주와 같은 상황에 처하면 어떻게 했을 것 같은지 친구들과 이야기해 보세요.

What would you have done if you were faced with a situation like that of Princess Bari? Discuss this with your friends.

Notes on Korean culture

If you go hiking in Korea, you'll often come across natural springs that contain various minerals that are thought to be really good for your health. In Korean folk beliefs, spring water is thought to not only cure bodily illnesses, but even to possess mysterious powers. For this reason, in Korean folktales people often pray beside a spring.

자라와 토끼

옛날 깊은 바닷속에 용왕이 살고 있었어요. 어느 날부터 용왕은 이유도 모르는 병 때문에 앓기 시작했어요. 신하들은 용왕님의 병을 고치기 위해서 잘 고치기로 소문난 의원을 데리고 왔어요. 용왕의 상태를 살펴본 후 의원이 말했어요.

"용왕님의 상태가 너무 심각해서 바다의 약으로는 나을 수가 없습니다."

그러자 한 신하가 의원에게 물었어요.

"그럼 용왕님의 병을 낫게 할 방법이 전혀 없다는 말입니까?"

신하의 말을 듣고 의원이 대답했어요.

"방법이 하나 있는데 그것은 육지에 사는 토끼의 간을 드시는 것입니다."

그러자 자라가 말했어요.

"제가 육지에 가서 토끼의 간을 가지고 오겠습니다. 그런데 저는 지금까지 토끼를 본 적이 없으니 토끼의 그림을 하나 그려 주세요."

자라는 토끼의 그림을 가슴에 품고 육지로 올라갔어요. 자라는 육지 이곳저곳을 다니며 토끼를 찾았어요. 그런데 어느 날 자라 앞으로 뭔가 빠르게 지나갔어요. 자라는 가슴 속에 품고 있던 그림을 꺼내서 봤어요.

The Turtle and the Rabbit

Long ago, deep under the sea, lived the Dragon King. One day, the Dragon King fell ill from some unknown cause. The ministers brought a doctor who was renowned for his effective cures.

After assessing the Dragon King's condition, the doctor said, "The Dragon King's illness is so serious that it cannot be cured by the medicines of the sea."

At that, one of the ministers asked the doctor, "Then do you mean there is no way to cure the Dragon King's illness at all?"

The doctor replied, "There is one way: he must eat the liver of a rabbit, which lives on the land."

Then a turtle spoke up.

"I will go to the land and bring back a rabbit's liver. But as I have never seen a rabbit, please draw me a picture of one."

Clutching the picture of a rabbit to his chest, the turtle went up to the land. He went here and there, looking for a rabbit. One day something passed by rapidly in front of him. He looked at the picture he had been holding to his chest.

"지금 내 앞을 지나간 것이 토끼구나!"

자라는 바위에 앉아서 쉬고 있는 토끼에게 다가가서 말했어요.

"토끼 선생님!"

그러자 토끼가 고개를 돌렸어요.

"지금 저를 부른 거예요?"

자라가 대답했어요.

"처음 뵙겠습니다. 저는 바다 용궁에서 온 자라라고 합니다. 토끼 선생님을 만나서 영광입니다."

토끼는 한 번도 만난 적이 없는 자라가 자기를 아는 것이 이상했어요.

"그런데 저를 만난 적이 있나요? 어떻게 저를 아세요?"

자라는 토끼에게 더 가까이 다가갔어요.

"토끼 선생님이 육지에서 가장 훌륭하신 분이라서 바다에서도 아주 유명하십니다."

자라의 말을 듣고 토끼는 기분이 좋아졌어요.

"하하. 아, 그래요?"

자라는 토끼가 좋아하는 모습을 보면서 생각했어요.

"토끼가 내 거짓말에 속아 넘어오는 것 같군."

자라는 토끼 앞에 넙죽 엎드리며 말했어요.

"사실 바다의 왕이신 용왕님께서 꼭 한번 토끼 선생님을 뵙고 싶어 하십니다. 그래서 용왕님께서 토끼 선생님을 용궁으로 모셔오라고 특별히 저를 육지로 보내셨습니다."

자라의 말을 듣고 토끼는 귀가 솔깃했지만 걱정도 됐어요.

"육지 동물은 물 속에 들어가면 숨을 쉴 수 없는데 제가 어떻게 바닷속 용궁에 갈 수 있겠어요?"

"제 등에 타면 바닷속에 있을지라도 숨을 쉴 수 있을 테니까 걱정하지 않으셔도 됩니다. 게다가 바닷속 풍경은 아름답기가 이를 데 없어서 가시면 정말 좋아하실 겁니다."

"그래요? 그럼 한번 가 보지요."

토끼는 자라 등에 올라타서 바닷속으로 들어갔어요. 자라가 말한 대로 자라 등에 타고 있으니까 바닷속에서도 숨을 쉴 수 있었어요. 그리고 태어나서 처음 본 바닷속 풍경은 정말 아름답고 신비로웠어요.

용궁에 도착해 토끼가 자라 등에서 내리자마자 자라가 소리쳤어요.

"토끼를 잡아왔습니다!"

"So the thing that passed in front of me just now was a rabbit!"

The turtle went up to the rabbit, which sat resting on a rock.

"Mr. Rabbit!"

The rabbit turned its head.

"Did you call me just now?"

The turtle replied, "It's nice to meet you. I am what's called a turtle, from the Underwater Palace in the sea. It's an honor to meet you, Mr. Rabbit."

The rabbit thought it was strange that the turtle knew him although they had never met.

"Have you met me before? How do you know me?"

The turtle went up closer to the rabbit.

"Since you're the most outstanding creature on land, you're very famous in the sea too."

The rabbit was pleased to hear what the turtle said.

"Ha, ha! Is that so?"

Seeing that the rabbit liked this, the turtle thought, "The rabbit seems to be completely taken in by my lies."

The turtle prostrated himself in front of the rabbit and said, "The fact is, the Dragon King, who is the king of the sea, particularly wants to meet you, Mr. Rabbit. So the Dragon King sent me specially to the land to escort you to the Underwater Palace."

On hearing this, the rabbit's ears pricked up, but he also had a concern.

"If a land animal goes under the water, it can't breathe, so how can I go to the Underwater Palace in the sea?"

"If you ride on my back, you'll be able to breathe even under water, so you don't need to worry. What's more, the scenery in the sea is extremely beautiful and if you go you'll really like it."

"Really? Then I guess I'll go."

The rabbit got on the turtle's back and went into the sea. Just as the turtle had said, while riding on his back the rabbit was able to breathe even under water. And the underwater scenery that he saw for the first time in his life was truly beautiful and mysterious.

As soon as they arrived at the Underwater Palace and the rabbit got off the turtle's back, the turtle shouted, "I've caught a rabbit!"

그러자 신하들이 나와서 토끼를 붙잡아서 용왕 앞으로 데리고 갔어요. 용왕은 토끼에게 말했어요.

"내가 큰 병에 걸렸는데 네 간을 먹으면 내 병이 낫는다고 해서 너를 이리로 데리고 왔다."

용왕의 말을 듣고 토끼는 깜짝 놀랐지만 전혀 놀라지 않은 척하면서 용왕에게 말했어요.

"아이고, 이를 어떡하나. 그럼 미리 말씀해 주셨어야지요."

용왕이 의아해하면서 물었어요.

"그게 무슨 말이냐?"

토끼가 대답했어요.

"오늘 아침에 간을 씻어서 말려 놓은 채 나와서 지금 제 몸에 간이 없습니다. 원래 토끼는 아침마다 간을 꺼내 잘 씻은 후 말려서 다시 몸 속에 넣어야 하거든요."

용왕은 토끼의 말이 의심스럽다는 듯한 표정으로 토끼에게 물었어요.

"그 말이 사실이냐?"

"사실이고말고요. 제가 어떻게 감히 용왕님께 거짓말을 하겠습니까? 다시 육지에 가서 얼른 간을 가지고 올 테니까 잠시만 기다려 주시기 바랍니다."

용왕은 자라더러 토끼를 데리고 다시 육지에 다녀오라고 했어요.

육지에 도착해서 자라가 토끼에게 말했어요.

"나는 여기에서 기다릴 테니까 어서 간을 가지고 오거라."

그러자 토끼가 말했어요.

"멍청한 자라야! 간을 뺄 수 있는 동물이 어디에 있냐? 용왕이 내 거짓말에 속았기에 망정이지 하마터면 죽을 뻔했네."

토끼는 깡충깡충 뛰어서 멀리 가 버렸어요.

토끼를 놓친 자라는 멍하게 그 자리에 있었어요.

"이대로 용궁으로 돌아가면 용왕님한테 큰 벌을 받게 될 게 뻔해. 토끼 없이 돌아가느니 차라리 여기에서 죽어버려야겠다."

자라가 죽으려고 바위에 머리를 찧으려던 바로 그때 신령이 나타났어요.

"자라야, 무엇을 하고 있었느냐?"

"용왕님의 병을 낫게 하기 위해서 토끼의 간을 가지고 가야 하는데 제 실수로 그만 토끼를 눈 앞에서 놓치고 말았습니다. 용궁에 돌아가면 큰 벌을 받을 게 뻔해서 차라리 여기에서 죽으려고 했습니다."

Then the ministers came out, seized the rabbit and took him before the Dragon King.

The Dragon King said to the rabbit, "We've brought you here because I'm suffering from a serious illness and they say I'll get better if I eat your liver."

When he heard the Dragon King's words, the rabbit was shocked, but he pretended not to be surprised at all.

"Oh my, what's to be done?" he said to the Dragon King. "You should have told me beforehand."

Bewildered, the Dragon King asked, "What do you mean by that?"

The rabbit answered, "This morning I washed my liver and left it to dry when I came out, so right now there's no liver in my body. Rabbits have to take their liver out every morning to wash it, then dry it and put it back in their body."

With a doubtful look, the Dragon King asked the rabbit, "Is that true?"

"Sure it's true. How would I dare lie to the Dragon King? I'll go back to the land and bring my liver right back, so please just wait a while."

The Dragon King ordered the turtle to take the rabbit back to the land. On arriving there, the turtle said to the rabbit, "I'll wait here, so hurry up and bring your liver."

"Stupid turtle!" the rabbit replied. "What animal can take its own liver out? It's a good thing the Dragon King was taken in by my lies—I could have died!"

And the rabbit hopped off into the distance.

Having lost the rabbit, the turtle stood dazed where he was.

"If I go back to the Underwater Palace like this, I'm sure to get a heavy punishment from the Dragon King. Rather than go back without the rabbit, I prefer to die right here."

Just as the turtle was about to hit his head on a rock to kill himself, a spirit appeared.

"Hey, turtle, what were you doing?"

"I have to take a rabbit's liver to cure the Dragon King's illness, but through my own fault I've let the rabbit escape right before my eyes. If I go back to the Underwater Palace I'm sure to get a heavy punishment, so instead I was about to kill myself right here."

자라의 말이 끝나자 신령은 자라에게 산삼을 주면서 말했어요.

"네 사정이 딱하구나. 이 산삼을 가지고 용궁으로 가거라. 용왕이 이 산삼을 먹으면 병이 나을 것이다."

"정말 감사합니다, 신령님."

자라는 신령에게 받은 산삼을 가지고 서둘러 용궁으로 갔어요. 산삼을 먹은 용왕은 병이 나아서 건강해졌어요. 자라 덕분에 목숨을 건진 용왕은 자라에게 큰 상을 내렸어요.

☆ ☆ ☆

Vocabulary

자라 **jara** turtle

바닷속 **badatsok** under the sea

용왕 **yongwang** the Dragon King

앓다 **alta** to be ill

소문나다 **somunnada** a rumor circulates

상태 **sangtae** condition

심각하다 **simgakada** to be serious

낫다 **natda** to recover

육지 **yukji** land

그림 **geurim** picture, painting

그리다 **geurida** to draw, to paint

가슴에 품다 **gaseume pumda** to clutch (something) to one's chest

이곳저곳을 다니다 **igotjeogoseul danida** to go around everywhere

빠르게 **ppareuge** fast

고개를 돌리다 **gogaereul dollida** to turn one's head

처음 뵙겠습니다 **cheoeum boepgetseumnida** Nice to meet you.

용궁 **yonggung** Underwater Palace (of the Dragon King)

영광이다 **yeonggwangida** to feel honored

가까이 다가가다 **gakkai dagagada** to come closer

속아 넘어오다 **soga neomeoooda** to be completely deceived

넙죽 엎드리다 **neopjuk eopdeurida** to prostrate oneself

특별히 **teukbyeolhi** specially

귀가 솔깃하다 **gwiga solgithada** to prick up one's ears, be tempted

게다가 **gedaga** besides

풍경 **pungkyeong** scenery

등에 올라타다 **deunge ollatada** to ride on the back

신비롭다 **sinbiropda** to be mysterious

내리다 **naerida** to get off, to come down

붙잡다 **butjapda** to seize

이리로 **iriro** here

의아해하다 **uiahaehada** to wonder

말리다 **mallida** to dry

의심스럽다 **uisimseureopda** to be doubtful

표정 **pyojeong** expression

감히 **gamhi** impudently

잠시만 **jamsiman** for a moment

When the turtle finished speaking, the spirit gave him some wild ginseng.

"Your case is a hard one," the spirit said. "Take this wild ginseng and go to the Dragon King. If the Dragon King eats this wild ginseng, he will recover."

"Thank you so much, dear Spirit."

The turtle took the wild ginseng and hurried back to the Underwater Palace. After eating the ginseng, the Dragon King got over his illness and became well. For saving his life, the Dragon King gave the turtle a great reward.

☆　☆　☆

멍청하다 **meongcheonghada** to be stupid

하마터면 **hamateomyeon** almost, nearly

놓치다 **notchida** to miss, to lose

머리를 찧다 **meorireul jjitda** to hit one's head

실수 **silsu** mistake

그만 **geuman** just like that

사정 **sajeong** circumstances, situation

딱하다 **ttakada** to be pathetic

상을 내리다 **sangeul naerida** to award a prize

Selected grammar points

- 고 싶어 하다 **Expressing a wish or hope; "want to"**
  This form is used with an action verb stem to indicate someone's desire, wish or hope in the third person.
  용왕님께서 꼭 한번 토끼 선생님을 **뵙고 싶어 하십니다.**
  The Dragon King wants to meet you, Mr Rabbit.

- (으)ㄹ지라도 **"even though," "regardless of"**
  This is used to indicate that even if one acknowledges or hypothesizes the situation or state of affairs described in the preceding clause, the situation in the following clause won't be affected by it.
  제 등에 타면 바닷속에 **있을지라도** 숨을 쉴 수 있을 테니까 걱정하지 않으셔도 됩니다.
  If you ride on my back, you'll be able to breathe even under water, so you don't need to worry.

- 기에 망정이지 **"it's a good thing that"** (expressing relief)
  용왕이 내 거짓말에 속았**기에 망정이지** 하마터면 죽을 뻔했네.
  It's a good thing the Dragon King was taken in by my lies—I could have died!

- 느니 차라리 **"I'd (much) rather . . ."**
  This indicates that you would rather do one action than another.
  토끼 없이 돌아가느니 차라리 여기에서 죽어버려야겠다.
  Rather than go back without the rabbit, I prefer to die right here.
- (으)ㄹ게 뻔하다 **"it's obvious that . . . ," "sure to . . ."**
  This is used to speculate about something negative that is obvious.
  용궁에 돌아가면 큰 벌을 받을 게 뻔해서 차라리 여기에서 죽으려고 했습니다.
  If I go back to the Underwater Palace I'm sure to get a heavy punishment, so instead
  I was about to kill myself right here.

After reading the story

1. 용왕의 병을 낫게 할 방법이 무엇이에요?
   How could the Dragon King's illness be cured?
2. 자라는 어떻게 토끼를 용궁으로 데려갔어요?
   How did the turtle take the rabbit to the Underwater Palace?
3. 토끼는 어떻게 죽을 위기를 넘겼어요?
   How did the rabbit escape from the danger of death?
4. 자라는 왜 죽으려고 했어요?
   Why did the turtle want to die?
5. 용왕은 왜 자라에게 상을 내렸어요?
   Why did the Dragon King give the turtle a reward?

Let's talk!

자라와 토끼 모두 거짓말을 했는데 둘의 거짓말 중 누구의 거짓말이 나쁜지 토론해 보세요.

The turtle and the rabbit both tell lies. Discuss which of their lies you think is worse.

Notes on Korean culture

The Dragon King, a spirit that rules the sea and the fish, often appears in traditional Korean folktales. The place where the Dragon King lives is called the Underwater Palace and is portrayed as a magnificent place full of jewels. At seaside villages there is a custom of performing rites to the Dragon King to pray for a big catch of fish, gentler waves and the safe return of the fishermen.

단군 이야기

옛날 옛날 아주 먼 옛날, 사람들이 나무 열매를 따 먹고 사냥을 하면서 살던 시대가 있었어요. 하늘나라에 환인이라는 신이 살고 있었는데 환인에게는 환웅이라는 아들이 있었어요. 환웅은 하늘에서 땅을 내려다보는 것을 좋아했어요. 땅에 있는 온갖 것들을 좋아했는데 그 중에서도 사람을 가장 좋아했어요. 그러던 어느 날 환웅은 환인에게 말했어요.

"세상으로 내려가서 사람들에게 도움을 주고 싶습니다."

그러자 환인이 말했어요.

"내가 세상을 살펴보니 태백산이 가장 아름답고 평온하구나. 그 곳으로 가서 나라를 세워 사람들에게 널리 도움을 주거라."

환웅은 비, 구름, 바람을 다스리는 세 신하를 데리고 태백산에 내려와서 나라를 세웠어요.

환웅은 사람들에게 농사를 짓는 방법을 알려주고 착하고 올바르게 사는 법을 가르쳤어요. 사람들은 환웅의 말을 잘 따랐고 환웅이 다스리는 나라는 언제나 평화로웠어요.

How Korea Came to Be

Long, long ago, in the very distant past, there was a time when people lived by picking the fruit off the trees and hunting.

In Heaven there lived a god called Hwanin, and Hwanin had a son named Hwanung. Hwanung liked looking down from Heaven to Earth. He liked all kinds of things that were on Earth, and among them all he liked the people most.

One day, Hwanung said to Hwanin, "I want to go down to Earth and help the people."

Hwanin replied, "When I look over the Earth, the Taebaek mountain range seems the most beautiful and peaceful place. Go there and found a nation and help the people far and wide."

Hwanung took the three heavenly ministers who ruled the rain, the clouds and the wind and went down to the Taebaek mountains where he founded a nation. Hwanung taught the people how to grow crops and how to live a good and upright life. The people followed Hwanung's teachings well and the nation that Hwanung ruled was always peaceful.

어느 날 곰과 호랑이가 환웅을 찾아와서 말했어요.

"환웅님, 저희는 사람이 되고 싶습니다. 제발 사람이 되는 방법을 가르쳐 주세요."

환웅은 곰과 호랑이에게 마늘과 쑥을 주면서 말했어요.

"백 일 동안 빛을 보지 않고 이 마늘과 쑥을 먹으면서 지내면 사람이 될 것이다. 그렇게 할 수 있겠느냐?"

곰과 호랑이가 대답했어요.

"할 수 있고말고요. 저희는 사람만 될 수 있다면 뭐든지 할 수 있습니다."

곰과 호랑이는 마늘과 쑥을 가지고 깊은 산 속 동굴로 들어갔어요. 빛 하나 들어오지 않는 곳에서 마늘과 쑥만 먹으며 지내는 것이 쉽지 않았지만 곰과 호랑이는 참고 견뎠어요. 그렇게 며칠이 지난 어느 날 호랑이가 말했어요.

"고기가 먹고 싶어서 죽겠어. 난 이제 동굴 밖으로 나갈래."

그러자 곰이 말했어요.

"사람이 되기로 결심한 이상 아무리 힘들어도 참을 수밖에 없잖아. 조금만 더 견디자."

호랑이는 곰의 말을 듣고 참아 보기로 했어요. 그런데 며칠이 지난 후 호랑이는 또 동굴에서 지내는 것이 힘들어졌어요.

"이렇게 괴로울 바에야 차라리 사람이 되는 걸 포기하겠어!"

곰이 말릴 새도 없이 호랑이는 동굴을 뛰쳐나가 버렸어요.

동굴에 혼자 남은 곰은 너무 외롭고 무서웠어요. 하지만 사람이 될 날을 기다리면서 매일 마늘과 쑥을 먹으면서 참았어요.

그렇게 시간이 흘러 곰이 동굴에 들어온 지 백 일째 되는 날이었어요. 신성한 빛이 동굴 속을 비추더니 곰을 감쌌어요. 그러자 곰이 아름다운 여자로 변했어요.

"내가 진짜 사람이 됐다니!"

여자가 된 곰은 너무 기뻐서 사람들이 사는 마을로 내려갔어요.

One day, a bear and a tiger came to see Hwanung.

"Lord Hwanung," they said, "we want to become human. Please teach us the way to become human."

Hwanung gave the bear and the tiger some garlic and mugwort.

"If you live on this garlic and mugwort for one hundred days without seeing daylight, you will become human. Do you think you can do that?"

"We are sure we can," said the bear and the tiger. "If we can only become human, we'll do anything."

The bear and the tiger took the garlic and mugwort and went into a cave deep in the mountains.

They lived in the cave eating nothing but the garlic and mugwort, as Hwanung had instructed them. It wasn't easy to live on nothing but garlic and mugwort in a place where no light came in, but they endured it with determination.

After spending a few days like this, the tiger said, "I'm dying to eat some meat. I'm going out of the cave now."

Then the bear said, "Since we've decided to become human, we have to stick with it no matter how hard it is. Let's just endure it a little longer."

On hearing the bear's words, the tiger decided to try and endure it.

But a few days later, the tiger got tired of staying in the cave again.

"This is so hard, I'd rather give up becoming human!"

And before the bear could stop him, the tiger ran out of the cave.

Left alone in the cave, the bear was terribly lonely and scared. But she went on eating garlic and mugwort every day and stuck with it, waiting for the day when she would become human.

And so time went by, until it was the one-hundredth day since the bear had entered the cave. A holy light shone into the cave and around the bear. Then the bear turned into a beautiful woman.

"I really have become a human!"

Overjoyed, the bear that had become a woman went down to a village where humans lived.

사람들은 여자가 된 곰을 웅녀라고 불렀어요. 웅녀란 곰이 변한 여자라는 뜻이에요. 웅녀는 이제 자기도 사람이 됐으니까 남편도 얻고 아이도 낳고 싶었어요. 웅녀는 마을의 남자들에게 자신의 남편이 돼 달라고 했어요. 그런데 마을의 어떤 남자들은 웅녀의 남편이 되는 것은 고사하고 웅녀 곁에 오는 것조차 꺼렸어요. 웅녀는 아름답지만 너무 신비로워서 마을의 남자들은 웅녀를 보고 겁을 냈어요.

웅녀는 마을의 신성한 나무에 가서 빌었어요.

"저도 남편이 생기게 해 주세요."

환웅은 하늘에서 웅녀가 비는 것을 보고 땅으로 내려왔어요.

"웅녀야. 고개를 들거라."

웅녀는 자기 앞에 환웅이 서 있는 것을 보고 깜짝 놀랐어요.

"환웅님께서 여기에 무슨 일로 오셨습니까?"

"웅녀야. 네가 빌고 있는 것을 하늘에서 봤다. 네 신비로운 기운 때문에 사람들 중에 네 남편이 될 자가 없으니 내가 너를 아내로 삼겠다."

환웅의 아내가 된 웅녀는 얼마 후 아들을 낳았어요. 환웅은 기뻐하며 사람들에게 자신과 웅녀 사이에 아들이 태어났음을 알렸어요. 이 아들의 이름은 단군왕검이었어요.

단군왕검은 환웅으로부터는 하늘의 기운을 받고 웅녀로부터는 땅의 기운을 받아서 아주 용감하고 지혜롭기가 이를 데 없었어요.

세월이 흘러 청년이 된 단군왕검은 환웅에게 말했어요.

"저도 아버님처럼 사람들이 행복하게 잘 사는 나라를 세우고 싶습니다."

"알겠다. 그럼 좋은 곳으로 가서 사람들이 서로 돕고 살 수 있는 나라를 세우거라."

단군왕검은 만 명의 백성을 데리고 새 나라를 세우기 위해 길을 떠났어요. 말을 타고 달리다가 밝은 기운이 있는 곳에 멈춰서 새 나라를 세웠어요. 단군왕검은 온 세상에 새 나라가 세워졌음을 알렸어요.

"이곳에 새 나라가 생겼으니 이름을 조선이라고 하겠다. 조선의 모든 백성은 크게 사람을 도울 것이다."

단군왕검은 조선을 잘 다스려서 모든 백성들에게서 존경을 받았어요. 단군왕검은 조선을 천오백 년 동안 다스린 후 산신이 되었다고 해요.

☆ ☆ ☆

The people called the bear that had turned into a woman Ungnyeo, which means a woman transformed from a bear. Now that she was human, Ungnyeo wanted to get a husband and have a child. She asked the men in the village to become her husband. But far from becoming her husband, the men in the village avoided even coming close to her. Although she was beautiful, Ungnyeo was so mysterious that the men of the village were afraid when they saw her.

Ungnyeo went to a holy tree in the village and prayed.

"Please let me have a husband."

From Heaven, Hwanung saw Ungnyeo praying and came down to Earth.

"Ungnyeo, lift your head up."

Ungnyeo was amazed to see Hwanung standing before her.

"What have you come here for, Lord Hwanung?"

"Ungnyeo, I saw you praying from Heaven. Because of your mysterious energy, there's no husband for you among the humans, so I will take you as my wife."

Having become Hwanung's wife, some time later Ungnyeo gave birth to a son. Hwanung was delighted and told the people that a son had been born to him and Ungnyeo. The son's name was Dangun Wanggeom.

Dangun Wanggeom inherited the energy of Heaven from Hwanung and the energy of Earth from Ungnyeo, and he was as brave and wise as can be.

Time went by and when Dangun had become a young man, he said to Hwanung, "I too want to found a nation where people live happily and well, as you did, Father."

"I see. Then go to a good place and found a nation where people can live helping each other."

Dangun took ten thousand people with him and set off to found a new nation. While riding his horse he stopped at a place where the energy was bright, and established his kingdom there. Dangun announced to the whole world that he had founded a new state. "A new nation has arisen here and its name will be Joseon. All the people of Joseon will help other people greatly."

Dangun ruled Joseon well and won the respect of all the people. They say that after ruling Joseon for 1,500 years he became a mountain spirit.

☆ ☆ ☆

Vocabulary

열매 **yeolmae** fruit, berry

사냥하다 **sanyanghada** to hunt

시대 **sidae** age

평온하다 **pyeongonhada** to be tranquil

나라를 세우다 **narareul seuda** to found a nation

널리 **neolli** widely

비 **bi** rain

구름 **gureum** cloud

다스리다 **daseurida** to govern

말을 잘 따르다 **mareul jal ttareuda** to obey someone's words well

평화롭다 **pyeonghwaropda** to be peaceful

곰 **gom** bear

마늘 **maneul** garlic

쑥 **ssuk** mugwort

백 일 **baek il** one hundred days

빛 **bit** light

견디다 **gyeondida** to endure

고기 **gogi** meat

포기하다 **pogihada** to give up

말리다 **mallida** to stop

뛰쳐나가다 **ttwichyeonagada** to dash out

신성하다 **sinseonghada** to be holy

비추다 **bichuda** to shine

감싸다 **gamssada** to wrap

곁 **gyeot** beside, by

겁을 내다 **geobeul naeda** to be afraid of

고개를 들다 **gogaereul deulda** to raise one's head

기운 **giun** energy

자 **ja** person

알리다 **allida** to inform

용감하다 **yonggamhada** to be brave

지혜롭다 **jihyeropda** to be wise

청년 **cheongnyeon** young man

만 **man** ten thousand

밝다 **bakda** to be bright

천오백 **choenobaek** 1,500

산신 **sansin** mountain spirit

Selected grammar points

- (으)ㄴ 이상 **"since," "now that"**

  This indicates that due to the content of the preceding clause being already described or certain, then the next course of action is clear or obvious.

  사람이 되기로 **결심한 이상** 아무리 힘들어도 참을 수밖에 없잖아.

  Since we've decided to become human, we have to stick with it no matter how hard it is.

- (으)ㄹ 바에야 **"I would rather," "it would be better to"**

  This is used when stating a preference between two options when neither is ideal.

  이렇게 괴로울 **바에야 차라리** 사람이 되는 걸 포기하겠어!

  This is so hard, I'd rather give up becoming human!

- 은/는 고사하고 **"let alone," "far from"**

  This is used when the event in the preceding clause is unlikely to happen, if not impossible, while the event in the following clause which is better, is still not easy.

  마을의 어떤 남자들은 웅녀의 남편이 되는 **것은 고사하고** 웅녀 곁에 오는 것조차 꺼렸어요.

  But far from becoming her husband, the men in the village avoided even coming close to Ungnyeo.

- 기가 이를 데 없다 **""couldn't be more . . . ," "as . . . as can be"**

  This is used to express that something is so extraordinary or excessive that it cannot be conveyed in words.

  용감하고 지혜롭기가 **이를 데 없었어요**.

  He was as brave and wise as can be.

After reading the story

1. 환웅은 왜 세상에 내려가고 싶어 했어요?

   Why did Hwanung want to go down to Earth?

2. 곰과 호랑이가 왜 환웅을 찾아왔어요?

   Why did the bear and the tiger come to see Hwanung?

3. 호랑이는 왜 동굴을 뛰쳐나갔어요?

   Why did the tiger run out of the cave?

4. 웅녀에게는 어떤 고민이 있었어요?

   What was Ungnyeo troubled about?

5. 단군왕검은 무엇을 했어요?

   What did Dangun Wanggeom do?

Let's talk!

여러분의 나라가 어떻게 세워졌는지에 대한 전래동화가 있나요?

Is there a traditional story about how your country was founded?

Notes on Korean culture

The story of Dangun is the national foundation story of Korea. The kingdom of Joseon that was founded by Dangun Wanggeom is commonly called Gujoseon or "Old Joseon" to distinguish it from the later Joseon era of the Yi Dynasty. The foundational philosophy of Dangun's Joseon was "devotion to the welfare of humanity." This concept implies benefiting humanity widely, helping people greatly, and, more broadly, benefiting the whole world including nature. In these words we can clearly see the Korean spirit of peace that respects all nature and loves all people.

English to Korean Glossary

For ease of search, all verb meanings are listed under T: "to —"

100th	백 번째
1,500	천오백

A

a little	조금
a lot	많이
about	대해서
actually	정말, 막상
adopted child	양자
after	후, 후에
after a while	얼마 후
again	또, 다시
age	시대
alcohol	술
all	다
all, every	온갖
all, everyone	모두 다
all day	하루 종일
all the while	그동안
almost, nearly	하마터면
alone	혼자(서)
along	따라서
already	벌써, 어느덧, 어느새, 이미
also, as well, too	도
although, even if	비록
always	늘
am, is, are	이다
among, between	중에는
and then	그리고
animal	동물, 짐승
anxiously	애타게
anyway	어차피
appearance	모습
appearance from behind	뒷모습
are, is, am	이다
around	주위
as … as	만큼
as expected	역시
as it is	그대로
as long as one likes	언제까지나
as time goes by	갈수록

as well, too, also	도
as you please	마음대로
at all	도저히
at any moment	금방이라도
at last, finally	드디어
at this rate	이러다가
autumn	가을

B

bachelor	총각
back (of a person or animal)	등
bag	자루
bag of millet	조 한 자루
banquet, feast	잔치
barely	겨우
basket	바구니
bear	곰
because of	때문에
before	전에
before, originally	원래
beginning of a month	월초
behavior	행동
behind	뒤
bell	방울
berry, fruit	열매
beside, by	곁
besides	게다가
be that as it may	그렇다고
between, among	중에는
Big Dipper	북두칠성
bird	새
black ox	검은 소
blood	피
body	몸
bottle	병
bottom	밑바닥
bowl	그릇
boy	남자 아이
bridge	다리
broom	빗자루
brother	형제
brush	붓

Buddha	부처님
but, by the way	그런데
but, however	그렇지만, 하지만
button	단추
by, beside	곁
by any chance	혹시
by chance	우연히
by mistake	잘못해서
by the way, but	그런데

C

carefully	조심스럽게
carefully, thoughtfully	곰곰이
carelessly, thoughtlessly	함부로
carp	잉어
cauldron	솥
cauldron lid	솥뚜껑
cave	동굴
center, middle	가운데
centipede	지네
certainly	그럼요, 틀림없이
certainly, obviously	당연히
chance, opportunity, occasion	계기
character, personality	성품
chief minister	정승
child	아이
children	아이들
circumstances	사정
city	도시
cliff	벼랑
cloud	구름
coat	외투
coin	동전
comb	머리빗
come in, welcome	어서 오세요
comfortably	편하게, 편히
complexion	얼굴색
concern	근심
condition	상태
conditions	형편
consequently	그 바람에
continuously	계속, 계속해서
counter for animals	마리
counter for inanimate objects	개
counter for people	명

counter for people (honorific)	분
country, nation	나라
county magistrate	원님
crescent moon	초승달
crisis	위기

D

darling, dear	부인, 여보
daughter	딸
daughter-in-law	며느리
day	날
day before yesterday	그저께
daytime	낮
difficulty	어려움
diligently	부지런히
dinner	저녁
district magistrate	사또
doctor (medical)	의사, 의원
dongdongju rice wine	동동주
door	문
door, of a room	방문
door handle	문고리
Dragon King	용왕
dream	꿈

E

each	각자, 씩
each other	서로
eagle	독수리
early, soon	일찍
Earth	땅
earthworm	지렁이
eight	여덟
elderly person	노인
energy	기운
entire	온
entire country	전국
entirely	온통
envoy	사신
equally, evenly	똑같이
especially	별로
even more	더욱더
even if, although	비록
even one	하나도
even though	아무리
evenly, equally	똑같이
every, all	온갖

every day	날마다, 매일매일
everyone, all	모두 다
exactly the same	똑같이
excessively, too	너무나
expression	표정
eye	눈
eyebrow	눈썹

F

face	얼굴
fact, truth	사실
fairy	선녀
family	가족
family member	식구
far away	멀리
farm, field	밭
farmer	농부, 농사꾼
farting person	방귀쟁이
fast	빠르게
father	아버지
feast, banquet	잔치
field, farm	밭
fifteen	십오
fifth day	오 일째
fifty	쉰
finally	이제야
finally, at last	드디어
finely	곱게
fireplace, hearth	아궁이
first	첫째
first day	첫날
fish	물고기
fist	주먹
five days	오 일
flame	불길
folktales	옛날 이야기
fool	바보
foot	발
footstep	발소리
for a long time	오래오래, 오랫동안
for a moment	잠시만
for some time	당분간, 한참
for a while	잠깐
forcibly	강제로
forest	숲
fox	여우

friend	친구
from	부터
from (a person)	에게서
from the beginning	처음부터
from now on	앞으로
front gate	대문
fruit, berry	열매
full moon	보름달
fully	가득

G

garlic	마늘
general (military role)	장군
giant	거인
ginseng, wild	산삼
glass of (alcohol)	한 잔
goblin	도깨비
god	신, 하느님
god, spirit	신령
gold mine	금광
gold nugget	금덩이
goldfish	금붕어
good-for-nothing, wastrel	건달
government officer	신하
gradually	점점
grain	곡식
grandfather, old man	할아버지
grandmother, old woman	할머니
grave	무덤
Great Jade Emperor	옥황상제
great reward	큰 상
greed	욕심
greedy person	욕심쟁이
green leaf	파란 잎
growl	어흥
guest	손님

H

half	반
hand	손
happily	행복하게
hard, diligently	열심히
health	건강
heart, mind	마음
hearth, fireplace	아궁이

heaven	하늘나라	**J**	
height	높이	jewel	보석
help	도움	joyfully	재미있게
here	여기, 이리로	just	그냥, 막
here and there	여기저기	just, only	그저
hill	고개	just in time	마침
hill at the back of one's house	뒷산	just like that	그만
		just now	방금 전에
hobby	취미		
hole	구멍	**K**	
home, house	집	kindling (for a fire)	불씨
hope, wish	소원	king	왕, 임금님
horse	말	kitchen	부엌
house, home	집	knowledge	지식
housekeeping	살림	Korea	한국
how much	얼마나	Korean language	한국어
however, but	그렇지만, 하지만	Korean traditional clothes	한복
hundred	백		
hunter	사냥꾼		
hurriedly	허겁지겁	**L**	
husband	남편, 서방님	lake	호수
husk	껍질	land	육지, 땅나라
		last night	어젯밤
I		last time	지난번
I	나, 내가	lastly	마지막으로
I (humble)	저	later	나중에
ice	얼음	less	덜
immediately	당장	letter	편지
immediately, right away	얼른	life	삶, 인생
impudently	감히	light	빛
in the end	결국	like that	그렇게
in front of, next to	앞	like this	이렇게
in a hurry	서둘러(서)	liver	간
in an instant	순식간에	livestock	가축
in the meantime	그 사이에, 그러는 사이에	long ago	옛날에
		look	눈빛
in the morning	아침에	lots of	수많은
in the past	전에는	loudly	큰 소리로
in person	직접	luck	재수
in vain	괜히		
injured area	다치신 데	**M**	
inside, in	안, 속	machine	기계
instead	그 대신	madam, sir	님
interest	관심	magic	요술
iron	쇠	makgeolli rice wine	막걸리
is, am, are	이다	mandarin duck	원앙새
it seems	아무래도	market	장
item, object, thing	물건	married couple	부부

married woman's parents' home	친정
meal	끼니
meaning	뜻
meanwhile	한편
meat	고기
medicine	약
merchant	상인
middle	중간
middle-aged man, "mister"	아저씨
mind, heart	마음
mineral water	약수
minister, government officer	신하
mirror	거울
mistake	실수, 잘못
"mister," middle-aged man	아저씨
money	돈
monk	스님
month	달
moon	달님
more	더
more than usual	다른 때보다 더
most	제일
mother	어머니
mother-in-law	시어머니
mountain	산
mountain animal	산짐승
mountain spirit	산신
mountainous district	산골
mourning dress	상복
mouth	입
much more	훨씬 더
mugwort	쑥
my (humble)	제

N

name	이름
nation, country	나라
nearly, almost	하마터면
neck	목
neighbor, neighboring	이웃
neighborhood	근처
never	절대로
new	새
New Year's Day (lunar)	설날

newly	새로
next	다음
next to, in front of	앞
next year	내년
Nice to meet you.	처음 뵙겠습니다.
night	밤
nine	아홉
no longer	이제 더 이상
no matter how, even though	아무리
no use	쓸모 없다
no way	설마
none other than	바로
not at all	전혀
nothing	아무것도
now	이제, 지금
nyang, unit of old Korean coinage	냥

O

object, item, thing	물건
obviously, certainly	당연히
occasion, chance, opportunity	계기
Oh my!	아이고
Oh my God!	에구머니나
Oh my! What a surprise!	깜짝이야
old man, grandfather	할아버지
old woman, grandmother	할머니
older brother	오빠, 형
[what] on earth	도대체
on the one hand	한편으로는
one	한, 일, 하나
one, a certain	어느, 어떤
one day	어느 날
one hundred days	백 일
one kind	한 가지
one night	하룻밤
one of a pair	한 짝
one's whole life	한평생
oneself	자기
only	만
only, just	그저
only then	그때서야
openly	솔직히
opportunity, chance occasion	계기

opposite side of the street	길 건너편	**R**	
ordinary	보통	rabbit	토끼
originally, before	원래	rain	비
other	다른	rather	차라리
other people's business	남의 일	reading	독서
otherwise	그렇지 않으면	real	진짜
our	우리	really	참
outside	밖에서	red bean porridge	팥죽
owner	주인	relief	안도
		repay one's kindness	은혜를 갚다
P		repeatedly	자꾸
painting, picture	그림	rice cake	떡
palace	궁궐	rice-cake pot	떡시루
parents	부모님	rice-cake soup	떡국
particularly	별로	rice paddy	논
pea patch	콩밭	rich person	부자
pen	우리	right away	얼른
people	사람들, 백성	ring	반지
persimmon tree	감나무	river	강
person	자, 사람	river water	강물
personality, character	성품	roadside	길가
personality, temper	마음씨	rock	바위
picture, painting	그림	room	방
piece	조각	rope	밧줄
pig	돼지	rudely	버릇없이
pillar	기둥	ruin	폐허
pine tree	소나무	rumor, hearsay	소문
pipe (musical)	피리		
please	부디, 제발	**S**	
Pleased to meet you.	만나서 반가워요.	sadly	슬프게
pocket, purse	주머니	sandy field	모래밭
pot	항아리, 독	scenery	풍경
present, gift	선물	scholar	선비
previous day	전날	sea	바다
price, value	값	seat, spot	자리
princess	공주	second	둘째
properly	제대로	secretly	몰래
property	재산	self-introduction	자기소개
		seller, merchant	장수
Q		servant	하인, 머슴
queen	왕비	servants' quarters	행랑채
quickly, fast	빨리	seven	일곱
quietly	살금살금, 조용히	several	몇
quite	꽤	several times	몇 번
		shade of a tree	나무 그늘
		shape	모양
		sheaf of unhusked rice	볏단
		shepherd boy	목동

shop, store	가게	**T**	
shortcomings	단점	tail	꼬리
shovel, spade	삽	talk	얘기, 말
side	옆	tavern	주막집
sincerity	정성	teacher	선생님
sir, madam	님	temper, personality	마음씨
situation	상황, 사정	temple	절
six	여섯	ten	열
skirt	치마	ten thousand	만
sky	하늘	thanks to	덕분에
slowly	천천히	that, it	그것
snake	뱀	That's great!	잘 됐다!
so, then	그러니까	then	그러면, 그럼,
so, therefore	그래서		그랬더니
so, very	너무, 아주	(and) then	그러자
soil	흙	there	거기서, 저기에
something new	새로운 것	therefore	그래서
son	아들	thief	도둑
sons and daughters	자식	thing, item, object	물건
soon	곧	third	셋째
soul, spirit	혼	this	이것, 이
sound	소리	this and that	이것저것,
southern province	남쪽지방		이런저런
spade, shovel	삽	This is lucky!	잘 됐다!
sparrow	참새	this time	이번
spear	창	this way and that	이리저리
specially	특별히	this way	이쪽
spirit	신령	this year	올해
spring (season)	봄	thornbush	가시덤불
spring water	약수	thoroughly	샅샅이, 찬찬히
stack of rice straw	볏가리	thoughtfully, carefully	곰곰이
stepmother	새어머니	thoughtlessly, carelessly	함부로
stick, cane	지팡이	thousand	천
still	가만히, 아직도	three	삼, 세 (셋)
store, shop	가게	thunder	천둥
stone	돌	tiger	호랑이
stone field	돌밭	time	세월
stork	황새	to (a person)	에게, 한테
story	이야기	to act, to behave	행동하다
straw rope	새끼줄	to act harshly	못살게 굴다
stream	시냇물	to allot, share	나누어 주다
stream water	개울물	to answer	대답하다
strong person	장수	to apologize	사과하다
suddenly	갑자기	to appear	나타나다
summer	여름	to arrive	도착하다
sun	해	to ask	물어보다
surely	꼭, 분명히	to ask (a question)	묻다
sweat	땀	to ask a favor	부탁을 하다

to ask for help	도와 달라고 하다	to be distressed	괴롭다
to assess the situation, test the water	사정을 살피다	to be doubtful	의심스럽다
		to be dumbfounded	어이가 없다
to attack	달려들다	to be early	이르다
to avoid, to escape	피하다	to be easy	쉽다
to award a prize	상을 내리다	to be embarrassed	당황하다,
to bang, hit	쾅 치다		부끄럽다,
to be, to have	있다		창피하다
to be (honorific)	계시다	to be enough	충분하다
to be admiring, to be respectful	존경스럽다	to be exactly the same	똑같다
		to be exasperated	기가 막히다
to be afraid	겁먹다	to be excited	신이 나다
to be afraid of	겁을 내다	to be expensive	비싸다
to be alright	괜찮다	to be fake	거짓
to be amazed	기가 막히다	to be famous, to be popular	유명하다
to be amazing, magical	신기하다		
to be angry	화가 나다	to be filled	차다
to be bad	나쁘다	to be filled with	들어있다
to be beautiful	아름답다	to be flabbergasted	어이가 없다
to be the best	최고이다	to be fooled, tricked	속다
to be better	낫다	to be formed	생기다
to be blocked, plugged	막히다	to be frightened, to be surprised	놀라다
to be blown	날아가다		
to be blue	시퍼렇다, 파랗다	to be frozen	얼어붙다
to be bored	심심하다	to be full	배가 부르다
to be born	태어나다	to be fun, interesting	재미있다
to be brave	용감하다	to be funny	우습다
to be bright	밝다, 환하다	to be gentle, dignified	점잖다
to be broad	넓다	to be glad	기쁘다, 반갑다
to be broken	깨지다, 부러지다	to be good	좋다
to be bumped into	부딪히다	to be great	훌륭하다
to be burned to death	타 죽다	to be greedy, to covet	욕심을 내다
to be careful	조심하다	to be happy	행복하다
to be certain	틀림없다	to be hard	힘들다
to be changed	바뀌다	to be healthy	건강하다
to be clean	깨끗하다	to be holy	신성하다
to be close	들이대다	to be hot	덥다
to be cold	춥다	to be huge	커다랗다
to be completely deceived	속아 넘어오다	to be humble, lowly	천하다
		to be hung	달리다
to be contained	들어있다	to be hungry	배가 고프다
to be deep	깊다	to be hunted and preyed on	잡아먹히다
to be delighted, enjoy oneself	즐거워하다		
		to be ill	앓다
to be difficult	곤란하다, 어렵다	to be impressed	감탄하다
to be dignified, gentle	점잖다	to be in a bad mood	기분이 나쁘다
to be diligent	부지런하다	to be in a good mood	기분이 좋다
to be disappointed	서운하다, 실망하다	to be in trouble	큰일이다

to be in uproar	발칵 뒤집히다	to be round	둥글다
to be inevitable	어쩔 수(가) 없다	to be rugged	험하다
to be insufficient	부족하다	to be sad	슬프다, 안타깝다
to be intelligent, smart	똑똑하다	to be satisfied	만족하다
to be interested	관심을 가지다	to be scary	무섭다
to be interesting, fun	재미있다	to be scolded	혼나다
to be jealous	배가 아프다,	to be seen, to appear	보이다
	질투가 나다	to be serious	심각하다
to be kind-hearted	착하다	to be a shame, to be	아쉽다
to be late	늦다	regretable	
to be lazy	게으르다	to be silly	어리석다
to be lonely	외롭다	to be sleepy	졸리다
to be lowly, humble	천하다	to be small	작다
to be lucky	운이 좋다	to be smart, intelligent	똑똑하다
to be magical, amazing	신기하다	to be smashed	산산조각이 나다
to be magnificent	굉장하다	to pieces	
to be many,	많다	to be sole	유일하다
to be much		to be sorry	미안하다,
to be meaningless	의미없다		죄송하다
to be mighty	힘이 세다	to be startled	깜짝 놀라다
to be mysterious	신비롭다	to be strange, unusual	이상하다
to be natural	당연하다	to be strong, mighty	힘이 세다
to be nearby	가깝다	to be stupid	멍청하다
to be nice	잘해주다	to be supreme, the best	최고이다
to be old	늙다, 오래되다	to be surprised	놀라다
to be on good terms	사이가 좋다,	to be frightened	
	의좋다	to be tasty	맛있다
to be pale	창백하다	to be tempted	귀가 솔깃하다
to be pathetic	딱하다	to be thin and pale	핼쑥하다
to be peaceful	평화롭다	to be thirsty	목이 마르다
to be piled up	쌓이다	to be this much	이만하다
to be plugged, blocked	막히다	to be a thousand	천 년 묵다
to be poor	가난하다	years old	
to be popular,	유명하다	to be tired	피곤하다
to be famous		to be topsy-turvy	발칵 뒤집히다
to be praised	칭찬을 듣다	to be tranquil	평온하다
to be pregnant	임신을 하다	to be tricked, fooled	속다
to be pretty	예쁘다	to be true	정말이다
to be punished by God	천벌을 받다	to be unusual, strange	이상하다
to be red	빨갛다, 붉다	to be urgent	급하다
to be regrettable,	아쉽다	to be valuable	귀하다
to be a shame		to be warm	따뜻하다
to be a relief	다행이다	to be weak	약하다
to be respectful,	존경스럽다	to be well-to-do	넉넉하다
admiring		to be white	하얗다
to be right	맞다, 옳다,	to be wise	지혜롭다
	올바르다	to be wrong	잘못되다

to be young	젊다
to be young, little	어리다
to bear patiently	꾹 참다
to become, be formed	되다
to beg for mercy	손이 발이 되도록 빌다
to begin, to start	시작하다
to behave, to act	행동하다
to bend	숙이다
to blaze	불이 활활 타다
to block	막다
to blow	불다
to boast	뽐내다
to borrow	빌리다
to break	깨뜨리다
to break a habit	버릇을 고치다
to break out (fire)	불이 나다
to breathe	숨을 쉬다
to bring (a person)	데리고 오다
to bring (something)	가지고 오다
to bring back (a person)	데려다 주다
to bully	괴롭히다
to bump into	딱 마주치다
to burgle	도둑이 들다
to bury	묻다
to burst (stomach)	배가 터지다
to buy	사다
to call	라고 하다, 부르다
to capture and bring	잡아오다
to carry on one's back	업다
to carry water	물을 긷다
to catch	잡히다
to catch, to kill	잡다
to change	바꾸다
to change, turn into	둔갑하다
to chase	쫓아가다
to check	확인하다
to cherish	아끼다
to choose, to select	고르다
to climb a hill	산을 오르다
to close	닫다
to clutch (something) to one's chest	가슴에 품다
to collapse	무너지다
to come	오다
to come at, attack	덤비다
to come back	돌아오다
to come closer	가까이 다가가다, 다가오다
to come down	내려오다
to come in, to join	들어오다
to come into one's mind, have an idea	생각이 나다
to come on foot	걸어오다
to come out	나오다
to come out with it	달려 나오다
to come to mind	생각이 들다
to command	명령하다
to commit a sin	죄를 짓다
to complete	마치다
to console	위로하다
to continue on a journey	계속 길을 가다
to cook	요리하다
to cook rice	밥을 하다, 밥을 짓다
to cover	감싸다
to covet, be greedy	욕심을 내다
to cross	건너다
to cry, to squawk (or other animal sounds)	울다
to cut	베다
to dash	달려가다, 달려오다
to dash out	뛰쳐나가다
to deceive	속이다
to decrease	줄어들다
to deepen (the night)	밤이 깊어지다
to deliver	갖다 주다
to deliver (humble)	갖다 드리다
to depart from this life	세상을 떠나다
to die	죽다
to die of hunger	굶어죽다
to dig	파다
to dig for gold	금을 캐다
to dig out	캐다
to disappear	사라지다
to discover	발견하다
to dislike, hate	밉다
to do	하다
to do one's best	정성을 다하다
to do something well	잘하다
to draw, to paint	그리다
to drink	마시다

to drive	몰아오다	to flounder	허우적대다
to drop	떨어뜨리다,	to fly	날아다니다,
	빠뜨리다		날아오다
to dry	말리다	to fly high	날아오르다
to eat	먹다	to fly into	날아들다
to eat (honorific)	드시다	to follow	따라오다
to eat/drink for free	거저 먹다	to forget	잊어버리다
to eavesdrop	엿듣다	to forgive	용서하다
to embrace, hold in	부둥켜 안다	to found a nation	나라를 세우다
one's arms		to freeze	얼다
to empty	비우다	to gather	모여들다, 모이다
to endure	견디다	to gather firewood	땔나무를 하다
to enjoy (a drink)	맛있게 마시다	to get a meal ready	밥을 차리다
to enjoy oneself	즐거워하다	to get angry	화를 내다
to enter	들어가다	to get hurt	다치다
to envy	부럽다	to get ill	병에 걸리다, 병이
to escape	빠져나오다		나다
to escape, to avoid	피하다	to get lost	길을 잃다
to escape, to run away	도망(을) 가다	to get money	돈이 생기다
to examine	살펴보다	to get off, to come	내리다
to exceed	넘다	down	
to experience	경험하다	to get revenge	복수하다
to face	처하다	to get scared	무서워지다
to fall	떨어지다, 빠지다	to get worried	걱정이 되다
to fall in love	반하다,	to get, to gain	얻다
	사랑에 빠지다	to give	주다
to farm	농사를 짓다	to give birth to	낳다
to fart	방귀를 뀌다	to give for free	그냥 주다
to feel flattered by	우쭐해지다	to give a reason	이유를 대다
to feel fresh	시원하다	to give up	포기하다
to feel frustrated	답답하다	to go	가다
to feel honored	영광이다	to go around	다니다,
to feel sleepy	졸음이 오다		돌아다니다
to feel sorry for	불쌍하다, 안되다	to go around	이곳저곳을
to feel uncomfortable,	답답하다	everywhere	다니다
frustrated		to go back	돌아가다
to fight	싸우다	to go by	지나가다
to fill	채우다	to go down	내려가다
to find	찾다	to go out	나가다
to find out	알아내다	to go to sleep	잠이 들다
to find something	황당하다	to go up, to rise	올라가다
absurd, be amazed		to govern	다스리다
to finish	끝나다	to grant wishes	소원을 들어주다
to fish	낚시하다	to greet	인사하다
to fish, to catch	잡다	to grow bigger	커지다
to fit perfectly	딱 맞다	to grow loud	커지다
to float	둥둥 뜨다	to guard, protect	지키다
to flop	주저앉다	to guide	안내하다

to hand over the throne	왕위를 물려주다	to know/to not know	알다 / 모르다
to hang	매달다	to laugh	웃다
to hang in clusters	주렁주렁 열리다	to learn	배우다
to harvest	수확을 하다	to leave	떠나다
to hate, dislike	밉다	to leave (something)	두고 가다, 두고 오다
to have	가지다, 지니다		
to have, to be	있다	to leave (something) as it is	이대로 두다
to have an aching heart	마음이 아프다		
to have another drink	한 잔 더 하다	to leave home	집을 나서다
to have the courage	용기가 나다	to lend	빌려주다
to have a good harvest	농사가 잘 되다	to let (someone) know	알려주다
to have an idea	생각이 나다	to let someone live in comfort	호강시키다
to have sons	아들을 두다		
to head for, set off for	향하다	to lie, speak falsely	거짓말을 하다
to hear, to listen	듣다	to lift	들어올리다, 올려 주다
to heave a sigh	한숨을 쉬다		
to help	돕다	to lift up effortlessly	번쩍 들어올리다
to help someone on with their clothes	입혀 주다	to light a fire	불을 붙이다
		to like	마음에 들다, 좋아하다
to hesitate	망설이다		
to hide	숨기다, 숨다	to listen, to hear	듣다
to hit, bang	쾅 치다	to live	살다, 살아오다, 지내다
to hit one's head	머리를 찧다		
to hold	들다, 붙잡다, 잡다	to look at, to watch	쳐다보다
		to look carefully	자세히 보다
to hold (a person)	안다	to look down	내려다보다
to hold in one's arms, embrace	부둥켜 안다	to look for	찾다
		to look in	들여다보다
to hold out	내밀다	to look like	생기다
to hold (something) tight to one's chest	가슴에 꼭 안다	to lose	잃어버리다
		to love	사랑하다
to hop	깡총깡총 뛰어오다	to make	만들다
		to make a deep bow	큰 절을 하다
to hunt	사냥하다	to make an effort	애를 쓰다
to idle, shirk	놀다	to make an excuse	핑계를 대다
to imprison, shut up	가두다	to make a fire	불을 피우다
to inform	알리다	to make a hole	구멍을 내다
to invent	발명하다	to make money	돈을 벌다
to invite people	사람들을 부르다	to make somebody do	시키다
to join, to come in	들어오다	to make war	전쟁을 하다
to jump into	뛰어들다	to marry	결혼을 하다
to keep alive	살아 있다	to marry (for a woman)	시집오다
to keep coming and going	왔다 갔다 하다	to meet	만나다
		to meet (humble)	뵙다
to kick out	내쫓다	to miss	보고 싶다
to kill	죽이다	to miss, to lose	놓치다
to kneel	무릎을 꿇다	to move	움직이다
to knock on the door	문을 두드리다	to move (house)	이사를 가다

to mutter	중얼거리다	to put on	올려 놓다
to name	이름을 짓다	to put one's heart into, do one's best	정성을 다하다
to need	필요하다	to raise	일으켜다,
to not be, to not have	없다		일으키다, 키우다
to not know	모르다	to raise one's head	고개를 들다
to obey someone's words well	말을 잘 따르다	to read	읽다
to obtain	구하다	to realize	깨닫다
to offer to Buddha	공양을 하다	to realize one's wish	소원을 풀다
to open	열다	to receive	받다
to open one's eyes	눈을 뜨다	to receive recognition	인정을 받다
to open one's mouth	입을 벌리다	to receive respect	존경을 받다
to pass	흐르다	to recover	낫다
to pass, to go by	지나다	to reflect, reconsider	반성하다
to pass away (honorific)	돌아가시다	to regain one's health	다시 건강해지다
to pass down	물려주다	to regret, be sorry	후회하다
to pass out	쓰러지다	to rely only on one's strength	힘만 믿다
to pay back	갚다	to remain	남다
to peck	쪼다	to request	부탁하다
to pick	따다	to rest	쉬다
to pick up	줍다	to return	돌려주다
to pity	불쌍하다	to revive	살아나다
to play	놀다	to ride	타다
to plough a rice field	논을 갈다	to ride on the back	등에 올라타다
to pluck up courage	용기를 내다	to ring loudly	크게 울리다
to point	가리키다	to ripen	익다
to poke, to stab	찌르다	to rise	뜨다
to pound	찧다	to rise (smoke)	연기가
to pour	따라 주다, 붓다		피어오르다
to pour (out of)	쏟아지다	to rise (wind)	바람이 불다
to pour down	줄줄 흘러내리다	to rise high	솟아오르다
to pray	빌다	to rot	썩다
to prepare	준비하다	to rub one's eyes	눈을 비비다
to prepare for death	죽음을 각오하다	to run	달리다, 뛰어가다
to press	누르다	to run away	도망치다
to prey on	잡아먹다	to run out	뛰어나오다
to prick up one's ears, be tempted	귀가 솔깃하다	to run out of	떨어지다
to propose	청혼하다	to rush back	달려 돌아오다
to prostrate oneself	넙죽 엎드리다	to save	구하다, 살리다,
to pull out, to take out	꺼내다		살려 주다
to pull out, to tear out	뽑다	to save money	돈을 모으다
to pull up weeds	풀을 뽑다	to say, to speak, to tell	말하다
to push through	뚫다	to say, to speak (honorific)	말씀하다
to put	놓다, 두다		
to put down	내려놓다	to say nothing	아무 말도 안 하다
to put in	담다, 넣다	to scold, punish	혼을 내다

to see, to watch	보다	to stick to	달라붙다
to seize	붙잡다	to stop	말리다, 멈추다
to select, to choose	고르다	to study	공부를 하다
to sell	팔다	to stupefy	멍하다
to send	보내다	to suffer hardship	고생을 하다
to send back	돌려보내다	to suppress one's anger	화를 참다
to set off for, head for	향하다	to survive dangers	죽을 고비를
to shake	흔들흔들거리다		넘기다
to shake one's head	고개를 흔들다	to swallow	삼키다
to share	나누다	to swim	수영하다,
to share, to allot	나누어 주다		헤엄치다
to shed	흘리다	to swing	휘두르다
to shed tears	눈물을 흘리다	to take	맞다
to shell	까다	to take (a person)	데리고 가다
to shine	비추다	to take (something)	가지고 가다
to shirk, idle	놀다	to take (something)	뜯다
to shoot with a bow	활로 쏘다	apart	
to shout	소리치다	to take away	빼앗다
to shut up, imprison	가두다	to take care of a baby	아기를 보다
to sink	가라앉다	to take a close look at,	자세히 보다
to sit	앉다	look carefully	
to sleep	자다	to take a look	둘러보다
to sleep (honorific)	주무시다	to take off	떼다
to smack one's knee,	무릎을 탁 치다	to take out	내놓다, 빼다
slap one's leg		to talk	이야기하다
to snow	눈이 오다	to teach	가르치다
to soak (something)	담그다	to tear out, to pull out	뽑다
in water		to tell, to say, to speak	말하다
to sound	소리가 나다	to test the water,	사정을 살피다
to sound, be heard	들려오다	assess the situation	
to sow seeds	씨를 뿌리다	to thank	감사하다, 고맙다
to spare a life	목숨을 살리다	to think	생각하다
to speak to say, to tell	말하다	to throw	던지다, 벌이다
to spend, to use	쓰다	to throw away	버리다
to spend time	보내다	to tie	매다, 묶다
to spread	뿌려 놓다	to tie (something)	나무에 묶다
to spread (of a plague)	전염병이 돌다	to a tree	
to squawk, to cry	울다	to tip (something)	머리에
(or other animal sounds)		on its head	뒤집어쓰다
to stack up	쌓아올리다	to travel	여행하다
to stand	서다	to treat, to cure	고치다
to stand up	일어나다	to turn	변하다
to start, to begin	시작하다	to turn into, change	둔갑하다
to starve, have	굶다	to turn one's head	고개를 돌리다
nothing to eat		to turn round and	뱅글뱅글 돌다
to stay	머무르다	round	
to steal	훔치다, 훔쳐가다,	to turn yellow	노래지다
	도둑질하다	to understand	이해하다

to use	사용하다
to use, to spend	쓰다
to visit	찾아가다
to wait	기다리다
to wake from sleep	잠에서 깨어나다
to walk	걷다
to want	원하다
to watch	지켜보다
to wear	입다
to wear (shoes)	신다
to weave cloth	옷감을 짜다
to weed a field	밭을 매다
to wish, to desire	바라다
to wonder	궁금하다, 의아해하다
to work	일하다
to work hard	수고하다
to worry	걱정하다, 고민이 되다
to wrap	감싸다, 싸다
to wrestle	씨름을 하다
to write	쓰다
toad	두꺼비
today	오늘
together	같이, 함께
tomorrow	내일
too, also, as well	도
too, excessively	너무나
tooth marks	이빨 자국
town, village	마을
trace, mark	흔적
traveler	나그네
treasure	보물
tree	나무
trowel, hand-held hoe	호미
truth, fact	사실
turtle	자라
twenty	이십
two	두 (둘)
typhoon	태풍

U

unavoidably, without a choice	할 수 없이
uncooked rice	쌀
under	아래, 밑
Underwater Palace (of the Dragon King)	용궁
unhusked rice	벼
unmarried woman	처녀
unnecessarily	쓸데없이
unusual thing	이상한 일
upper side	위쪽
upwards	위로

V

value	짜리
various	여러 가지
venom	독
very, none other than	바로
very, so	너무, 아주
village, town	마을

W

wall	벽
wastrel, good-for-nothing	건달
water	물
way, means	방법
weather	날씨
welcome, come in	어서 오세요
well	글쎄, 잘
what	무엇
What a surprise!	깜짝이야!
What do you mean?	무슨 소리요?
[what] on earth	도대체
when	언제
where	어디
while	동안
whisper	귓속말
who	누구
whoever	누구든지
why	왜
widely	널리, 크게
wife	아내
wild ginseng	산삼
winter	겨울

wish, hope	소원	yo-ho	영차
woman	여자	you	너, 당신
word	말 한마디, 단어	you all	너희
world	세상	young (animals)	새끼
worry	걱정	young lady	아가씨
Wow, oh my goodness!	와, 세상에	young man	청년
wrapping cloth	보자기	young person	젊은이
writing	글	younger brother	동생
		younger sister	여동생
		youngest	막내

Y

yard	마당
year	해, 년
years of age	살
yellow ox	누런 소

Z

zelkova tree	느티나무

"Books to Span the East and West"

Tuttle Publishing was founded in 1832 in the small New England town of Rutland, Vermont [USA]. Our core values remain as strong today as they were then—to publish best-in-class books which bring people together one page at a time. In 1948, we established a publishing office in Japan—and Tuttle is now a leader in publishing English-language books about the arts, languages and cultures of Asia. The world has become a much smaller place today and Asia's economic and cultural influence has grown. Yet the need for meaningful dialogue and information about this diverse region has never been greater. Over the past seven decades, Tuttle has published thousands of books on subjects ranging from martial arts and paper crafts to language learning and literature—and our talented authors, illustrators, designers and photographers have won many prestigious awards. We welcome you to explore the wealth of information available on Asia at **www.tuttlepublishing.com**.

Published by Tuttle Publishing, an imprint of Periplus Editions (HK) Ltd.

www.tuttlepublishing.com

Copyright © 2022 Sukyeon Cho, Yeon-Jeong Kim and Andrew Killick.
Illustrations © 2022 Minjee Kim.

ISBN 978-0-8048-5463-4

26 25 24 23   7 6 5 4 3 2

Printed in China   2307CM

Distributed by

North America, Latin America & Europe	**Asia Pacific**
Tuttle Publishing	Berkeley Books Pte. Ltd.
364 Innovation Drive	3 Kallang Sector #04-01
North Clarendon, VT 05759-9436 U.S.A.	Singapore 349278
Tel: 1 (802) 773-8930	Tel: (65) 6741-2178
Fax: 1 (802) 773-6993	Fax: (65) 6741-2179
info@tuttlepublishing.com	inquiries@periplus.com.sg
www.tuttlepublishing.com	www.tuttlepublishing.com

TUTTLE PUBLISHING® is a registered trademark of Tuttle Publishing, a division of Periplus Editions (HK) Ltd.

Are you living your most authentic life? Are you leaning into your purpose or running away from it? Is this the story you want your future self to tell or do you ache for something more?

Through his breakthrough discoveries, *New York Times* best-selling author Lewis Howes reveals how you can rewrite your past to propel yourself into a powerful and abundant future.

With these raw and revealing personal stories, science-backed strategies from industry-leading experts, and step-by-step guidance, you will learn how to:

- Clearly define a Meaningful Mission to enhance your purpose for this season of life

- Identify the root causes of self-doubt and conquer the fears that hold you back

- Transform your mind to end self-sabotaging thoughts to live a rich life

- Manifest your greatness to make the maximum positive impact on those around you

By applying the lessons and strategies found inside *The Greatness Mindset*, you will be able to design the life of your dreams and turn it into reality.

Are you ready? Your journey to greatness begins now!

Lewis Howes is a *New York Times* best-selling author, keynote speaker, and industry-leading show host. Howes is a two-sport All-American athlete, former professional football player, and member of the U.S.A. Men's National Handball Team. His show *The School of Greatness* is one of the top podcasts in the world with over 1 billion downloads. He was recognized by the White House and President Obama as one of the top 100 entrepreneurs in the country under 30. Lewis has been featured on *Ellen*, the *Today* show, *The New York Times*, *People*, *Forbes*, *Fast Company*, *ESPN*, *Entrepreneur*, *Sports Illustrated*, *Success*, and *Men's Health*. Learn more by visiting **LewisHowes.com**.